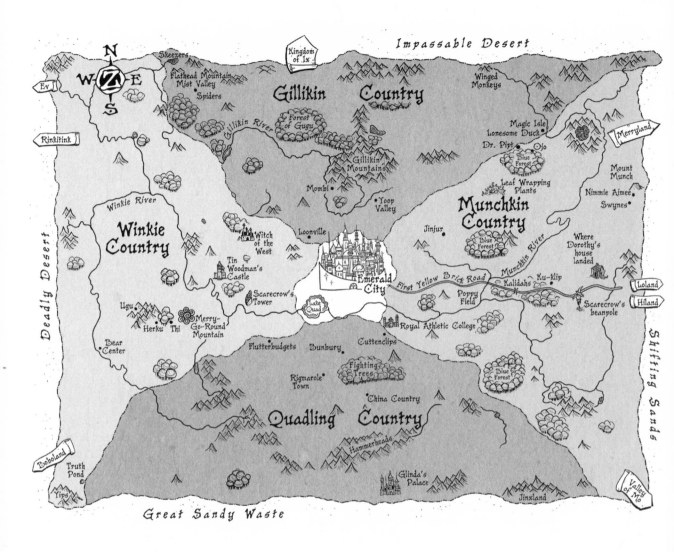

A Guide to Wisdom, Heart, and Courage

The Way of Oz

Robert V. Smith

Illustrations by Dusty Higgins

Texas Tech University Press

This book is typeset in Monotype Dante. The paper used in this book meets the minimum requirements of ANSI/NISO Z39.48-1992 (R1997). ∞

Designed by Kasey McBeath
Cover illustration by Dusty Higgins
Videos by Scott Irlbeck
QR Codes and credits by Rachel Pierce

Library of Congress Cataloging-in-Publication Data

Smith, Robert V., 1942–
    The way of Oz : a guide to wisdom, heart, and courage / Robert V. Smith ; illustrations by Dusty Higgins.
        p. cm.
    Summary: "A model for personal and professional development based upon the story and characters of the Wizard of Oz and the life of its author, L. Frank Baum. Discusses the intellectual, moral, and ethical value of life-long learning, loving, and serving others with humility and a focus on the future"—Provided by publisher.
    Includes bibliographical references and index.
    ISBN 978-0-89672-739-7 (hardcover : alk. paper) — ISBN 978-0-89672-740-3 (pbk. : alk. paper) — ISBN 978-0-89672-762-5 (e-book) 1. Baum, L. Frank (Lyman Frank), 1856–1919. Wizard of Oz. 2. Self-realization in literature. 3. Literature and morals. I. Higgins, Dusty. II. Title.
        PS3503.A923W6376 2012
        813'.4—dc23   2012013928

Printed in the United States of America
12 13 14 15 16 17 18 19 20 / 9 8 7 6 5 4 3 2 1

Texas Tech University Press
Box 41037 | Lubbock, Texas 79409-1037 USA
800.832.4042 | ttup@ttu.edu | www.ttupress.org

To the Daughter of Mars and the spirit of youth in us all

Contents

I
Oz and Its Creator: Inspiration for *The Way of Oz*

II
The Way of Oz and Learning

III
The Way of Oz and Loving

IV
The Way of Oz and Serving

V
The Way of Oz and a Focus on the Future

VI
The Way of Oz and Humility

Enhanced Video Content

Enhanced Video Conent..........................x

Learn More with QR Codes
Download a QR reader from your smartphone's app store and use it
to scan codes like this one. Need Help? Visit www.thewayofoz.com.

Preface

In 1956 (the one hundredth anniversary of L. Frank Baum's birth), when I was fourteen, the classic 1939 film *The Wizard of Oz* began to be shown yearly on television. I was not a great fan of the movie—at first. But, as Oz aficionados know, the movie grows on you. It is rated the number one fantasy film and is tenth among the 100 Greatest Movies of All Time by the American Film Institute. Starring Judy Garland as Dorothy, Ray Bolger as the Scarecrow, Jack Haley as the Tin Woodman, Bert Lahr as the Cowardly Lion, and Frank Morgan as the Wizard, *The Wizard of Oz* is one of the all-time favorite films of Americans of all generations.

I didn't read Baum's 1900 book, *The Wonderful Wizard of Oz*, on which the movie was based, until 1997, when I was interviewing for a job at the University of Kansas. I thought since the classic work was set in Kansas I should be familiar with it and perhaps I could create intriguing links between the development of Baum's book and the position for which I was interviewing. One thing I learned from that interview, however, was that the Kansans I met didn't seem to know much more about Baum's book than people in any other state. I didn't get an offer from KU, but it was on that April 1997 trip that I began thinking about the possible broader implications of the Oz stories. As a bonus, in preparing for the interview I also read Michael Patrick Hearn's original annotated work, *The Annotated Wizard of Oz*. Hearn's wonderfully detailed book had enough in it about the life and times of Frank Baum to pique my interest in the author and the potential of the larger Oz story.

It seemed to me that in our contemporary world, educated people should aspire to integrate the intellectual, moral, and ethical lessons Baum's characters come to represent: learning, loving, and serving others through humility and a focus on the future. I thought that by extension, Baum's book could serve as a model for integrated scholar faculty members—individuals who are able to blend teaching, research, and service in extraordinary ways—to the benefit of students and themselves. And it could serve bright high school and college students in similar ways. From these musings evolved the bases for *The Way of Oz*, specifically the linkages among learning (wisdom), loving (heart), and serving (courage), with one caveat. Learning in and of itself does not necessarily lead to wisdom. But in the philosophical construct of *The Way of Oz*, the integration of learning, loving, and serving can indeed lead to wisdom. And, when combined with the Dorothy figure as leader and the Wizard as the champion of humility and related virtues, a powerful complex, or model, evolves for lifelong learning, loving, and serving. Thus, it became my hope that *The Way of Oz* might assist the "youth of all ages."

Acknowledgments

Numerous people have influenced me in the development of *The Way of Oz*, including the authors of many books I have read on Oz and L. Frank Baum, along with the authors of many books on human development. But other people I've known through my teaching and administrative careers have enriched the Oz landscape and helped to shape my outlook and insight. To all who contributed to my effort with their goodwill and graciousness, I offer a metaphorical toast.

A few friends and colleagues deserve specific mention: I have long admired John A. White, chancellor emeritus of the University of Arkansas, who uses references to Oz to inspire students and families about the power and value of education. James Harris, president of Widener University, may be the first to have proposed the concept of Dorothy as a leader (with the attendant notion of her focus on the future), which I've adopted for *The Way of Oz*.

Several friends and colleagues at Texas Tech University and the Lubbock community read parts of this manuscript and were sources of encouragement: Randy Christian, Susan Hendrick, Grace Hernandez, Linda Hoover, Juan Muñoz, and Aliza Wong. Librarians and other friends or colleagues were helpful, including Sean Carroll (a member of the Club of Madrid), Richard Jackson (who was at the time living in Thessaloniki, Greece), George Matthews (from Peabody, Massachusetts), Trish Patrick (of Greensboro, North Carolina), and Kat Paulson (from Fayetteville, Arkansas), who offered encouragement and suggestions for specific portions of the text. In addition, I have greatly appreciated the assistance of Texas Tech reference librarians, especially Laura Heinz, Kimberly Vardeman, and Rob Weiner.

During the journey toward publication, a number of education, economics, and literary scholars, the TTU Press Advisory Board and the press's director, Robert Mandel, reviewed the *Way of Oz* manuscript. The recommendations and suggestions of this group, especially those of director Mandel, enhanced measurably the quality of work. The keen and thoughtful editing by Kathryn Lang added further value to the final work. Arkansas cartoonist Dusty Higgins brilliantly conceived and crafted the illustrations for *The Way of Oz*, and I am most appreciative of his graciousness in accepting suggestions for changes and additions. Katherine Pickett (POP Editorial Services) did masterful work in copyediting, for which I am most appreciative. I am also grateful to Texas Tech colleagues Sally Post, Katie Allen, Scott Irlbeck, and Rachel Pierce for their extraordinary efforts in producing the videos linked to the work. Overall, I am truly grateful for the represented assistance and support.

I leave for last the person who is first and foremost in my life—Marsha June Day Smith. She is my confidante, my muse, and my unstinting supporter—in all ways; she is a person who enriches my life.

Introduction

If you take the basic *Wizard of Oz* story, mix it with the life, loves, and trials of its author, L. Frank Baum, and then blend in themes from his Oz characters—the Scarecrow, who stands for Learning and Wisdom; the Tin Woodman, for Loving or Heart; the Cowardly Lion, for Serving and Courage; Dorothy, for a Focus on the Future; and the Wizard, for Humility—you have the basis for *The Way of Oz*. This book, representing such a synthesis, begins with an overview of Baum's original 1900 Oz book, *The Wonderful Wizard of Oz*, and the later acclaimed film made from it and is followed by a chapter on the life and times of L. Frank Baum.

The positive attributes of his characters emanate from the life of L. Frank Baum himself. He was a man of many interests and notable creative talents: he was at different times in his life an actor, a breeder of rare chickens, a director, a gardener, a lyricist, a merchant, a movie producer, a philatelist, a photographer, a playwright, a printer and newspaper publisher, a salesman, a theater manager, a window dresser, and, of course, a celebrated author. Baum had a great capacity for loving and serving; his focus on the future is reflected in many of his creative works, and his humility can be seen as a result of several business failures and personal setbacks. What I call *The Way of Oz* derives from Baum's original tale and its sequels, the life story of its creator, and the derivative lessons for you and me from all of these elements. As you will come to see, successes evolve for those who embrace the tenets of *The Way of Oz*, whether they know it or not.

The two introductory chapters are followed by five sections on learning, loving, serving, focusing on the future, and humility and related virtues—all connected to the Oz story and its author and all crafted as a guide to adolescents—in

Education professor
Patricia Patrick
comments on the value
of *The Way of Oz*.

particular for students enrolled in gifted and talented programs and those aspiring to enroll in college. All of these students will find their lives enriched and assuming special meaning through self-directed learning, a caring engagement with the world and its inhabitants, and a drive for service.

Throughout the chapters, I hope you will enjoy the illustrations masterfully created by Dusty Higgins along with a unique feature of this book. Imbedded in the text are quick response (QR) two-dimensional barcode icons and uniform resource locators (URLs) that will link you to a series of more than a dozen videos related to the substance and messages in *The Way of Oz*. The videos, produced by a team of colleagues at Texas Tech University, portray students and colleagues for whom *The Way of Oz* or its antecedent literature and cultural influences, not least of all the life and times of Frank Baum, have influenced their own outlooks and successes in navigating their lives' yellow brick roads. For those less familiar with QR technology, we offer help at www.TheWayofOz.com on downloading a linking application (app) into a smart phone. For those of you who are reading *The Way of Oz* through an electronic version, the URLs should help you connect directly to the video messages.

In essence, *The Way of Oz* is intended as a guide and a set of tools for lifelong learning, loving, serving, and leadership. It is a guide for personal and professional development, and it represents a highly integrated paradigm that can be useful to people of all ages.

There are countless books about human development. I refer to several in *The Way of Oz*. But I'm unaware of another book that ties literature, biography, and personal and professional development into a cohesive and compelling whole. The Oz story contains many important lessons for the intellectual, emotional, and social development of Americans and others in our international community.

The gestalt of *The Way of Oz* includes powerful archetypal themes embedded in the basic Oz story and its sequels; it taps into imagery that has had a powerful influence on the modern American psyche, experience, and parlance; and it gives me the opportunity to help advance the cause of women's rights, which, as it was for Frank Baum, has been a personal passion for many years.

A history professor at Texas Tech who read an earlier version of the manuscript of this book wrote me: "The work truly touched me in a way that I did not expect—as a person and an educator, and perhaps most fundamentally, as a mother who will share the lessons of Oz with her child." This is my hope, then, that *The Way of Oz* will touch a universally responsive chord in its readers, giving them an understanding of the powerful Oz-inspired triad of learning, loving, and serving.

So, take the trip down the yellow brick road with me to learn about the life and times of L. Frank Baum and see how you can incorporate the intriguing and helpful perspectives embedded in *The Way of Oz*—a new model for personal and professional development—into your own life.

History professor Aliza Wong offers a personal view on *The Way of Oz*.

I

Oz and Its Creator:
Inspiration for *The Way of Oz*

Survey of the Original Oz Book and the 1939 Film

Having this thought in mind, the story of "The Wonderful Wizard of Oz" was written solely to pleasure children of today. It aspires to being a modernized fairy tale, in which the wonderment and joy are retained and the heart-aches and nightmares are left out.

L. Frank Baum (1856–1919), from his introduction to
The Wonderful Wizard of Oz (1900)

The original Oz book and its derivative stories have intrigued children and adults for generations. The tale of a midwestern girl sojourning to the fantasy world of Oz embodies powerful messages and imagery, bolstered by the 1939 film, which brilliantly contrasts the gray dust-bowl appearance of Aunt Em and Uncle Henry's farm on the Kansas prairie with the colorful Land of Oz. With its pastoral appearance and the apparent kindly culture of the Munchkins, Oz, to some readers, epitomizes an agrarian model, which originated in Greek philosophy but was reborn during the time of Thomas Jefferson. Emphasizing rugged individualism, self-reliance, sustenance through agriculture, closeness to nature, love of family and place, wariness of modern technology, and minimal interest in national or international affairs, this model of agrarianism would have been recognizable to many people during Frank Baum's lifetime.

The Oz story begins with Dorothy (in later works she's given the apt last name of Gale), who is portrayed as a five- or six-year-old when she is first transported to Oz. In his 1964 essay on Oz as a parable for populism, history

Attorney Charlotte Bingham comments on the effects of the Oz stories on her as a child.

teacher Henry M. Littlefield suggests Dorothy represents "little Miss innocent everybody"; she is "levelheaded and human . . . good, not precious,
and [she] thinks quite naturally about others." Oz scholar Michael Patrick
Hearn writes that "Dorothy is American through and through . . . spunky
and tenacious." Economist Hugh Rockoff adds, "Dorothy represents America—honest, kindhearted, and plucky." She may also be emblematic of the
daughter Frank Baum and his wife, Maud, never had, though having four
sons may well have desired. Dorothy is the archetypal heroine who journeys
forth, has impressive adventures, and returns home triumphantly, with powers to share, or as Evan Schwartz notes: "The special object or piece of
wisdom that signifies transformation." She symbolizes American optimism
and its moral sense of the conquest of good over evil—themes that perme-
ate Baum's works.

I align Dorothy with what I call the future focus tenet of *The Way of Oz*.
She is a symbol of leadership. Along with other female leaders who emerge
in the Oz series, Dorothy offers an important role model for women. Clini-
cal psychologist Madonna Kolbenschlag writes, "I have been amazed at the
number of times the Dorothy-script surfaces in the consciousness—sometime in the dreams—of women in transition or undergoing a major transformation in self-image," in part because Dorothy comes from humble beginnings, reaches out to others in need, and lifts them and herself up while
becoming, in her translocation and venturing forth, "one of the most wonderful wish fulfillments in all of literature."

Dorothy was accompanied from the start by her faithful companion,
Toto, a Cairn terrier in the 1939 film but variously drawn in the Oz books as
a Cairn, a Boston bulldog, or a French bulldog. In mythology, dogs are
guides, offering safe passage among real and supernatural worlds. Given
Frank and Maud Baum's belief in theosophy, it's been suggested that the
name Toto may be a contraction of *totality*—a word that embraces the Eastern philosophical concept of totality, or a natural "unity of matter and energy . . . both real and imagined."

Dorothy ventures forth with the help of a Kansas tornado to Oz, a land
that becomes much more developed in Baum's many Oz sequels.

You might recall the vivid scene in the now-classic 1939 movie of the legs
and feet of the Wicked Witch of the East crushed by the tornado-assisted

descent of Dorothy's house into Munchkin land. The scene is significantly different from Baum's 1900 book in that the film portrays the Wicked Witch's enchanted slippers as ruby red. The sparkling red slippers that Dorothy inherits from the witch make a vivid visual contrast against Munchkin land's meandering Yellow Brick Road. (As an aside, one pair of the original ruby slippers sold at auction for $666,000 in 2000; another pair is on display in the American History Museum of the Smithsonian Institution in Washington, DC.) The slippers in Baum's book, however, were silver. Some critics have suggested a link between the silver slippers and the intense political debate during the 1890s about silver and gold standards for US currency.

Dorothy isn't fully aware of the magic of the slippers at the time they appear on her feet, but when the Good Witch of the North bestows a kiss on her forehead, she receives a mark that promises to shield her from harm. The potential for harm, of course, is anticipated by the Good Witch of the North and the Munchkin people who encourage Dorothy to travel to the Emerald City to seek the Great Wizard's help in returning to her native Kansas. This short episode contains another difference between the book and the film. In the film, the Good Witch of the North is referred to as Glinda, who is clearly associated with the Good Witch of the South (and the Quadling people) in the 1900 book and subsequent sequels, including Baum's last Oz book, *Glinda of Oz*.

Armed with the silver (or ruby red) slippers, the Good Witch of the North's magic forehead mark, and the farewell wishes of the Munchkin

people, Dorothy, accompanied by her faithful Toto, begins a journey west on the Yellow Brick Road toward the Emerald City. You might not fully realize, unless you read the thirteen Baum sequels, that Oz is a country composed of four lands with their associated colors: Munchkin land in the east (blue), Winkie land in the west (yellow), Quadling land in the south (red), and Gilligan land in the north (purple), all surrounding the capital—

Emerald City—at the center. Oz has been variously associated with America, a place beyond the borders of the United States, or a land beyond the realm of earth. The Yellow Brick Road may reflect Baum's childhood memories of yellow-brick-paved roads in upstate New York, where he grew up.

Dorothy encounters three important companions on her trip to Oz. Baum associated her companions with time-honored character traits, and critics have subsequently linked them with symbols relevant to the sociopolitical events of the 1890s when Baum was crafting his fairy tale masterpiece. The Scarecrow, for example, has been thought to represent Midwest farmers and their problems with drought and finances, particularly during the severe economic depression that became widespread in 1893.

Others have seen this character as a metaphor for intelligence or faith. The Scarecrow's request for a brain from the Wizard is logical but at times paradoxical, since the straw-stuffed character frequently exhibits remarkable insight and wisdom. If you read Baum's *The Marvelous Land of Oz*, you'll delight in the Scarecrow's wise pronouncement: "I am convinced that the only people worthy of consideration in this world are the unusual ones. For the common folks are like the leaves of a tree, and live and die unnoticed." I have associated the Scarecrow with learning and wisdom in *The Way of Oz*.

The Scarecrow, in search of a brain, and Dorothy, in search of a way back to Kansas, proceed down the Yellow Brick Road, although the road is more and more in disrepair as they proceed. In short order, they encounter the Tin Woodman. His origin in the film is obscure, but in Baum's book and its sequels we learn he was placed under a spell by the Wicked Witch of the East to deflect his affections for a Munchkin girl (Nimmie Amee), an apparent ward of the witch. The Wicked Witch desires the girl's services and fears she may fall in love with and marry the woodman. Because of the spell, the woodman, in great distress, cuts off his arms and legs and head with his ax and ultimately strikes his torso, causing him to lose his heart. After each of the woodman's self-mutilating acts, a tinsmith's services are engaged to fashion new body parts for him, but his virtual aching heart continues to long for the Munchkin maiden. In the original Oz book the Tin Woodman yearns for her: "While I was in love I was the happiest man on earth; but no one can love who has not a heart, and so I am resolved to ask Oz to give me one. If he does, I will go back to the Munchkin maiden and marry her."

Some observers have associated the Tin Woodman with the dehumanization of the working class by the eastern establishment in Baum's day. Here in *The Way of Oz*, I have aligned him with "heart" or love.

Now the expanded Oz group continues its journey west. We know from the book and the 1939 film that they soon meet up with the Cowardly Lion, who, like the Scarecrow and the Tin Woodman, reveals traits opposite his name: the Cowardly Lion, who bemoans his lack of bravery, is often courageous and helpful in extricating himself and his fellow travelers from threatening situations. I designate the Cowardly Lion as a model not only for courage but also for service in *The Way of Oz*.

The four seekers and Toto are now on their way to the Emerald City. In Baum's book, they next encounter the Kalidahs (ferocious beasts, part bear and part tiger), who attempt to devour them but are thwarted by quick thinking on the part of the Cowardly Lion, assisted by the Scarecrow and the Tin Woodman.

After defeating the Kalidahs, in Baum's book the Oz team encounters a river they must ford on their journey west. The Tin Woodman comes to the rescue by chopping down trees to construct a raft and poles to cross the river. The Scarecrow and the Tin Woodman volunteer to pole the raft, but during the crossing they encounter a swift current, and the straw-packed hero's pole becomes stuck in the muddy bottom—lifting him from the raft and stranding him in the middle of the river. The others make it to the opposite side of the river, thanks to the swimming ability of the Cowardly Lion, whose tail becomes a tether for the Tin Woodman, who, along with the raft, is pulled to shore. But now the Oz team minus one must find a way to rescue the Scarecrow. Fortunately, a passing stork stops to chat with the crew on the riverbank. She agrees to fly out to the middle of river to rescue the Scarecrow, and when she does, the team is once again intact.

Dorothy and her friends' next adventure takes them to a poppy field, which is portrayed differently in Baum's book and the 1939 film. Poppies, well known in the late nineteenth century as a source of opium and its derivatives, are depicted in Baum's book as having deadly sleep-inducing

properties. The Oz troupe's flesh-and-blood members, including Dorothy, the Cowardly Lion, and Toto, are in mortal danger when they fall asleep in the poppy field. But the Scarecrow and the Tin Woodman, unaffected by biological poisons, are able to rescue Dorothy and her faithful canine by carrying them away from the deadly flowers.

Rescuing the huge Cowardly Lion, however, presents a more formidable challenge. The Scarecrow and the Tin Woodman seek the help of an army of field mice led by its kindly queen. An alliance is struck in part because of the Tin Woodman's earlier killing of a wildcat that had endangered the life of the queen mouse. Now, at her command, thousands of mice, each holding a piece of string connected to a wooden cart the Tin Woodman has crafted for the Cowardly Lion, pull the mighty beast to safety.

In the 1939 movie, the deadly poppy field episode is portrayed as an intervention of the Wicked Witch of the West who, with Nikko the lead Winged Monkey, is watching the travelers through a crystal ball. Dorothy, Toto, and the Cowardly Lion are imperiled as they are in the book, but in the movie (and in the 1902 musical *The Wizard of Oz*), with Glinda's help, the effects of the poppies are reversed by a snowfall, and Dorothy and her crew set off again to the Emerald City.

Passing out of the dangerous territory of the poppies, the Oz team finally comes to the Emerald City (which some critics say is named for Ireland, a country Baum loved) at the end of the Yellow Brick Road. In the Oz movie, relatively little attention is paid to the arrival of the group, but instead the focus is on the striking scene of the city's Art Deco design (a style unknown at the time of the original Oz book's publication) and the friendly gatekeeper's greeting of the Oz troupe. In Baum's book, the Emerald City is depicted with the domes, towers, and spires of Victorian Orientalist design. Studded with emeralds, the city appears to cast a shining green sheen over everything, but visitors and residents are required to wear green-tinted glasses in and around the city to complete the "emerald aura." The Oz gatekeeper outfits our traveling friends (including Toto) with spectacles and admonishes them not to remove them. Otherwise, of course, the Emerald City would appear principally (and unmagically) white. This mandatory wearing of green spectacles suggests what we learn later of the Wizard's duping of the residents of Oz.

If you are a student of history, you will recall that Chicago was the site of the 1893 World's Columbian Exposition, noted for its "White City," built from cement and fiber of different types (hemp, jute, sisal). Various scholars have suggested that Baum (and his illustrator, W. W. Denslow) used the White City of the Chicago exhibition as the model for his Emerald City.

Now in Oz, our traveling friends have come to solicit help from the Great Wizard. And like the character in the film and the book, he is a difficult man to see. Eventually, however, they are granted an audience because of the Wizard's interest in Dorothy's silver shoes and the mark on her forehead the Good Witch of the North had given her. The travelers' collective encounter with the Wizard of Oz in the film is frightening, but the individual meetings Dorothy and her friends have in Baum's book with the Emerald City bully are even more so. The Wizard appears in mean-spirited incarnations to each of them—a disembodied head (to Dorothy), a beautiful yet gruff woman (to the Scarecrow), a five-eyed wooly beast (to the Tin Woodman), and an intimidating ball of fire (to the Cowardly Lion). The Wizard's consistent message is this: You get nothing for nothing; kill the Wicked Witch of the West and I will grant you your wishes.

In *The Way of Oz* I align the Wizard with humility because he is eventually humbled through his interactions with the Oz troupe. In the Oz sequels he is redeemed when Oz's new ruler, Ozma, invites him to become a citizen of Oz, and he subsequently develops true wizard-like abilities (through the mentoring of Glinda, the Good Witch of the South), which he uses with humility and a spirit of beneficence.

Seeking Out the Wicked Witch of the West

It is hard to imagine how any unempowered group would feel setting out to kill as implacable a foe as the Wicked Witch of the West, but Dorothy and her fearless crew continue their journey west toward Winkie land. You might recall the vivid kidnapping scene in the film involving the Winged Monkeys. In Baum's book, life is much more difficult for the Oz team. The Wicked Witch of the West, who has only one eye, is endowed with telescopic powers, which allow her to see the advancing group. She attempts to kill them with waves of fierce wolves, wild crows, black bees, and armed Winkie slaves. When the Scarecrow, the Tin Woodman, and the Cowardly Lion, using various strategic moves, defeat the combatants, the Witch sends the Winged Monkeys to kidnap the crew.

In Baum's book, much of the Witch's power is vested in a Golden Cap she keeps in her cupboard. The cap offers its possessor three wishes. By the time she encounters Dorothy and friends, the Witch has already used the cap twice—first, commanding the Winged Monkeys to defeat the Winkies and take over Winkie land, and second, using the Monkeys' skills to oust the Great Wizard from her domain. The Witch's third wish is to destroy or capture Dorothy and her compatriots, which she proceeds to do, disemboweling the Scarecrow's straw, causing the Tin Woodman to crash to earth during a flight over rocky terrain, abducting and imprisoning the Cowardly Lion, and kidnapping Dorothy and Toto, who end up at the Witch's castle. With the Witch's last wish fulfilled, the Winged Monkeys take their leave, happy to be no longer under her command.

Dorothy spends several days as an indentured servant in the castle of the Wicked Witch of the West, who is fearful of harming the little girl because of the charmed mark on her forehead. However, the Witch lusts for Dorothy's silver (or ruby red) shoes and their purported power. Thus, one day, the Witch sets a trap involving an invisible iron bar that causes Dorothy to fall and lose one of her shoes. In retaliation, Dorothy tosses a bucket of water on the mean old Witch. In the book as well as the film, the Wicked Witch of the West dissolves, to exist no more.

With the Wicked Witch of the West dead, Dorothy and her colleagues regroup and plan a trip back to the Emerald City. In Baum's book, the queen of the mice tells Dorothy to use the Golden Cap for a wish of her own. Dorothy enlists the help of the Winged Monkeys, who ferry her and the other members of her troupe back to the Emerald City.

At the gate to the Emerald City the travelers meet, once again, the Guardian of the Gates, who is surprised and pleased to learn about the demise of the Wicked Witch of the West. After receiving their green spectacles, the troupe walks through the gate and into the Emerald City, where they encounter citizen gawkers, who have apparently been informed of the troupe's success in killing the Wicked Witch of the West. The citizenry of Oz joins Dorothy and her companions in their march. In the film, as you might recall, the march to the palace is accompanied by a rousing chorus of "Ding-dong! The Wicked Witch is dead!"

Word now is sent to the Wizard of the troupe's arrival at the palace, but the Wizard does not respond for three days. On the third frustrating day, the Scarecrow requests that a message be sent to the Wizard. If the Wizard does not respond immediately, the Scarecrow threatens to send for the Winged Monkeys to harass the Emerald City's ruler as they had in the past. The Wizard then sends a message to the Oz travelers that he will see them at four minutes past nine the next morning.

After a sleepless night, the four travelers are escorted to the gem-studded Throne Room, where they encounter a domed structure covered by a curtain. In this detail, Baum's book and the film are consistent. Also consistent are the intimidating voice from the top of the dome and the pleas of Dorothy's group for the Wizard to deliver on his promises. The Wizard's request for another day's delay in their meeting prompts agitated dialogue among the group and a threatening roar from the Cowardly Lion. In the book, the Lion's roar frightens Toto, who tips over a screen in a corner of the Throne

Room, revealing the Wizard. In the film, you may recall, Toto drags the curtain aside to expose the embarrassed Wizard.

Here the book and the film deviate. In the book, a lengthy dialogue ensues in which the Wizard is reminded of his promises, after which he is forced to confess his phoniness. He goes on to describe the illusions he created when each member of the troupe visited him last. The Wizard talks about his roots in Omaha, Nebraska, and his work with a circus as a ventriloquist and balloonist. He tells them how a "run-away balloon" took him to Oz one day and, upon his descent through the clouds, he was acknowledged as a great wizard. For his amusement, he claims, he ordered the citizenry to construct the Emerald City, where they find themselves this day.

In both the book and the film, members of Dorothy's troupe declare that the Wizard is a humbug. In both, Dorothy says, "I think you are a very bad man." To which the Wizard replies, "Oh, no, my dear; I'm really a very good man; but I'm a very bad wizard, I must admit." The Wizard is embarrassed and makes an attempt to fulfill the wishes of the Oz travelers. In Baum's book, the Scarecrow receives a mixture of bran and pins and needles (to make him sharp) as a replacement for the straw in his head. In the film, he is awarded an honorary degree—the Th.D., or Doctorate of Thinkology—and immediately tries out his new brain by reciting the Pythagorean Theorem, albeit incorrectly.

In Baum's book, the Wizard places in the Tin Woodman's chest a sawdust-filled silk heart (which Baum later referred to as "a kind but not loving heart"). In the film, the Tin Woodman receives "a testimonial" in the form of a pocket watch and the Wizard's wise advice: "A heart is not judged by how much you love, but by how much you are loved by others."

To the Cowardly Lion, in Baum's book, the Wizard gives a bowl filled with green liquid dispensed from a square-shaped green bottle along with the admonishment: "You know, of course, that courage is always inside one; so that this really cannot be called courage until you have swallowed it." The "green liquid" is, of course, liquor—possibly gin. In the film, which was aimed primarily at a children's audience, instead of liquor the Cowardly Lion is awarded the Triple Cross for "meritorious conduct, extraordinary valor, [and] conspicuous bravery against wicked witches." Thus, the "humbug Wizard's" gifts acknowledge what their recipients have demonstrated, rather than what they needed, during their adventures in Oz. Or, as Patrick Hearn sums up: "The value of their journey to the Great Oz does not lie in the gifts of a brain, a heart, and courage. The journey itself is more important than its conclusion, for it forced them to discover within themselves what they always possessed. They just had to test the virtues through experience. They learned how to use the gifts of the great Oz, and in doing that they never really needed what he had to give them."

Both in Baum's book and the film, the Wizard promises to take Dorothy back to Kansas via hot-air balloon, although in the book it takes him four days to dream up the scheme. In the book, Dorothy and the Wizard construct the balloon of silk, glue, and a wash basket. In the film, the Wizard claims to have saved the balloon in which he traveled to Oz. In both cases, a time is set for the balloon's launching. Before the ascent, the Wizard (in the book) proclaims to his subjects: "I am now going away to make a visit. While I am gone the Scarecrow will rule over you. I command you to obey him as you would me." Dorothy and the Wizard climb into the balloon's basket, but Dorothy realizes Toto has disappeared. She jumps out of the basket to retrieve him, but before she can get back, the balloon's tether is released. The Wizard alone ascends, crying out for Dorothy to come on board. She's unable to catch Toto in time because of his adventure with another woman's cat, and she and Toto are stranded on the ground. The Wizard in the balloon floats out of sight, and Dorothy is once again in distress.

In the film's next scene, Glinda returns to give Dorothy instructions on an easy passage to Kansas.

The Final Part of the Journey

In Baum's book, the Scarecrow and the Tin Woodman are apparently happy with their respective situations following the Wizard's exit. But Dorothy is distraught that she's lost her chance to return to Kansas. The Scarecrow suggests she invoke the help of the Winged Monkeys through the second wish vested in the Golden Cap Dorothy inherited from the Wicked Witch of the West. After Dorothy speaks the conjuring words printed in the hat, a group of Winged Monkeys appears. When she requests their help to get back to Kansas, the lead Winged Monkey proclaims, "We belong to this country alone, and cannot leave it."

With the second Golden Cap wish wasted, the troupe seeks advice from Oz's lone bearded soldier. He recommends seeking help from Glinda because "she is the most powerful of all the witches and rules over the Quadlings." The Oz troupe resolves to proceed to Quadling land.

The next morning, Dorothy and her companions, in renewed good spirits, begin their journey to the Land of the South. After an uneventful first day, they come upon a thickly wooded area with a front row of trees that grab passersby. Soon the Scarecrow is in their clutches. Fortunately, the Tin Woodman is able to use his trusty ax to gain his release. The troupe musters the collective courage to proceed and passes through the remaining trees without incident.

As the troupe exits the stand of trees, they encounter a high wall that appears to be made of white china. The Tin Woodman comes to their aid by crafting a ladder to scale the wall. At the top of the wall, the Oz group gains a good view of the Dainty China Country where the floor and all of the houses and inhabitants are made of white china. The houses are brightly painted but only half the size of Dorothy, and the painted china citizens and their animals are half again as small. After a few encounters with the china people, including a mishap with a milkmaid and her cow that breaks its leg and must be glued back together, the troupe proceeds farther south, where they encounter a low china wall they can scale by climbing over the back of the Cowardly Lion. He is able to leap over the wall, but not without accidently damaging a china church with his tail.

On the other side of the wall, the Oz troupe passes through marshy country for some time before entering an old forest inhabited by many large animals, including tigers, elephants, bears, and wolves. One of the tigers approaches the Cowardly Lion with the greeting, "Welcome, King of Beasts!" The Cowardly Lion learns later that the forest animals have been threatened for some time by a large spiderlike creature—"with a body as big as an elephant and legs as long as a tree trunk"—that has been devouring many of them. The tiger asks if the Cowardly Lion would take on the spiderlike creature and, if he's successful, assume the role of "King of the Forest." The Cowardly Lion agrees and ventures forth to find what turns out to be an exceedingly ugly creature. Fortunately for the Cowardly Lion, the creature is asleep, and he's able to mount the creature's back, and with his powerful paw, he knocks its head from its body (so much for Baum's claim of "night-mares . . . [being] left out").

The Cowardly Lion returns to his friends, who have been safely guarded by the forest animals. He promises the forest animals he will return to assume his kingship once he has helped Dorothy return to Kansas.

The troupe's march south continues out of the woods into a clearing, but then the travelers are confronted by a rock-laden hill they must climb to continue their journey. Among the rocks, they encounter hundreds of arm-less Hammer-Head people. These strange creatures are able to propel their heads into the air several feet to intimidate or strike blows to intruders. After violent "head attacks" to the Scarecrow and the Cowardly Lion, the Tin Woodman suggests that Dorothy again summon the help of the Winged Monkeys. She does, and they appear quickly. She asks the Monkeys to whisk the troupe away, and soon they are delivered to Quadling land, which is beautiful to behold, populated by friendly people who are short and stocky, dressed in red outfits, and living in red houses.

Literary critics have not been complimentary of the Fighting Trees, Dainty China Country, old forest, and Hammer-Head sections of Baum's original Oz book. None of these sections, apparently perceived as boring and irrelevant, appear in the 1939 film, except for a short fighting apple tree episode (instigated by the Wicked Witch of the West) right after Dorothy meets the Scarecrow. The film contains at least three other brief scenes in which the Wicked Witch of the West either threatens Dorothy and her friends or directly intervenes in their travails. Baum, in his 1900 classic, places more obstacles in Dorothy and her friends' path. The challenges to the Oz crew are due—as in all of our lives—to a myriad of characters and events. And, as Patrick Hearn asserts: "Each of Dorothy's friends now has what he has so long desired, but . . . each had to test himself to see what he is capable of doing. Only experience can do that."

In Baum's story, the Oz troupe, continuing their march south (through Quadling land), comes upon a beautiful castle guarded at its gate by "three young girls, dressed in handsome red uniforms trimmed with gold braid," reminiscent of Baum's time in South Dakota and the lance-carrying drill team there known as the Aberdeen Guards (these were Civil War veterans' daughters who wore uniforms consisting of red skirts and hats and blue jackets with gold piping). Dorothy asks the young women if Glinda resides in the castle and whether the Good Witch of the South might receive her crew. The girls go to find out, and the troupe is soon admitted to the castle.

Sitting on a throne of rubies, the beautiful Glinda, with red hair and blue eyes and clad in a long white dress, greets Dorothy and her friends with great kindness and solicitude. When Dorothy explains her wish to return to Kansas, Glinda asks for the Golden Cap. Now that Glinda is the new possessor of the cap, she is entitled to three wishes. She summons the Winged Monkeys and instructs them to carry the Scarecrow back to the Emerald City, where he may assume his leadership position, fly the Tin Woodman to Winkie land where he has been invited to become their ruler, and return the Cowardly Lion to the old forest where he's been asked to become king.

The climax of the Quadling land episode in Baum's book is similar to the film's, when Glinda instructs Dorothy to pick up Toto, click the heels of her silver (ruby red) shoes three times, and make a wish ("Take me home to Aunt Em" in Baum's book and "There is no place like home" in the film).

In both the book and the film, Glinda tells Dorothy that she could have returned to Kansas at any time after she inherited the silver (ruby red) shoes, but Dorothy is consoled by the fact that her harrowing sojourn has benefited her new friends greatly. In the scenes that follow, Dorothy is back in Kansas on Aunt Em and Uncle Henry's farm. In Baum's book, Uncle Henry has built a new home to replace the one the cyclone carried away. In the film, Dorothy ostensibly awakens from sleep and the dream of Oz—surrounded by Aunt Em and Uncle Henry, Professor Marvel, and the farmhands Hunk, Hickory, and Zeke. Although Dorothy insists her adventure was not a dream—that Oz was a real place with people just like those surrounding her bed—moviegoers are left with the notion that it was all a dream.

Connecting the Oz Story to the Way of Oz

Dream or not, Baum's original Oz story offers three major characters whose positive personal traits (the Scarecrow—wisdom, the Tin Woodman—love, and the Cowardly Lion—courage) you can acquire if you pursue life's journey using what I call the Way of Oz—thoughtfully, caringly, and unselfishly. These traits are potent, particularly when coupled with Dorothy's focus on the future and the Wizard's sense of humility. The power of the Way of Oz comes from within. As Glinda says at the end of the 1939 film, "You need to find things out for yourself."

Or, as Mariah Carey would sing years later, "… a hero lies in you." You have no need for shamans, clerics, gurus, or others to dictate to you the precepts of the Way of Oz, although teachers, family members, friends, and colleagues can all contribute to your pursuit of positive practices and character traits. As Matilda Gage, Frank Baum's mother-in-law, wrote in 1891 during the last days of her life to her daughters and granddaughters, "You have got to do it for yourself. . . . Look within your own soul for light."

Frank Baum believed in the tenets of theosophy, which include an acknowledgment of the power of the Buddha's Golden Road, or path to self-understanding and enlightenment through a life of study and struggle. Baum's life exemplifies this struggle—in his seeking out many different career paths (of necessity) and in pursuing his many and varied avocational interests. He came to recognize, particularly as he neared death, that his talent for storytelling was his best gift all along. In the final reckoning, it ensured his immortality.

2

L. Frank Baum: An American Polymath

When I was young I longed to write a great novel that should win me fame. Now that I am getting old my first book is written to amuse children. For, aside from my evident inability to do anything "great," I have learned to regard fame as a will-o'-the-wisp which, when caught, is not worth the possession; but to please a child is a sweet and lovely thing that warms one's heart and brings its own reward.

L. Frank Baum (1856–1919), from a letter
written to his sister Mary Louise in 1897

Frank Baum spent the last fifteen months of his life confined to his bed—writing—being productive even though he was afflicted with a fatal heart condition that had its roots in his childhood. In his book about the fantasy world of Oz, Michael O. Riley says that Baum's stamina and dedication served him to the end: "For him, his whole life long, living had meant creating—to stop would be to die."

During his final months, weeks, and days, Baum may well have experienced the circular aspect of his life, about which philosopher Harold Rosen has said, "When you come to the end you think of the beginning." So, we'll begin our pursuit of the Way of Oz by looking at Baum's life, starting at the beginning.

Lyman Frank Baum, or L. Frank Baum as he chose to be called (he passionately disliked his first name), was born on May 15, 1856, in Chittenango, New York. Chittenango is an Erie Canal town in central New York, fifteen miles east of Syracuse, thirty-five miles east of the easternmost portion of the state's Finger Lakes region. Baum was the seventh of nine children born to Cynthia (Stanton) Baum, who was of Scotch-Irish descent, and Benjamin Ward Baum, whose ancestors had emigrated from Germany to central New York state in the mid-eighteenth century. Of the nine children, only four, besides Frank, lived to adulthood, including two brothers (Benjamin William and Henry "Harry" Clay) and two sisters (Harriet "Hattie" Alvena and Mary Louise). Baum would dedicate various books to members of his family, including his favorite sister, whom he immortalized in a series of volumes (*Mary Louise in the Country* [1916], *Mary Louise and the Liberty Girls* [1918]) that he wrote under the pen name Edith Van Dyne.

At the time of Baum's birth and during his early years in Chittenango, his father (trained as a cooper) had a barrel factory, which later fell on hard times, causing the Baums to move to Syracuse, New York, in 1861. Not long thereafter, Benjamin Baum hit it big in oil recovery and sales in Pennsylvania, near Titusville. Baum's father invested in real estate, was active in stock trading in Manhattan, where he maintained an office, and in 1863 founded the Second National Bank in Syracuse. With some of his recently acquired wealth, in 1866 Baum senior purchased a manicured four-acre estate about four miles north of Syracuse, near the Erie Canal. Because of the hundreds of rose bushes on the estate, Frank's mother called it "Rose Lawn." Rose Lawn—with its many plantings, including "every variety of fruit tree and grapevine that would flourish in upstate New York"—would serve as a model for places Baum later created in his books, including most notably the mansion and grounds in *Dot and Tot in Merryland*.

Although his family maintained a townhouse in Syracuse, both Frank and his mother preferred their days at Rose Lawn. Just north of Rose Lawn his father acquired a 240-acre agricultural spread, which included an 80-acre tract known as Spring Farm. The farm produced grain, and there the family raised cattle and horses. Frank Baum's farm experiences were central to his later writings, including his creation of the Scarecrow character and his many allusions to crows, which held special fascination for him.

In the years just before his birth and a month thereafter, Baum's parents lost three children, probably to infectious diseases, and, worried about their new young son's apparent congenital heart condition, they were predisposed to spoil him. There's some confusion in the literature about the exact nature of Baum's heart condition, whether it was congenital, as his son

Frank Joslyn Baum suggested, or the result of rheumatic fever, or a combination of the two. In any case, young Baum had an infirmity that inspired the solicitous treatment of his parents and inhibited much outdoor play for him—both of which encouraged his dedication to the creative life of the mind and his early devotion to books, including the imaginative works of Charles Dickens, Charles Reade, William Shakespeare, and William Thackeray, the allegorical works of John Bunyan, the American legendary tales of James Fennimore Cooper, the fantasies of Jonathan Swift and Lewis Carroll, and fairy tales of various types, but particularly those of the Grimm brothers and Hans Christian Andersen.

Moving into His Teens

Like his siblings, Baum was schooled at home by English tutors until he was twelve. Then, with the approval of physicians, his parents decided to send him away to boarding school. They selected the Peekskill Military Academy, founded in 1833 (and closed in 1968) in the Hudson River village of Peekskill, New York, 220 miles southeast of Syracuse. Young Baum didn't want to go, but his father evidently believed it would be good for him. It's hard to imagine the precocious and coddled Frank Baum in an institution fostering a culture of strict discipline and training, whose motto was "Stand Firm as An Oak, Quit You Like Men."

Baum lasted just two years at Peekskill, suffering greatly during that time, although many years later he donated signed first editions of all his Oz books to the academy. It's thought that the many yellow brick roads of the heavily Dutch city of Peekskill (paved with the abundant yellow bricks used as ballast in merchant ships coming to this country from Holland) were the inspiration for the Yellow Brick Road in Baum's original 1900 Oz book.

During the period of Baum's attendance at the military academy, Peekskill village in the 1860s was also the site of piloted balloon races, and hot-air balloon journeys, of course, are of great importance to the 1900 Oz story. Baum's interest in balloon events, possibly stemming from his years in Peekskill village, was likely reinforced by others he witnessed in his adolescent and adult years in Syracuse, Aberdeen, and Chicago.

Back at home at Rose Lawn in 1870, Baum once again continued his education through tutors. The fourteen-year-old cultivated a love of English literature and developed an interest in printing and publishing, following a chance visit to a printing shop in Syracuse. Baum's instant fascination for and immediate involvement in printing and publishing would become a pattern for other interests he developed in many areas throughout his life.

This newfound passion for printing inspired his now wealthy parents to buy costly printing equipment for him, and Baum began some notable projects, the first of which was the *Rose Lawn Home Journal*, which he published in 1870 and 1871. As Katharine M. Rogers notes in her 2003 biography of Baum, "The *Journal* was filled with works by Frank and other members of his family, together with pieces drawn from national magazines and books. His father contributed the first installments of a 'History of the Oil Company,' describing the beginning of the petroleum industry in Pennsylvania. His sister Mary Louise contributed at least two poems." It became typical of Baum to involve others in his ventures and to give them opportunities to contribute to his creative and productive projects.

Baum's interest in printing and publishing continued through the early 1870s when he established and published a journal called *The Stamp Collector*, along with an eleven-page publication called *Baum's Complete Stamp Dealer's Directory*, which supported a foreign postage stamp mail-order business he developed with William Norris, a traveling salesman from Albany, New York. In 1873 he teamed up with his brother Harry and Thomas Alvord, Jr., the son of New York's former lieutenant governor, to publish *The Empire*, a multipurpose journal that included literary pieces and contributions on practical matters such as stamp collecting. Baum continued his interest in philately throughout his life and had a formidable stamp collection at the time of his death.

In 1873 Baum interrupted his publishing activities to attend Syracuse Classical School, but this only lasted a year before he was back to his creative and entrepreneurial activities. His formal schooling, not counting his home tutoring, included just two years at Peekskill Military Academy and a year at Syracuse Classical School. His innate talents, coupled with his diligence and enthusiasm for learning, guided his intellectual and professional development, notwithstanding his tendency to jump from one interest to another, which occasionally threatened his ability to focus his efforts at different times in his life.

One example of Baum's predilection for venturing precipitately into new interests was his fascination for the theater, which began sometime around 1874. Syracuse in the 1870s was a theater town, with professional troupes performing plays that might eventually make it to the New York City stage. When Baum was about eighteen, he began frequenting local theaters. He visited some of the theaters his father had acquired and managed in several small cities in New York and Pennsylvania. Baum was smitten, and he worked earnestly to become part of a professional group. A Shakespearean theater troupe signed him on in 1874 with the promise that he might be called on to assume several roles if he would acquire costumes appropriate to each of the characters he was to play. In this instance, Baum became the quintessential dupe. His parents paid several thousand dollars for elegantly fabricated costumes that were expropriated by members of the theater troupe under the guise of borrowing them. Baum returned home from this experience disillusioned and embarrassed. This early failure, a portent of many others to come in his life, was perhaps one of his first lessons in humility.

Despite this first bitter experience with the theater, Baum didn't give up his love for theatrical productions, which permeated much of his later life and work. But at nineteen, with the recent humiliation of the appropriated costumes fresh in his mind, Baum moved onto a more practical path and took a clerk's position for a year or two with the family-owned Neal, Baum & Company dry-goods store in Syracuse. This is another hallmark of Baum's life: when life presented him challenges, particularly in his creative or esoteric ventures, he turned to practical alternatives to bridge difficult times. Baum used this strategy many times in his life, which has also been true of many other creative people throughout history.

Into His Twenties

After his clerking experience at Neal, Baum & Company in Syracuse, Baum teamed up with his father and his brother Harry at Spring Farm to establish B. W. Baum & Sons, a company specializing in breeding fine poultry. Baum's contribution consisted primarily of raising Hamburg chickens, a small but handsomely plumaged variety of Dutch and German fowl. Baum became an expert on the breed, and his efforts helped make B. W. Baum & Sons stand out in the state.

In addition to his attention to the Hamburgs, Baum became active in regional and national poultry circles. He helped found the Empire State Poultry Association and served as its first secretary. He also founded a monthly trade journal, *The Poultry Record*, which he later sold to the *New York Farmer and Dairyman*.

Baum's expertise with Hamburgs led to a lengthy article he published in serialized form in *The Poultry Record* from July through November of 1882. This article became the basis for his first book, which Connecticut-based H. H. Stoddard published in 1886, allegedly without Baum's knowledge. This may seem like a peculiar start for the creator of the Oz books, but when you know of Baum's interest in poultry, it isn't hard to see how it fits into his repertoire of published works.

Even though Baum was still involved in his Spring Farm poultry work, around 1878 he began to study acting more seriously, first under the tutelage of his aunt, Katherine Gray, an elocution teacher in Syracuse, and then later in New York City at the Union Square Theater. He appeared in the New York City production of *The Banker's Daughter*, which played between November 1878 and early March of 1879.

After short stints writing for the *New York Tribune* and the *Bradford Era* (a newspaper published in Bradford, Pennsylvania), in 1880 Baum became manager of a string of his father's theaters along the southwestern New York–Pennsylvania border. During the next year or so, Baum formed an acting company to produce plays for audiences in the small oil-producing communities of the region.

Baum's work in the poultry and theater-management businesses not only exemplifies his changing vocational interests but also highlights another important feature of his life—a commitment to reach out to the communities connected with his various areas of endeavor. This is another way of saying "service," and Baum, even in his teens and early twenties, had a knack for offering his services and talents to those who might benefit from his insight, creativity, and expertise. This trait helped him make the transition from one area of his creativity and efforts to another.

Baum's knowledge of theater management led in part to his writing plays, three of which he completed in 1882. The most notable of these, written under the pen name of Louis F. Baum, was *The Maid of Arran*, based on the Scottish novelist William Black's *A Princess of Thule* (1874). In her book *Wonderful Wizard, Marvelous Land*, Raylyn Moore characterizes Baum's play as an "Irish musical comedy with highly sentimental dialogue, plot, and music." It's been suggested that Baum chose to highlight Irish characters and life to appeal to the predominant ethnic group in the area where *The Maid of Arran* premiered. Being attuned to the local community in this instance typified many of Baum's later endeavors.

Baum wrote the script as well as the music and lyrics for *The Maid of Arran*. He assisted in the set design and development, organized the theater company, and produced the show. He also played the lead character, Hugh Holcomb, continuing to use the pseudonym Louis F. Baum. The show opened in 1881 at one of his father's theaters in Gilmor, Pennsylvania, and went on to Syracuse for a performance on May 15, 1882. It was such a hit that Baum took it on the road, where it played several midwestern venues, including Columbus, Milwaukee, and Chicago, before moving on to Toronto, Canada.

During the creation and production of *The Maid of Arran*, Baum met Maud Gage, a Cornell University student who became his lifelong companion, supporter, confidante, and "genius of practicality." They fell in love and immediately planned to marry. Maud was the daughter of Henry and Matilda Joslyn Gage of Fayetteville, New York, which is just ten miles east of Syracuse. Matilda Gage, a key figure in the women's rights movement, eclipsed her husband, Henry, a successful dry-goods merchant and prominent Erie Canal boat operator. Matilda was a significant collaborator (maybe even the primary author) with Elizabeth Cady Stanton and Susan B. Anthony of the formidable trilogy *History of Women's Suffrage* (written between 1881 and 1886), in addition to being an author of several works of her own. She opposed her daughter's marrying an actor, whose uncertain life would include considerable travel. But Maud Gage was stubborn in her resolve, and Matilda gave in, partly out of respect for her daughter's inherent right as a woman to choose her own husband.

Despite her initial reservations, Matilda Gage soon grew fond of Baum, in part because of his affable and kindly nature. She appreciated his creative talents and introduced him to theosophy, a religious movement brought to the United States by the Ukrainian psychic Helena Petrovna Blavatsky, whose writings were embraced by notables such as Elizabeth Cady Stanton and Thomas Alva Edison. Adherents of theosophy believe in the inalienable rights of all people, regardless of race, religion, sex, or class. Theosophists seek truth through a blended understanding of philosophy, religious beliefs from all faiths, and science. Theosophists also believe science helps in the continuing illumination of religious belief. This enlightened interdisciplinary orientation and worldview influenced and informed much of Baum's lifelong learning and writing, with a few notable exceptions.

The Maid of Arran was on the road when Baum and Maud married (November 9, 1882), and the newlyweds traveled through early 1883 in the Midwest, where the play was performed in Kalamazoo, Michigan; Elkhart and South Bend, Indiana; and Lawrence and Topeka, Kansas. The latter performances probably mark Baum's first contact with the state that would become central to his 1900 Oz book.

During the spring of 1883, Maud became pregnant, and the couple decided to return to Syracuse to establish a home for their first child, Frank Joslyn Baum, who was born on December 4, 1883. Baum continued his theater work into 1884 from his base in Syracuse. He oversaw productions of *The Maid of Arran* at venues in Connecticut, Massachusetts, New Jersey, and Pennsylvania. In mid-1883 he became involved with the family oil business and in 1884 helped to found a new company, Baum's Castorine Company, a joint venture with his chemist brother Benjamin William Baum and his uncle Adam Baum. Frank served as a production superintendent in the new company from 1884 to 1888, but he was occupied with many other personal and professional matters during these years. His theater foundered around 1884 due to the misdeeds of a bookkeeper and a fire that destroyed the theater in Gilmor along with several properties associated with the production of *The Maid of Arran*.

During 1885, Baum's father was injured in a horse-drawn vehicle accident and remained sickly for the two years before his death in 1887. Baum's brother and business partner, Benjamin, became sick and died in February of 1886. Around this same time, Maud suffered a serious and painful case of peritonitis and nearly died, following the birth of their second son, Robert Stanton Baum, on February 1, 1886. Maud's birth-related illness continued for two years.

These were traumatic events for Baum, who was spending considerable time on the road promoting Baum's Castorine products. But his circumstances became even more difficult with his uncle Adam's illness and his own unfortunate hiring of a clerk who apparently embezzled funds from the company to support his gambling habit. The episode came to a head in early 1888 when Baum returned from a sales trip to find the clerk dead—the victim of a self-inflicted gunshot wound. Baum sold the Castorine business later in 1888.

Because of the financial and personal travails the young family experienced from 1884 to 1888, Baum and his wife decided they needed to make a change. Three of Maud's siblings (her brother T. Clarkston "Clark" Gage and her sisters Julia Gage Carpenter and Helen Leslie Gage) a few years earlier had moved to the Dakota Territory, in the vicinity of Aberdeen and Edgeley, which is now in southeastern North Dakota, sixty-five miles north of Aberdeen. Baum listened to their reports of the good prospects they had found in the West after emigrating to land Maud's father owned, and he set his sights on property available there through the US Homestead Act.

With the expansion of the United States and the economic prospects offered in the Midwest through rich agricultural development, many easterners were attracted to the idea of going west. The presence of Maud's relatives in Aberdeen and Edgeley, especially her brother Clark (a member of the first graduating class at Cornell University and an early settler in Aberdeen), created a special lure for the struggling young Baum family. The Dakota Territory had been considered a land of opportunity after the arrival of the railroad in 1873 and the Black Hills gold rush of 1875–1876. The beleaguered Baums planned to move to Aberdeen in September of 1888.

At this juncture in Frank Baum's life, it is intriguing to consider the national events that may have influenced his thinking up through his thirty-second birthday and his family's move to the Dakota Territory.

In his youth and as a young man, Baum probably heard discussions and at times probably read about the formation of the Confederacy (1861), the Abraham Lincoln presidency (1861–1865), the American Civil War (1861–1865), Reconstruction (1865–1877), P. T. Barnum's rise to fame (1861–1881), President Andrew Johnson's impeachment (1868), the Ulysses S. Grant presidency (1869–1877), the Coinage Act of 1873, the depression of 1873–1879, the Rutherford B. Hayes presidency (1877–1881), the surrender of Sitting Bull (1881), the formation of the Oriental Telephone Company by Thomas

Edison and Alexander Graham Bell in 1881, the founding of the Standard Oil Trust by John D. Rockefeller in 1882, the James Garfield presidency and assassination (1881), the Chester A. Arthur presidency (1881–1885), and Grover Cleveland's first term as president (1885–1889).

Although we can't be certain of Baum's awareness of all these events as they unfolded, we know that he heard the horror stories of his uncle Adam Clarke Baum, a Union assistant surgeon physician during the Civil War (including the amputations that may have influenced his portrayal of the Tin Woodman). It is likely that he was aware of P. T. Barnum's promotion of tiny Tom Thumb, who was only eleven inches tall, and his marriage to twenty-two-inch-tall Mercy Lavinia Warren Bump in 1863 when Barnum's Grand Traveling Museum, Menagerie, Caravan, and Hippodrome (precursor to "The Greatest Show on Earth") came to Syracuse in 1871. It's probable that Barnum's productions influenced Baum's Munchkin imagery, along with the character of the Wizard and his Midwest counterpart, Professor Marvel, in his Oz writings.

We know that Maud's family would have had a great interest in the Cleveland presidency, since the Gage home in Fayetteville was just across the road from the house where Grover Cleveland grew up.

In addition, the senior Baum's oil recovery and sales business was adversely affected financially by the Standard Oil monopoly. Baum's father experienced losses in the stock market in the 1870s, just prior to the depression of 1873–1879. We know as well that Maud's grandfather was involved in abolitionist causes and, as we noted earlier, that her mother, Matilda, was a stalwart in the beginnings of the women's rights movement. We can't say with certainty how Baum was affected by these national events up to the time of his thirty-second birthday, but we are able to chart his interest in national affairs when he and his family moved to the Dakota Territory.

Continuing into His Thirties

Baum went to Aberdeen ahead of his family in June of 1888. There, he conferred with Clark Gage and practiced his lifelong avocational interest in photography. His photos of the Dakota Territory show a prairie and a town composed of flat clapboard stores and other buildings, raised wooden sidewalks and earthen streets. Although these photographs might suggest stereotypical backwater environs, historian Nancy Tystad Koupal notes in her book *Our Landlady* that the "atmosphere in Aberdeen in 1888 was one of boosterism and excitement. Lawyers, real estate brokers, bankers, doctors, and business owners of various types had relocated from the East, Midwest, and South." As was true of many areas of the upper Midwest, Dakota had its share of international immigrants, many from central and northern Europe. Aberdeen was also an attractive and engagingly small yet emerging hub where three railroad lines crossed.

After returning to Syracuse, Baum applied his creative and entrepreneurial talents to his future prospects. Writing to his brother-in-law Clark, he said that what Aberdeen needed was a variety store, patterned after the F.W. Woolworth "5 and 10 cent store" Frank had discovered in Utica, New York, during one of his many sales trips. Baum thought it should offer a range of products from china and housewares to stationery and books, camera supplies, sporting goods, and games.

With an investment of two thousand dollars, including his personal capital, loans from friends, and a note from the Northwestern National Bank of Aberdeen, on October 1, 1888, Baum's Bazaar opened on the ground floor of a building owned by Clark and Helen Gage, less than two weeks after the Baum family arrived in Aberdeen. Early business was brisk, and after a Christmas holiday slowdown caused by the loss of requisitioned goods on a ship that sank in Lake Huron, the Baums had continued mercantile success in the spring of 1889. Although Baum's Bazaar may have started out with a modest selection of items, it soon developed a reputation for a quality line of varied and sophisticated goods, excellent customer service, and always interesting displays, including fanciful window dressings that Baum himself designed.

During the spring of 1889, Baum showed his penchant for community involvement when he collaborated with other Aberdeen business owners to found the Aberdeen Baseball Club (Baum served as its first secretary) and the Hub City Nine, a professional baseball team. The Baums became prominent social figures in Aberdeen, and their prospects should have been rosy. Unfortunately, events were brewing to challenge this optimistic beginning.

The Dakota Territory had experienced droughts in 1886 and 1887; then more normal conditions returned in 1888. But drought conditions re-emerged in 1889, and with a depressed national economy, a decline in new residents, and an out-migration of recent arrivals to the area, Baum's business faltered and the bank foreclosed on the Bazaar. The store closed its doors on January 1, 1890.

Baum's Bazaar was sold on January 18, 1890, in a foreclosure sale to Baum's sister-in-law Helen, who reopened it as H. L. Gage Bazaar a month later. Helen Gage had a more focused and tightly managed vision for the store's operation and made the business a success for the next twelve years. This failed business venture was another lesson in humility for Baum.

Referring to the 1889–1890 period and the socioeconomic stresses on the citizens of Aberdeen, particularly those involved in farming and ranching, Baum joked ironically that horses should be outfitted with green goggles so they might be fooled into eating wood shavings—giving a premonitory hint of the green glasses to come in his first Oz book. On November 2, 1889, North and South Dakota were granted statehood (becoming the thirty-ninth and fortieth states), and the Baums' third child, Harry Neal Baum, was born on December 17, 1889. There were good reasons for the Baums to give Aberdeen and South Dakota another chance.

Baum decided to buy a weekly newspaper (*The Dakota Pioneer*) from John H. Drake, a Syracuse transplant who had recently been appointed US consul to Kiel, Germany, by President Benjamin Harrison. After changing the name to *The Aberdeen Saturday Pioneer*, Baum published his first issue on January 25, 1890.

Baum became a jack-of-all-trades in his work with *The Pioneer*. He assisted with the production and delivery of the paper and wrote editorials and other articles; collected news, legal notices, and other items of local interest; and imported nationally syndicated columns and related pieces (so-called boilerplate) to incorporate into the eight-page weekly editions. His wide-ranging editorials covered many areas but emphasized such topics as women's suffrage (he was a staunch supporter of a ballot measure required by the 1889 South Dakota constitution for women to get the vote), Prohibition (although no teetotaler, Baum believed the state constitutional clause should be obeyed to give the experiment a chance), and issues of faith and reason (highlighting theosophical principles and sharing concerns about traditional religious practices and beliefs). In one of his editorials, he commented that theosophists "are the dissatisfied of the world, the dissenters from all creeds. . . . They admit the existence of a God—not necessarily a personal god. To them God is Nature and Nature God"—thereby distancing himself from traditional Christian beliefs.

Baum's editorials often supported the Republican Party, endorsing Republican candidates and causes; he wrote articles on South Dakota's economic development, and he promoted the expansion of diverse industries in the state, influenced in part by Edward Bellamy's popular 1888 book *Looking Backward, 2000–1887*. His editorials were full of advice on improving human relations, particularly between men and women.

Many critics have suggested that the original Oz story is an allegorical treatment of the populist movement of the 1890s, which begs the question, was L. Frank Baum a populist? To answer this question requires a familiarity with populism and the formation and development of the Populist Party during the 1890s. I offer a brief review here, with apologies to those who are already well informed on this topic.

Starting in the 1870s but most importantly in the 1880s, through farmer-based organizations and alliances, the seeds of populism were sown. The movement revolved around government's role in controlling large industries such as communications and transportation (especially railroads) and fostering programs that would benefit agrarian interests. One populist proposal promoted government-backed loans for storehouses of grain and other farm commodities, which would allow the government to recover costs. The idea for such a program may have originated in Russia. A second "pre-populist" idea called for a graduated income tax to generate revenues that could be used for public works projects like those initiated many years later during the Franklin Delano Roosevelt administration.

These ideas represent a centrist, or socialist, approach to government, which was controversial at the time. But the most visible and contentious component of populism (beginning formally with the Independent Party, which became the Peoples' and then Populist Party in the early 1890s) was the issue of the financial backing of US currency. The commonly accepted standards—gold; silver and gold, called bimetallism; and government or fiat backing, based on the overall wealth of the nation—were thought to have differing effects on the economy, especially in the agrarian West. Although the US currency was based on a bimetallism standard from 1832 to 1900, the Populists and their progenitors blamed the "functional gold standard" of the 1890s as a reason for tight money policies and dollar deflation that had had disproportionally adverse effects on farmers and their allies in the West. William Jennings Bryan's passion for the "gold vs. bimetallism issue" including his famous "Cross of Gold" speech and his nomination for president by the Democrats and Populists in 1896 to oppose William McKinley, were extraordinarily important political events, as were Bryan's defeats in his bids for the presidency in 1896 and 1900. Ultimately, populism and the Populist Party were co-opted by the Democratic Party, and the populist movement eventually became progressivism that would become the mark of the Democratic Party and other political movements well into the twentieth century.

During Baum's time as editor-owner of *The Pioneer*, there's a strong indication from his writings that he was a Republican, although in today's parlance he was perhaps a middle-of-the-road type. Some authors have suggested that Baum was a Democrat and that he may even have voted for Democrat William Jennings Bryan in the 1896 and 1900 elections. Others argue that Baum was more of a skeptical independent at best. In any case, the Populist Party and the populist movement were such colorful and important events of the early 1890s that Baum wrote about them, especially in his "Our Landlady" column, a regular feature of *The Pioneer*.

There is one serious blot on Baum's editorial record that occurred at a difficult time in US government–Native American relations when Aberdeen and its surrounding area seemed to be threatened by violence from the death of Sitting Bull and the tragic events of Wounded Knee. In editorials he published on December 20, 1890, and January 3, 1891, Baum wrote about the need to consider the "total annihilation of the few remaining Indians" and a "total extermination of the Indians." Some of Baum's biographers believe these isolated though admittedly abhorrent remarks were the result of terrible misunderstandings and local hysteria. No further evidence of such egregious racial hatred appears in Baum's documented life or works. However, it must be said that Baum was not above using racial stereotypes, slurs, epithets, and ethnic humor in some of his later published works.

In his "Our Landlady" column, which resembled similar columns in magazines and newspapers in the northeastern United States, Baum crafted a brilliantly satiric piece that ran forty-eight times during the life of his newspaper. He based it on the life and times of a fictitious semiliterate widow, Mrs. Sairie Bilkins (with its play on the word *bilking*), who runs a boarding-house in Aberdeen. Baum portrayed dinner table conversations among her boarders: a cigar-smoking loan agent, referred to as the colonel; a store clerk, Tom, whose rent was always in arrears; and a softhearted physician. Their conversations not only included references to sociopolitical events of the day, particularly in the new state of South Dakota, but also contained veiled and at other times direct references to citizens of Aberdeen and their foibles and frailties. Baum's depictions used insightful humor, puns, and other plays on words. The column highlighted Mrs. Bilkins's propensity for malapropisms, misunderstandings, and misstatements. Her dialect, reminiscent of that of Mark Twain's characters in *The Adventures of Huckleberry Finn*, was patterned after accents that might well have been heard among Aberdeen's northern or central European (especially German) immigrants of the time. Baum used this fanciful column not only to comment on important contemporary events and movements—the economic hardships of farmers, women's suffrage, and populism—but also to poke gentle fun at the Aberdeen citizenry. In short, "Our Landlady" was a tour de force and offers a preview of Baum's creative talents that would be revealed in his later literary works.

There was a commercial aspect to the "Our Landlady" column, but its effectiveness in engaging community interest was a hint of Baum's future vocational efforts, as was Baum's storytelling, with which he entertained his children and their friends at home, in the Bazaar, and around town. He relished including his children in his love of national holidays—putting on amateur fireworks displays on the Fourth of July and dressing up and appearing as Santa Claus at Christmas family parties and gatherings.

The drought of 1889 persisted through 1890, causing continuing economic hardship to the citizens of Aberdeen, although there was a slight upturn around the time of the traditional fall South Dakota State Fair, which was held in Aberdeen. The illusory optimism of the economic turnaround may have inspired Baum to begin a new venture—the magazine *The Western Investor*. Unfortunately economic conditions soured toward the end of 1890, primarily because of the failed wheat crop, and Baum was forced to cease publication of the new magazine. At the same time, subscriptions to *The*

Pioneer diminished by more than half. Baum was discouraged by the failure of the women's suffrage amendment to pass in the November elections, the defeat of local Republicans to Independent candidates, and the selection of Pierre as the state capital over Aberdeen, among other cities contending for the designation. Economic conditions continued to worsen into the New Year, and Baum's financial woes were compounded in February 1891 when he had surgery to remove a tumor from under his tongue (he was an inveterate cigar smoker). In short, he needed to decide soon where his future fortunes might lie.

After looking into potential opportunities in Minneapolis and Chicago during March and early April of 1891, Baum chose the latter. In the meantime, Maud gave birth to their fourth and last child on March 24, a son they named Kenneth Gage Baum. On April 4, Baum closed down *The Aberdeen Saturday Pioneer* and planned for the relocation of his family to Chicago.

The move came at an extraordinary time in Chicago's history. Just a little more than a year before (on February 24, 1890) the US Congress had voted (on the eighth ballot) to accept Chicago's bid to be the site for the World's Columbian Exposition of 1893, meant to commemorate the four hundredth anniversary of Christopher Columbus's discovery of America. Chicago won over New York, St. Louis, and Washington, DC. The boisterous verbal expression of "Chicago spirit" was given credit for the city's successful bid to host the Exposition—as a result of which New York editor Charles Anderson Davis referred to Chicago as "the Windy City." (If you're like me, you thought the nickname had more to do with Chicago's notorious winds, especially in winter, rather than its outspoken boosterism.) In any case, the exposition was a plum. One of the major reasons Chicago was chosen to host the event was the city's impressive rebuilding and civic development efforts after the Great Fire of 1871. With the nod from Congress, the pressure was on to produce an outstanding fair. Expectations were high because of the extraordinary performance of the French, who had produced the *Exposition Universelle* in 1889—the fair that unveiled the Eiffel Tower.

In the early 1890s, Chicago was the second most populous city in America (after New York) with more than one million residents. But, as importantly, Chicago had transformed its mercantile wealth (to a large extent from its stockyards and meat-processing industries) into a booming metropolis, built largely through the creativity and engineering prowess of some of

America's architectural giants, including Daniel Hudson Burnham, Frederick Law Olmsted, John Wellborn Root, and somewhat later, Louis Henry Sullivan. In the 1890s, Chicago could claim the first skyscraper (the Montauk building), an elevator suited for tall buildings (developed by Chicago native Elisha Graves Otis), and other innovations that set a pattern for American urban development throughout the coming century. Chicago had heeded the advice of Columbian Exposition builder Daniel Burnham, who was fond of admonishing his contemporaries, "Make no little plans; they have no magic to stir men's blood."

With these developments, who could imagine a more exciting place than Chicago in the America of 1891? Frank Baum was drawn to the city, but it was far from easy for him to find employment there. After inquiring about work at nine local newspapers, he landed a job as a reporter and editorial writer for the relatively new *Chicago Evening Post*. At this time he joined the Chicago Press Club, where he maintained a membership well into his forties—a membership that would provide him crucial contacts for his later creative work.

He began at the *Post* on May 1, but he soon found that the pay (eighty dollars a month) was not enough to support a wife and four children. That fall he took a job as a china buyer for the department store Siegel, Cooper & Company. This job provided him a segue to a position as traveling salesman for the prestigious fine china and glassware firm of Pitkin and Brooks, a job Baum held from about 1893 to the late fall of 1897.

In preparing for his interview for the Siegel, Cooper & Company buyer's position, Baum read widely about china, impressing his prospective employers with his knowledge of their wares. In a similar manner, Baum later turned sales calls into opportunities to be creative. Baum's years of record sales during his time with Pitkin and Brooks were attributable largely to his interactions with the company's store-owner customers, helping them develop displays that would enhance their retail sales. These efforts later led Baum to create for china buyers and sellers a new journal, a book-length guide, and a national association.

Though he didn't relish being on the road away from his family for much of the week, Baum managed to put this time to good use. Despite the boredom of traveling (mostly by rail); unpacking, displaying, and repacking samples; and staying in hotels, Baum found himself creating themes, puns, and other ideas for his future writing. As Michael O. Riley notes in his discussion of Baum's life as a salesman, "While they [other salesmen] whiled away the tedious time on the train with card games and idle talk, he watched the landscape fly by and let his imagination wander freely; while they gathered around the stove in the hotel and told stories no lady could hear, he sat by himself and jotted down nonsense verse and stories with which to amuse his children when he returned home."

From the earliest days of his marriage to Maud, Baum was a devoted husband, father, and close friend to her relatives and friends. He had a reputation for gentleness, kindness, even-temperedness, and love for his wife and his children. He left disciplining the children to his wife, since he was never able to scold or correct his boys. Baum was kind and gracious to his mother-in-law, Matilda, who stayed in the Baums' home for extended periods during the family's years in Chicago. Matilda Gage greatly influenced Baum's writings, both by her direct encouragement ("You'd be a damn fool if you didn't write those stories down!") and through conversations full of interesting information on diverse subjects.

The biographical record reveals that the Baum family frequently visited the Columbian Exposition, which had many displays related to technological progress (the Electricity Building and the Movable Sidewalk, for example) and prospects for the future. The exposition included international buildings such as the Brazilian Building, the German Building and Castle, and the Temple of Luxor, along with cultural features like the Art Palace, the Café de la Marine, and the Women's Building, all of which would later influence the first illustrator of Oz, W. W. Denslow, in his portrayal of the Emerald City in the 1900 book.

No description of the World's Columbian Exposition, however, should omit mention of its main feature: the Ferris wheel, conceived by George Washington Gale Ferris, a native of Illinois, a practicing engineer educated at the Rensselaer Polytechnic Institute in Baum's home state of New York, and a business owner in Pittsburgh. The Ferris wheel was the tallest structure at the exposition. Outfitted with thirty-six cars, the bicycle-style wheel with spokes rotated on a seventy-ton forged steel axle forty-five feet long and thirty-two inches in diameter. The wheel itself was 250 feet in diameter. The individual cars were the size of a railroad passenger car and held sixty people each. Overall, the Ferris wheel was the largest device of its kind ever crafted until that time. When fully loaded, the Ferris wheel took 2,160 people for an unforgettable ride, and one of its passengers was likely to have been Frank Baum.

In considering the influences on Baum's later work, another aspect of the Columbian Exposition and its related events deserves mention: the Parliament of Religions was held in September of 1893 in the Hall of Columbus and attracted thousands of people. Attendees came to hear more than 190 representatives from ten of the world's most prominent religions: Buddhism, Christianity, Confucianism, Hinduism, Islam, Jainism, Judaism, Shintoism, Taoism, and Zoroastrianism. Although it was dominated by English-speaking Christian representatives (152 of 194), one Hindu representative, Swami Vivekanada from India, captured the rapt attention of the opening day (curiously, September 11, 1893) with these words:

> Sectarianism, bigotry, and its horrible descendant, fanaticism, have long possessed this beautiful earth. They have filled the earth with violence, drenched it often and again with human blood, destroyed civilization and sent whole nations to despair. Had it not been for these horrible demons, human society would be far more advanced than it is now. But their time is come; and I fervently hope that the bell that tolled this morning in honor of this convention may be the death-knell of all fanaticism, of all persecutions with the sword or the pen, and of all uncharitable feelings between persons wending their way to the same goal.

With his exotic presence and charisma, the Swami became an instant celebrity, with reports of his appearances at parliament reported widely in the popular press. At parliament's end, the Swami went on a three-year American tour from coast to coast and north to south, making him a rich man. His message (embodied in the metaphor of "the Golden Path") was this: "The philosophy of yoga tells us that the root cause of all our sorrows and sufferings is loss of contact with our true self." He taught that the "true self" comes alive through four great yoga meditations: Jnâna Yoga—receiving wisdom, Bhakti Yoga—opening the heart to compassion and love, Karma Yoga—gaining courage for action, and Raja Yoga—achieving serenity and inner harmony.

The Swami's message was enormously influential on Baum's conception of the characters and the themes of the Oz stories. In addition, Baum's early years in Chicago when he was in his thirties and early forties were probably the most significant years of his life, presaging the beginning of his career as a serious author.

Advancing through His Forties

Baum worked on fairy tales and manuscripts of children's tales from his earliest days in Chicago, but his first successful publication came as the result of a contact he made through his membership in the Chicago Press Club. Opie Read, a Western novelist and a member of the Press Club, introduced him to Chauncey L. Williams, a principal of the Way & Williams publishing firm. This association led to the acceptance and publication in 1897 of Baum's *Mother Goose in Prose* (with illustrations by the soon-to-be-famous American illustrator Maxfield Parrish). One of the stories in *Mother Goose in Prose*, "Little Bun Rabbit," introduced an attractive farm girl, Dorothy, who could communicate with animals. This character may well have served as a model for the Dorothy of the 1900 Oz story. Baum's conversion of classic children's poems ("Three Wise Men from Gotham" and "The Woman Who Lived in a Shoe," for example) into the twenty-two prose stories he crafted for *Mother Goose in Prose* came from his Aberdeen storytelling sessions that continued in Chicago. These story times, enlivened by treats for the children, gave Baum the opportunity to test his ideas and fairy tales, including those that would later appear in *The Wonderful Wizard of Oz*.

In the late 1890s, in addition to his writing for children, Baum worked on another project that came from his experience with theatrical productions, from the Bazaar in Aberdeen, and from his most recent work as a salesman. In 1897 he convinced Chauncey Williams to become his financial backer and to serve as the publisher of a new journal, *The Show Window: A Journal of Practical Window Trimming for the Merchant and the Professional*, which was launched on November 1, 1897. The aims of *The Show Window*, as the journal noted editorially, were to "teach the techniques of window trimming to its readers . . . [and] to raise the vocational standing as well as the standards of window trimmers." In his typically enthusiastic headlong manner, Baum also proposed the formation of a National Association of Window Trimmers of America. He served as secretary of the organization in 1898.

The Show Window was a success, and Baum's articles for it served as the basis for his full-length book that has the extraordinary title *The Art of Decorating Dry Goods Windows and Interiors: A Complete Manual of Window Trimming, Designed As an Educator in All the Details of the Art, According to the Best Accepted Methods, and Testing Fully Every Important Subject*. After the sale of the journal in 1902, *The Show Window* went on for many years in two other guises, most recently as *Display World*, which was published from 1922 to 1973.

About the time of the publication of *Mother Goose in Prose*, Opie Read introduced Baum to another Chicago Press Club member, the illustrator William Wallace Denslow (W. W. Denslow, as he called himself). Although Denslow was the same age as Baum, the illustrator had an established reputation, having contributed to Mark Twain's *A Tramp Abroad* (1880), P. T. Barnum's *Dollars and Sense* (1890), and many other commercial ventures. Denslow—bohemian, cynical, vain, and morose—was of a very different background and temperament than Baum. Nevertheless, they hit it off—at least for the first few years of their association.

Baum and his new friend and colleague collaborated on five projects. The first, *By the Candelabra's Glare*, was a collection of personal verses Baum wrote, printed, and published in limited edition (the ninety-nine copies were distributed primarily to family members, friends, and colleagues). Denslow contributed two illustrations of the several by other artists that appeared in the book.

Their second and more extensive collaboration was *Father Goose: His Book*, which was patterned after *Mother Goose in Prose* but contained Baum's original nonsense rhymes rather than work derived from well-established tales. This joint effort was unique in its artistically integrated character. Poets and playwrights, with talents Baum could also claim, look for the complementary blending of the meaning with the sound of words as they create their works—since these creative works are read or spoken aloud. As Katharine M. Rogers notes: "Baum and Denslow developed *Father Goose* together. Denslow found inspiration for comic illustrations in Baum's verses, and sometimes Baum invented verses to fit pictures Denslow drew." Theirs was a fruitful collaborative effort, despite their differing perspectives and character traits.

The *Father Goose* book, issued in September of 1899, was an artistic and commercial success. More than seventy-five thousand copies were sold by the end of the calendar year. However, there's one aspect of this work we should note: in the *Father Goose* book, as well as in some later works (*The Woggle-Bug Book* [1905] for instance), Baum uses the "N-word" along with commonly accepted stereotypical slurs of his time for people of Chinese, Irish, Swedish, and Arab descent. As Richard Tuerk notes in his important 2007 study, *Oz in Perspective*, "Baum seems to have accepted unquestioningly the prevalent racism of his day."

Baum has also been accused of sexism in his writings, including *The Wonderful Wizard of Oz*. This claim, however, seems spurious given his special relationship with his mother-in-law, pioneering women's rights advocate Matilda Gage, and his strong advocacy of women's rights in his *Aberdeen Saturday Pioneer* editorials. It's important to remember Baum's theosophical ideas, such as the inalienable rights of all people, regardless of race, religion, gender, or class. Tuerk says, "Baum's racism and the apparently justified assumption that his contemporary adult readers shared his racism, then, provide present day adult readers . . . insight into real people who read and wrote in America during the early part of the twentieth century." Context not only helps us assess earlier behavior and prejudices that are currently unacceptable but also reinforces the commitment of enlightened people today to the principles of equality, equity, and appreciation for diversity.

It's interesting to consider the many projects Baum was involved in about the time of his creation and publication of *The Wonderful Wizard of Oz* in 1900. Here's just a partial list:

- *Adventures in Phunniland*, originally copyrighted in 1896, later retitled and published in 1900 by R. H. Russell, New York, as *A New Wonderland*, with illustrations by Frank Verbeck; it was reissued in 1903 by Bobbs-Merrill as *The Surprising Adventures of the Magical Monarch of Mo and His People*. This work consists of fourteen fantastic stories set in a magical land where the ground is made of maple sugar, rain comes in the form of lemonade, and popcorn serves as snow.

- *Mother Goose in Prose*, published in 1897 by Way & Williams, Chicago

- *By the Candelabra's Glow*, self-published in 1898

- *Father Goose: His Book*, published in 1899 by Hill in Chicago

- Two "learning the alphabet" books: *The Army Alphabet* and *The Navy Alphabet*, with illustrations by Harry Kennedy, published in 1900 by Hill in Chicago

- *The Songs of Father Goose, for the Home, School and Nursery*, a third collaboration with Denslow, who created illustrations for the music written by Alberta N. Hall with lyrics adapted from Baum's rhymes, also published in 1900 by Hill

- *The Art of Decorating Dry Goods Windows and Interiors: A Complete Manual of Window Trimming, Designed As an Educator in All the Details of the Art, According to the Best Accepted Methods, and Testing Fully Every Important Subject*, published in 1900 (*The Show Window*, Chicago)

- Six poems published in the *Chicago Times-Herald*

- Eleven articles, essays, and short stories published in various magazines and the *Chicago Times-Herald*

- Several miscellaneous works or short pieces that may have been published but in unknown venues

Baum worked for Pitkin and Brooks from 1893 to 1897; from 1897 to 1900 he was involved with the publication of *The Show Window*—a job he gave up to devote full time to his work as an author of fiction. Baum's creative productivity during 1895–1900 was extraordinary, but it was soon to accelerate after the publication of the first Oz book.

Years after the publication of *The Wonderful Wizard of Oz*, Baum claimed that its inspiration came to him suddenly during one of his storytelling sessions for his sons and their friends: "I was sitting on the hatrack in the hall, telling the kids a story and suddenly this one moved right in and took possession. I shooed the children away and grabbed a piece of paper that was lying there on the rack and began to write. It really seemed to write itself. Then I couldn't find any regular paper, so I took anything at all, even a bunch of envelopes." The sudden inspiration and early draft material may well have come to Baum as he said, but the elaboration and illustration of the text—collaboratively with Denslow—occurred over many months. It's now generally believed that ideas for *The Wizard* whirled around in his head for at least a few years, beginning perhaps as early as 1893.

Baum finished the manuscript for *The Wonderful Wizard of Oz* on October 9, 1899, and mounted the nub of a pencil he used to write the work on paper. He framed the resulting collage, to which he added, "With this pencil I wrote the Ms. [manuscript] of 'The Emerald City.'" He ultimately abandoned his original title *The Emerald City*. In fact, he considered several titles for the book, including *From Kansas to Fairyland*, *The City of the Great Oz*, *The City of Oz*, *The Fairyland of Oz*, *The Great City of Oz*, and *The Land of Oz*. Baum's final choice was influenced in part by the superstitious publishing notion that the name of a gem in a book's title spelled commercial doom.

Several publishers rejected Baum's manuscript, and although Baum and Denslow were discouraged, they were not defeated and soon came to an agreement with the George M. Hill Co. to produce the book, albeit with a considerable subsidy by the author and illustrator.

At the time of the book's acceptance and publication, George Hill had in his employ Frank K. Reilly as production manager and Sumner S. Britton as secretary and head salesman, both of whom subsequently formed Reilly and Britton (after the failure of the Hill Company in 1902), which would publish many other of Baum's books.

That Baum set the book in Kansas may have reflected his aversion to offending his relatives and former friends in South Dakota, despite the fact that the landscape in *The Wizard* is similar to Aberdeen's. In fact, there is considerable evidence that the Kansas of Oz *was* South Dakota (particularly eastern South Dakota), which Baum knew well.

There have been various suggestions about the origin of the name Oz, but the most likely seems to be that when a child in one of Baum's storytelling sessions asked him the name of the fabled country where the magical tales took place, he happened to glance up and see a file drawer in the room that was labeled "O-Z." Some of his biographers dispute this story, but in an interview in the *Los Angeles Mirror* on January 27, 1904, Baum said it was true, that the name of the Land of Oz came from this fateful sighting of the file drawer label.

The creative, integrated meshing of Denslow's illustrations—coordinated with colors associated with the various lands in Oz—and Baum's text resulted in a classic work that has been described as forthright, all-American, having a sense of reality (in sometimes unreal places), and written in a non-condescending, informal, and humorous manner.

Although *The Wonderful Wizard of Oz* didn't sell as briskly as the *Father Goose* book, it was considered a success with sales of more than thirty-seven thousand copies in the first fifteen months after publication in September 1900. Mostly positive reviews of the book appeared in more than two hundred publications. Through vision, perseverance, and a basic belief in themselves, Baum and Denslow had a winner. These traits that ensured the success for *The Wonderful Wizard of Oz* would serve Baum well throughout the remainder of his life.

With the publication of *Father Goose* and the first Oz book, the first evidence of strain in the relationship between Baum and Denslow appeared, in part because the reviews seemed disproportionately to credit Denslow for the success of the works. Nevertheless, their collaboration continued through the development of Baum's next book, *Dot and Tot of Merryland* (1901), a travelogue-type of fairyland story involving Dot, the daughter of a well-to-do family who is sent from her urban residence to a country estate called Roselawn (after Baum's boyhood home). At Roselawn, Dot meets a boy named Tot, and the two of them plan a river journey in a small boat. During their adventure, they meet up with an assortment of odd characters and a kindly queen who makes Dot a princess and Tot a prince. The queen accompanies the princess and prince on the remainder of their boat journey, which ends where it began, at Roselawn. The book is not among Baum's best works, but it reinforced his and Denslow's reputation, which may have added to the tension between them. It's been suggested that they had now come to the point where their individual fame made it possible for them to go separate ways. Perhaps more important, however, were Denslow's apparent attempts to overshadow Baum through his cover illustrations for the *Father Goose* work and his assumption of credit for previous joint work in comic pages that he published under his name alone in the *New York World* in 1900.

The emerging rift between Baum and Denslow was complicated by the fact that they held separate copyrights for their respective contributions to their joint works. Their disagreements over credit came to a head in 1901 during the development of a musical stage version of *The Wonderful Wizard of Oz*. From this point on, Baum would not allow a copyright arrangement like the one he and Denslow had used in their five collaborative efforts. Baum resolved that his future works would be copyrighted exclusively in his name, with due credit given to illustrators.

With the critical and commercial success of *Father Goose* and *The Wizard*, Baum began thinking about new projects. Although he didn't attempt at this time to create sequels to *The Wonderful Wizard of Oz* or his other recent works, Baum wrote and published two other books in 1901 that added to his reputation: *American Fairy Tales*, which received mixed reviews, and *The Master Key: An Electrical Fairy Tale*.

The Master Key was inspired by Baum's fascination with science fiction and the exhibits celebrating the marvels of electricity he had seen at the 1893 World's Columbian Exposition. He dedicated the book to his second son, Robert Stanton, who was mechanically and scientifically adept. The book's hero is a boy named Rob Joslyn (Matilda Gage's maiden name was Joslyn), whose experiments with electricity and electrical devices cause him to conjure up a genie—the Demon of Electricity or Slave of the Master Key. The Demon offers Rob three wishes weekly, for three weeks, for gifts of devices run by electricity. These prescient gifts include oral tablets that can be used to take the place of daily meals (like food product concentrates, such as those used in NASA space missions); a stun tube to incapacitate would-be attackers for an hour (like modern TASER devices); an anti-gravitational wrist device, affording its wearer instant travel throughout the world (as in *Star Trek*); a Garment of Protection that foils weaponry (similar to modern bullet-proof vests); and an Automatic Record of Events that portrays in real time events happening around the world (like our twenty-four-hour television and Internet news services).

The boy's foolish use of his gifts, typified by his not working with the scientific community to ensure their adoption for the good of humanity, and the good and bad aspects of modern technological marvels were two themes Baum developed in this work. The double-edged sword theme, the positive and adverse effects of technological advances, permeates many of Baum's books.

During his work on the books published in 1901 and 1902, including *The Life and Adventures of Santa Claus,* Baum renewed his interest in theater. He collaborated with Chicago composer Paul Tietjens on a musical stage production of *The Wonderful Wizard of Oz.* Denslow was also involved in this project, and the three men spent time during the summer of 1901 at a summer home the Baums bought the following year in the resort area of Macatawa Park, along the shore of Lake Michigan, six miles west of Holland, Michigan. Baum was in charge of the libretto, Tietjens the music, and Denslow the costumes and scenic effects. An account from Baum's son Robert indicates that there was a notable esprit de corps among the three, and in September 1901 Baum and Tietjens copyrighted a script for the production. Later, however, there were contentious discussions among the trio about royalty splits. These negotiations signaled the end of any future collaboration between Baum and Denslow.

At this juncture, at the time of the family's purchase of the Macatawa summer home, Baum suffered from an attack of Bell's palsy, an acute paralysis of facial nerves. Despite his physicians' advice to rest, Baum designed and crafted stained-glass objects for their new home, built several pieces of furniture, and engaged in many other interior decorative efforts. In the end, the Baums christened their retreat "the Sign of the Goose," since its purchase was made possible through revenues from the *Mother Goose* and *Father Goose* books.

As Baum would soon learn, it was one thing to write and copyright a scenario for a musical, but quite another to see it produced faithfully according to the script. Collaborations among writers, producers, and directors often wreak havoc on an original text. So it was with the musical extravaganza of the Oz stage production. Producer Fred R. Hamlin (the son of the wealthy John Hamlin, who ironically made his fortune on sales of the quack cure-all, Wizard Oil), and director Julian Mitchell liked many of Baum's ideas, including making the Scarecrow (played by Fred Stone) and Tin Woodman (played by David Montgomery) the lead comedic focal points of the production, but they implemented many other changes to Baum's work, making the play more commercially viable. The stage production included many new conspiracies and romantic entanglements: they featured a grown-up Dorothy; instead of Toto, they brought in a cow named Imogen; they introduced Lady Lunatic (Cynthia Cynch) to Munchkin land, along with Sir Dashemoff Daily, who falls in love with Dorothy; they brought in a Snow Queen, who helps end the poppy field–induced intoxication through the use of a snowstorm (which was later copied in the 1939 *Wizard of Oz* film) along with armies of young, attractive chorus girls. They made other changes during the show's lengthy run. Katharine M. Rogers comments, "The resulting extravaganza was not a dramatization of *The Wizard of Oz*, but a hodge-podge of spectacular effects, comic romantic entanglements, slapstick routines, puns and wisecracks."

The show opened on June 16, 1902, at the Grand Opera House in Chicago. It was a great success, and performances continued in the Windy City for fourteen weeks before the play was taken west. The extravaganza played at several venues in Canada, then went on to New York's Majestic Theater, where it played for several months. Performances took place in various locations across the United States until 1911, and according to one report, the play generated revenues close to $5.5 million; Baum's royalties are said to have exceeded $100,000, an extraordinary sum in the first decade of the twentieth century.

Some have suggested that Baum was initially upset by the changes to his Oz book in the ultimate stage production. However, he eventually accepted the fact that what works in one medium didn't necessarily turn into profits in another.

Along with his published works during 1901–1903 (including *The Enchanted Island of Yew* in 1903), Baum continued working with Paul Tietjens and others on theatrical adaptations of his books, most of which were either unsuccessful or unproduced. During this period, however, he received hundreds of letters from children asking questions about Oz and pleading for more stories about the enchanted land. From the outset, Baum dutifully answered the children's letters and finally succumbed to the young fans' solicitations by writing *The Marvelous Land of Oz*, which was published in 1904. The book was dedicated to the stars of the *Wizard of Oz* stage production—Fred Stone and David Montgomery—and is the only Oz book in which Dorothy does not appear. The book's hero is a small boy, Tippetarius, or Tip, who in the end becomes Princess Ozma. The sequel includes many new characters that play roles in Tip's adventures, including an animated sawhorse (Saw-Horse); the wooden "stick man" Jack Pumpkinhead; Mombi the Witch, who raises Tip; a female General Jinjur and her all-woman army; Pastoria, a former ruler of Oz; Mr. H. M. (Highly Magnified) Woggle-Bug; T. E. (Thoroughly Educated); and others. Baum's new illustrator was Philadelphia-based John R. Neill.

It seems Baum wanted a varied and sufficiently eccentric sequel that might inspire a new stage production to rival the success of the *Wizard of Oz* production. As in his youth, he was once again enamored of the theater. On June 29, 1902, he told a *Chicago Sunday Record-Herald* reporter:

> Few people can understand the feelings of an author who for the first time sees his creations depicted by living characters upon the stage. Scarecrow, the Tin Woodman and the Cowardly Lion were real children of my brain, having no existence in fact or fiction until I placed them in the pages of my book. But to describe them in pen and ink is very different from seeing them actually live. When the Scarecrow came to life on the first night of *The Wizard of Oz* I experienced strange sensations of wonder and awe; the appearance of the Tin Woodman made me catch my breath spasmodically, and when the gorgeous poppy field, with its human flowers, burst on my view—more real than my fondest dreams had ever conceived—a big lump came into my throat and a wave of gratitude swept over me that I had lived to see the sight. I cannot feel shame at these emotions. To me they were as natural as the characters were real. Perhaps all authors have like experiences, and if so, they, at least, can sympathize with me.

It's widely believed Baum had no intention of creating a series of Oz sequels. He intended to produce just this one follow-up book for additional income and perhaps a "theatrical hook." But Baum seemed destined to find his greatest fulfillment in his role as an author. As he approached his fiftieth year, he was a prolific writer, publishing many titles in his own name as well as books under pen names such as Schuyler Stanton, Laura Bancroft, Captain Hugh Fitzgerald, and Edith Van Dyne. At this period in his life he could claim significant publishing success and somewhat mixed success in the theater, including a failed stage production of a Woggle-Bug play in Chicago. But there was the irrefutable evidence of his success through his royalties; the Baums had become wealthy.

As a result of their newfound wealth, the Baums toured the American Southwest, including New Mexico, Arizona, and California from San Diego to San Francisco, in February and March of 1904. During this trip, they discovered the Hotel del Coronado in San Diego—built in 1888 by Elisha Babcock and H. L. Story as a lavish seaside resort.

Beginning in 1905 and continuing through 1908 (excepting 1906), the Baums established new patterns in their lives. They would leave Chicago in January, stay at The Del until late March or early April, move on to their summer home at Macatawa Park in Michigan, and return to Chicago in November. During these years, Baum would write every morning and early afternoon, and while they were at The Del, he would play golf in the late afternoons.

The Fifties and Beyond—His Last Thirteen Years

By Baum's fiftieth birthday he was at the top of his game both personally and professionally, and he and Maud now ventured on what would be their only excursion abroad. The trip took nearly five months. They sailed from New York through Gibraltar, had extended stays in Egypt and Italy, and enjoyed shorter stops in Switzerland and France (mainly in Paris). For Baum, it was a working trip. For Maud, it was a vacation, and she corresponded with friends during the journey. In 1907 Baum edited and published a collection of her letters from the trip as *Other Lands Than Ours*, which included a preface he wrote and sixteen photographs he took of their travels.

It's difficult to determine which of Baum's books published between

1906 and 1908 were written during the Baums' 1906 travels, but it's clear from Maud's letters that Frank was writing all the time during the trip. At least three books, two in the Aunt Jane's Nieces series and *The Last Egyptian: A Romance of the Nile*, were clearly linked to his international experiences.

The 1906–1908 period was extraordinarily productive for Baum. During this time, he published twenty-three books and several other shorter works, including *John Dough and the Cherub*, which has some intriguing characters but is today ranked among Baum's weaker works because of its lack of a strong story line and quest theme. His apparent motive was to create a work that could be transformed into a comic stage production.

Most importantly, the 1906–1908 period witnessed the release of the third Oz book, *Ozma of Oz: A Record of Her Adventures with Dorothy Gale of Kansas, the Yellow Hen, the Scarecrow, the Tin Woodman, Tiktok, the Cowardly Lion and the Hungry Tiger; Besides Other Good People Too Numerous to Mention Faithfully Recorded Herein*, written in large measure because of the urgings of his young readers, who wanted to learn more about the Oz mythology and specifically more about Dorothy, who was left out of the second Oz book. In the appendix, I've summarized this second Oz sequel and the remaining eleven sequels Baum wrote during 1907–1919.

Avid Oz readers and critics alike expressed great appreciation for *Ozma of Oz*. In it Baum created a work with an ending that would lend itself to further sequels, including the third Oz sequel, which he had already been under contract to complete by 1911.

In 1908 Baum finished and published what some critics have called his strangest and darkest Oz sequel, *Dorothy and the Wizard of Oz*, the fourth book of the Oz series. It isn't clear what motivated Baum to write such a dark book, but the year of its publication was another turning point in his life, which began with his production of *Fairylogue and Radio-Plays*.

If we could turn back the clock and attend a performance of *Fairylogue and Radio-Plays*, we would probably leave the theater remarking how effectively Baum used multimedia. Picture a *Fairylogue and Radio-Plays* performance: Baum is dressed in an elegant white tuxedo-like suit (with silky lapels and woolen pants); he stands before a large screen. Near him is a live orchestra. The orchestra begins the action by playing music composed by Nathaniel Mann. Baum begins his portion of the production by talking about the Land of Oz; at appropriate times in the script, imagery from lantern slides or movie clips appears behind him on a screen. The lantern slides are hand colored, as are the film clips, produced initially in black-and-white and then sent to Paris for coloring. Since these movie clips predate "talkies," the only sounds we hear come from Baum's voice and the orchestra. Live actors made up as Oz characters appear at appropriate points in the script. The characters emerge from a prop that looks like a large book on stage, the cover of which is opened by actors dressed as fairies. As each character steps forward, an identical depiction in a film clip is shown simultaneously. This "movie trickery" was only one of several incorporated into the film clips—all Baum's conception.

The slides and film clips for the first half of the *Fairylogue and Radio-Plays* show were developed from Baum's books *The Wonderful Wizard of Oz*, *The Marvelous Land of Oz*, and *Ozma of Oz*, giving him a rich cast of characters. The second half of the show was devoted to segments from *John Dough and the Cherub* and Baum's then latest work, *Dorothy and the Wizard of Oz*. During intermission, Baum would sign and sell books to members of the audience.

The idea for *Fairylogue and Radio-Plays* apparently came to Baum when he attended a presentation of his son Frank Joslyn's after his travels to Asia (mainly to the Philippines), in which lantern slides illuminated the spoken descriptions. Baum was struck with the idea that a "fairylogue" could be analogous to a travelogue, and during the production of *Fairylogue and Radio-Plays*, he asked Frank Joslyn to participate.

Fairylogue and Radio-Plays opened in Grand Rapids, Michigan, on September 24, 1908. It went on to several venues in the Midwest and East before going to the Hudson Theater in New York City that December. Reviews of the show were uniformly positive. Critics were impressed with Baum's presence, his speaking voice, and his creativity. They said the show would delight children and parents alike.

Despite great reviews and the energy and enthusiasm Baum poured into the production, it quickly became a financial disaster. Ticket revenues and book royalties collectively were not nearly sufficient to meet the high cost of producing and performing *Fairylogue and Radio-Plays*. The show closed just before Christmas of 1908.

To pay off some of his debts, in 1910 Baum contracted with Selig Studios for the production of four of his properties—*The Wonderful Wizard of Oz*, *The Marvelous Land of Oz*, *John Dough and the Cherub*, and *Dorothy and the*

Scarecrow in Oz—which the company turned into one-reelers. He also worked on several plays in collaboration with Chicago and New York theater moguls and Chicago author Edith Ogden Harrison. At the same time, Baum turned over to the trustee of his estate the publishing rights to *The Wonderful Wizard of Oz* and several other earlier properties until his debts were cleared, at which time the rights would revert to Maud, to whom Baum had transferred all intellectual property rights, around 1904.

Baum's creative genius burned brightly from 1908 to 1911. During this period, he created or published fifteen books, along with a host of other writing projects, including articles, poems, scripts for movies and plays, and an opera. Most notably, Baum advanced the Oz book series with the fourth and fifth sequels, *The Road to Oz: In which is related how Dorothy Gale of Kansas, The Shaggy Man, Button Bright, and Polychrome the Rainbow's Daughter met on an Enchanted Road and followed it all the way to the Marvelous Land of Oz* in 1909 and *The Emerald City of Oz* in 1910. The latter is especially notable in that Dorothy writes a letter to Oz fans in which she announces there can be no more Oz books because Glinda has cast a barrier of invisibility over the Land of Oz to protect it from future intrusion. Baum invented this device—along with a preliminary comment in *The Road to Oz*—to extricate himself from the Oz series so he could go on to other interests. As Richard Tuerk notes, by 1909 Baum "really does seem to have been growing tired of writing Oz books." But his loyal readers would persuade Baum to reverse his decision not long after the 1910 declaration.

Once again faced with financial challenges, the Baums economized by giving up their homestead in Chicago, eliminating the sojourns to The Del, selling the summer home at Macatawa Park, and moving to rented quarters in Los Angeles. Despite these efforts, Baum had to declare bankruptcy in June of 1911. In 1910 Maud had spent some of her inheritance from her mother and borrowed additional funds to buy a lot in Hollywood on Cherokee Avenue, one block north of Hollywood Boulevard. There the Baums built a comfortable if not lavish home and christened it Ozcot. Baum designed and constructed several lighting fixtures for the dining room, using emerald green glass, emblematic of his favorite mythical city. As he had done for their Macatawa home, he did some other interior decorating as well.

Woody Allen has said, "If you're not failing every now and again, it's a sign you're not doing anything very innovative." Frank Baum's failures in business ventures were almost legendary, despite his focus on the future, in which he routinely looked for new challenges in the literary and theatrical worlds. Fortunately, he was able to place great faith and fiduciary responsibility in the capable hands of his beloved spouse, who had intuitive and astute financial sense and exhibited careful management practices. With Maud's guidance, Baum's fortunes turned around again during the last decade of his life.

The last ten years of Baum's life were turbulent times for the United States, both in domestic affairs, reflecting the socially progressive movements of these years, and internationally, with the advent of World War I. Baum would have been aware of President Theodore Roosevelt's (1901–1909) impact on social reform (trust-busting, food and drug quality, conservation) and on the culture and standing of the United States internationally (mediating the Russo-Japanese War, ordering the construction of the Panama Canal), along with his run for a third term in office on the Bull Moose ticket of 1912.

Baum would also have been aware of Roosevelt's successor, William Howard Taft (1909–1913), and of Woodrow Wilson (1913–1921), the wartime president who continued the mission of progressive government begun under Theodore Roosevelt.

Other than continuing problems with revenues and debts, the Baums' early life in Los Angeles was marked by great enjoyment and satisfaction. Baum was always good at handling ambiguity, an important aspect of life in Oz, especially in the character and actions of Dorothy. With some effort, the Baums managed to maintain the appearance of opulence and good fortune. They lived in a sizable two-story house that had large living and dining rooms, a library, a solarium, a well-equipped kitchen, and a maid's quarters, all on the first floor. The second level consisted of four bedrooms and a sun porch. On the large lot were a summerhouse and sundial in the backyard gardens, an aviary nearly twelve feet in diameter, a goldfish pond, a chicken yard (where Baum raised Rhode Island Reds), a two-car garage, and an archery range in the side yard.

The Baums frequently entertained in their home, and Frank enjoyed rich foods. He joined the Los Angeles Athletic Club and its companion group, the Lofty and Exalted Order of Uplifters, and became a serious gardener and accomplished amateur horticulturist through study and experimentation, winning more than twenty prizes for his flowers in shows all across Southern California.

Baum's routine at Ozcot was to alternate writing with physical activity. After rising around eight o'clock and having a full breakfast, he would, given satisfactory weather, move into the garden to work on his prize-winning dahlias and chrysanthemums. After a one o'clock luncheon he would either go to a second-floor bedroom he had transformed into a writing workshop or sit in the garden where he would write in longhand. As his third son, Harry Baum, noted, "He would make himself comfortable in a garden chair, cross his legs, and with a cigar in his mouth [because of his weakening heart, at this time in his life he would chew on rather than smoke cigars], begin writing whenever the spirit moved him. . . . When he had finished an episode or adventure, he would get up and work in his garden. He might putter around for two or three hours before returning to his writing." Baum revised his work only once, by typing a final version (entirely with two fingers) from his handwritten original draft. He was not a careful editor of his manuscripts, and there are many errors in his published works—misspellings, inconsistencies, incoherencies, and incongruities in the Oz sequels, which occurred in part because of the somewhat haphazard way Baum composed and typed these books and in part because they weren't subjected to careful copyediting. From the inconsistencies in different works (death versus no death in Oz, claims of no violence versus horrors that appear in several sequels) and the unfortunate reversal of geography in the Oz maps, it's clear that Baum didn't take the time to compare the elements in various sequels to ensure consistency and coherence with the original story. However, without modern data processing and computerizing of texts, it would have been difficult for Baum (or anyone for that matter) to remember all the stories he had concocted on his journey through Oz, from his original book through its thirteen sequels.

Given the stresses of his weakened financial position and the move to California, Baum's productivity from 1909 to 1911 was nothing short of spectacular. In 1912 his productivity fell off, although he managed to publish four books and was putting the last touches on the sixth Oz sequel, *The Patchwork Girl of Oz*. In its introduction Baum describes how he has reestablished communication with Dorothy in the Emerald City via wireless tele-graph (as one of his readers suggested) so he can learn of new stories, thus making the new sequel possible.

The Patchwork Girl of Oz was not as financially successful as *The Emerald City of Oz*; however, it was popular enough to encourage Baum's publisher to accept further titles in the Oz series. *The Patchwork Girl* was notable for another reason: it reintroduced the quest theme (with the modification that heroes—at the end—do not necessarily return home but stay gloriously in Oz), which many believe ultimately made *The Wonderful Wizard of Oz* and the 1939 Oz film so extraordinarily popular. The new work introduced at-tractive new characters to Oz readers, particularly the Patchwork Girl, whose evil mistress (Margolotte) wished her to remain a humble servant girl. Instead she became an outspoken, quick-witted, ingenious, and self-confident young woman. In this book, Baum mixed old and new characters, and through their travels, he reinforced the geography of Oz in the minds of his readers. The diverse elements in the *Patchwork Girl* book meshed well with Baum's reemerging interest in the world of theater and the rapidly emerging film industry.

Baum's resurrected interest in theater led to a new musical production, *The Tik-Tok Man of Oz*, which he developed with the famous American com-poser Louis F. Gottschalk. The new work opened in Los Angeles in March of 1913 and continued with performances in San Francisco and Chicago, among other venues. The show received mixed reviews and made only mod-est profits, but this didn't dampen Baum's enthusiasm for the performing arts.

Baum was excited about the prospect of contributing to the impressively evolving film industry in Hollywood. He hoped that the medium of film might offer him greater control over Oz productions, and he doubtless fan-tasized about seeing many of his literary creations in theater or films.

In 1914, as he had done so often throughout his life, he jumped headlong into a new venture. With significant backing ($100,000) from members of the Los Angeles Athletic Club, Baum and his fellow Uplifters (including prominent Hollywood personages such as Harold Lloyd and Sigmund Rom-berg), planned, organized, and implemented the development of The Oz Film Manufacturing Company, which had a film distribution office in New

York City run by Frank Joslyn. Baum was president and Louis Gottschalk vice president. Baum designed the complex and extensive facility, which incorporated a sixty-five-by-one-hundred-foot stage and concrete tanks for filming water scenes.

The company began operations in 1914, producing three movies: *The Patchwork Girl of Oz, His Majesty the Scarecrow of Oz*, and *The Magic Cloak* (based on Baum's 1905 book *Queen Zixi of Ix*). Only the first of the three films was shown publicly because of the actions of the major Hollywood studios to stymie the efforts of budding film companies. The Motion Picture Patents Company, which owned Thomas Edison's film projection patents, filed suit against The Oz Film Manufacturing Company for patent infringement. It would be many years before the US Supreme Court would declare the business of cross-sectional control illegal, but Baum became a victim of a system that suffocated the innovation and development of newcomers to the film industry. Baum may also have been a victim of public taste, which didn't give books or films with juvenile themes the same respect as adult-themed works.

If there was one positive aspect for Baum of the closure in 1915 of The Oz Film Manufacturing Company, it was that he had none of his own money tied up in the venture and thus wasn't faced with another devastating financial loss. No doubt Maud had had something to say about the ill-fated company's fiscal arrangements.

Because of his defeat in the film industry, Baum turned to other kinds of productions in the performing arts, such as the yearly satirical plays for which he wrote scripts and lyrics (the music was by Louis Gottschalk), for the Uplifters. He wrote such plays as *Stagecraft, or The Adventures of a Strictly Moral Man* and *The Uplift of Lucifer, or Raising Hell*. Baum derived great pleasure from these efforts and enjoyed his association with the Uplifters.

Baum continued to be prolific from 1914 up to his death in 1919. However, his health deteriorated markedly during this time. His early heart disease, his too-rich eating habits, and his deleterious use of tobacco finally caught up to him. He experienced symptoms of full-blown coronary heart disease and congestive heart failure. He also suffered periodic gall bladder attacks and a recurrence of trigeminal neuralgia, which causes intense pain to the face including the eyes, forehead, and jaw. Nevertheless, in the five years before his death, he wrote and published nineteen books, movies, several plays (including those in the Uplifters' Minstrel series), articles, and a poem. His new books included sequels in the Oz series—one a year: *Tik-Tok of Oz*, 1914, which contains a reversal of the map of Oz; *The Scarecrow of Oz*, 1915; *Rinkitink of Oz*, 1916, which was criticized for incoherence; *The Lost Princess of Oz*, 1917; *The Tin Woodman of Oz*, 1918, a revision of the Tin Woodman's story about his love for a Munchkin girl and her relationship with the Wicked Witch of the East rather than an "unsavory woman"; *The Magic of Oz*, 1919, which incorrectly designates the Shifting Sands Desert as the Deadly Desert; and *Glinda of Oz*, 1920, which uses the inexplicable term "Krumbic Witch." (Synopses of all of these works appear in the appendix.)

The last four Oz sequels—particularly the last two, *The Magic of Oz* and *Glinda of Oz* (both published posthumously)—are most important to our understanding of Baum and his final themes: Ozma's dedication to love and service to her people through outreach and understanding; Glinda's Council of State, which parallels the League of Nations (formed in 1919), the precursor to the United Nations, and promotes discussion and negotiation among those who wish to serve their constituents well; and the similarities between the Flathead and Skeezer war (*Glinda of Oz*) and World War I, with citizens on both sides of the conflict suffering whether they are ruled by an elected leader or a dictator. Through the dictators Su-dic and Coo-ee-oh, Baum displays a prescient notion of many disastrous twentieth- and twenty-first-century tyrants and their exploitation of their people—whether the officials are elected (for example, Mugabe in Zimbabwe) or come to power through coercion and force (Stalin, Hitler). Other of Baum's last themes dwell on the risks and benefits of science and technology and the importance of animal welfare.

L. Frank Baum died on the morning of May 6, 1919, having seen neither *The Magic*

of Oz nor *Glinda of Oz* published. But these works, along with his many other literary and creative works and deeds, are likely to have been in his mind during his last days. For as T. S. Eliot has so famously noted:

> We shall not cease from exploration
> And the end of all our exploring
> Will be to arrive where we started
> And know the place for the first time.

Just before he died, Baum expressed his lifelong devotion to Maud. Taking his last breaths on May 6, he said to her: "Now we can cross the Shifting Sands."

II

The Way of Oz and Learning

3

Learning: An Integrated Perspective

I perceived that you had acquired some knowledge . . . from others, and that you were perplexed and bewildered; yet you sought to find out a solution to your difficulty. I urged you to desist from this pursuit, and enjoined you to continue your studies systematically; for my object was that the truth should present itself in connected order, and that you should not hit upon it by mere chance.

Moses Maimonides (1135–1204), Talmudic scholar, philosopher, physician, and author of the broadly influential text *The Guide for the Perplexed* (1190)

The "connected order" Maimonides recommended in *The Guide for the Perplexed* is relevant to our twenty-first-century world, including his timeless advice to "observe, study and seek understanding." Division chief Rufus E. Miles, Jr. (1910–1996), of the US Bureau of the Budget, coined the aphorism that "where you stand is where you sit," meaning that your position in an organization shapes your views, whether they are related to personnel or program development, philosophic perspectives or policies. In the context of this book, you might consider a modification of Miles's law, that where you stand is related not only to where you sit but also to what you read, what you write, what you communicate, and what you experience.

Experiences come alive when they involve interactions among all the elements of learning, particularly as they relate to learn-

ing and wisdom, because learning in and of itself does not lead to wisdom. The eminent psychologist Robert Sternberg wrote:

> Wisdom is defined as the application of knowledge, successful intelligence, and creativity toward the achievement of a common good through a balance among intrapersonal, interpersonal, and extrapersonal interests, over the short and long terms, through the infusion of positive ethical values. That is, wisdom is the skill of using one's intelligence, as well as one's knowledge, for a common good, today and long into the future.
>
> Why is wisdom so important? Just consider what can happen when great intelligence is not accompanied by wisdom. Hitler, Stalin, and many other crackpot despots have shown how different intelligence and wisdom can be.

In short, your understanding—your learning—involves many activities. Indeed, effective learning comes from your integrated efforts that mutually reinforce and support combinations of learning, loving, and serving—wisdom, heart, and courage—guided by a focus on the future and humility.

In other words, learning is integral to and supported by what I have termed the Way of Oz.

Living in the Integrated Learning Model

You may know the work of jazz composer and performer Michael Franks, whose lyrics integrate learning and understanding from many fields. In Franks's song "A Walk in the Rain," for example, he writes, "I lived in a painting by Renoir" (*Barefoot on the Beach*, 1999). Consider this line and Pierre-Auguste Renoir's painting the *Luncheon of the Boating Party*, which portrays a group of friends who have been out in a boat, now enjoying a convivial lunch on the balcony of a restaurant in a Parisian suburb. Renoir, portraying his friends and acquaintances as subjects, depicts a variety of people and their interactions. One man is engaged in contemplation. Others are engaged in conversations with several people or with one specific other. The scene offers a metaphor for learning, which can occur through a combination of activities, from isolated study to dialogue to group interactions, in a safe environment that is diverse in composition, talent, and ambience.

The interactions among the people in the Renoir painting also suggest interdisciplinary learning, akin to that which occurred between the illustrator W. W. Denslow and writer Frank Baum when they collaborated on *Father Goose: His Book* and *The Wonderful Wizard of Oz*. Many other interdisciplinary interactions in more modern settings have led to unusual opportunities for learning and understanding, including discoveries and developments that would not have been possible otherwise. Consider the blending of mathematics and electrical engineering that resulted in an entirely new field of study—computer science. The interactions of biological, chemical, medical, and physical scientists and engineers made possible many recent discoveries in nanoscience, from electronic devices (nano-iPod devices) to new medicines (chemotherapeutic or imaging agents bound to polymeric nano-particles along with binding proteins to target cancer cells) to new industrial lubricants.

Earlier we considered how Frank Baum made productive use of his time as a traveling salesman for Pitkin and Brooks, when instead of playing cards, he began to think about the creative ideas he later put into his children's books. Baum seized opportunities for learning that created new vocational or avocational pursuits for himself, such as his chicken breeding or store window dressing, both of which were interests he reinforced by developing journals and professional associations.

Many other notable people have mixed vocational and avocational interests. Imagine the several years (1902–1909) of Albert Einstein's most creative period in developing his theories of relativity, when he also worked at his "day job" at the patent office in Bern, Switzerland. Or consider Nathaniel Hawthorne (1804–1864), who conceived four novels, including *The Scarlet Letter*, while he performed his routine duties in the Customs House in Salem, Massachusetts. Charles Ives (1874–1954) composed many of his avant-garde musical works while he was employed as an insurance clerk and co-founder of a school for training insurance agents; Edgar Lee Masters (1868–1950), a Chicago attorney, managed at the same time he was practicing law to write biographies, novels, and poetry; Alexander Borodin (1833–1887), a chemist, composed music as a divertissement, including the music for the opera *Prince Igor*, his symphonic poem *In the Steppes of Central Asia*, and his Second (*Heroic*) Symphony; and Gary Larson (1950–), the cartoonist extraordinaire and creator of *The Far Side*, used his early love of animals and his background in biology to inform many of his hilarious cartoons.

As you consider the integration of the components of learning, you might ask yourself the following questions:

- How can reading objectives and choices be dovetailed with other learning efforts such as writing and communicating?

- What approaches for preserving key ideas from reading can serve other learning activities?

- How can writing be integrated with other learning activities?

- How can interdisciplinary and other cross-disciplinary efforts be used to enhance oral communications?

- How can the benefits of travel be used for learning?

- Are there available substitutes to travel, such as service learning, digital video conferencing, video gaming, or virtual reality programs?

- How can synergy among the learning modes and their integration meet short-term and long-term goals?

I will address the first six questions in the following chapters on learning. The last question involves some broad-based perspectives, which prompt a consideration of three individualized aspects of integrated learning: personal environmental scanning; selective volunteerism, teaching, and self-reinforcing learning; and continuing and lifelong learning and professional development.

Personal Environmental Scanning

Personal environmental scanning is assessing your near- and long-term career goals and the education you'll need to reach your goals. Gifted and talented students in grades eight through twelve (and others) will need an understanding of the future labor market to determine their near-term goals about college-level and postgraduate education. Here are some facts and predictions to think about:

- In the 1940s and 1950s only 10 percent of jobs in the United States required college education.

- In 2008, 38 percent of all American jobs required college preparation.

- By 2018, 85 percent of all jobs in the United States are projected to require a college degree.

- From 2008 through 2018, it is estimated that the percentage of jobs requiring a master's or doctoral degree will increase by more than 15 percent.

Earning a bachelor's degree is a critical consideration for all students; in some professions, earning a graduate degree is becoming just as important.

When Steven Sample, longtime president of the University of Southern California, addressed a recent class of incoming freshmen, he predicted that beginning students "will still be working in their nineties, either by choice or necessity. And as a result, they will need to reinvent themselves and their careers several times during their lifetimes. Most of them will have three or four different careers. Not jobs—but careers. And essentially all of them will eventually go on to some kind of postgraduate education, many of them more than once."

President Sample went on to describe the learning environments and experiences necessary to develop the type of baccalaureate degree that will serve the educational needs of twenty-first-century professionals:

Professor of theater Dorothy Chansky and professor of mechanical engineering Michelle Pantoya speak about their integrated scholarship.

- Breadth with depth: a rigorous curriculum containing multiple majors or sets of minors

- Interdisciplinarity: programs that blend links and connections among disparate fields, as, for example, among institutions and programs that afford undergraduates opportunities to participate in research and original scholarship

- Opportunities to serve society: implementing service learning courses, providing a milieu in which the ethos of serving and learning are integrated

- A global perspective: the creation of study-abroad programs, both short and long term; and opportunities to earn degrees from two or more institutions, even continents apart

Fortunately, there are institutions that offer the richness in opportunity President Sample describes, and you can find out about many of them through Internet resources, including the Voluntary System of Accountability (VSA) Program, which requires participating public institutions to prepare objective and standardized College Portraits of Undergraduate Programs, which are published on the VSA website and updated regularly.

For practicing professionals with prior college experience and one or more degrees, personal environmental scanning takes on different dimensions. For example, imagine yourself as a professional in an entry-level position within a nongovernmental agency (NGO) such as the American Cancer Society or Boys & Girls Clubs of America. Imagine what it might take for you to move into middle management or upper administrative positions in the same or similar organizations. By thoughtful observation or scanning, you can assess the management skills of supervisors. You will note that successful NGO managers need grant-writing skills, which require a proficiency in communication as well as an understanding of the scientific, social, cultural, economic, and legal aspects of the projects being proposed. No one can know all these things, but anticipating your move up a potential career ladder will suggest to you new areas for study, which will be enhanced through selective volunteerism, teaching, and self-reinforcing learning.

Selective Volunteerism, Teaching, and Self-Reinforcing Learning

Environmental scanning can lead not only to an understanding of areas for study but also special opportunities for learning. These opportunities, more often than not, are created rather than happening by chance. For example, imagine yourself as an NGO professional seeking opportunities to head a project that requires the preparation of a significant grant proposal. By volunteering for such a task, you've created an opportunity that could represent some risk but that provides great impetus for you to learn and succeed.

It's a common belief among students that college or university professors are experts in their fields. This is frequently untrue. University instructors, especially new ones, are often only a few steps ahead of their students. For beginning instructors, it becomes a powerful intellectual growth experience to learn the subject material as well as how to present it to students with varying abilities. Many if not all students have taken classes from teachers who weren't adequate to the task. To be a successful teacher requires study, keen intuition, understanding, and a belief that teaching can become an important route to personal learning. J. William Fulbright, a five-term US senator and author of the legislation that led to the Fulbright Fellowship Program, began his professional career in the late 1930s as a teacher in the law school at George Washington University. Of this part of his professional life, he said, "I learned much more teaching than I did in school."

In our knowledge-based world, most professionals need to acquire teaching skills before they can reap the benefits of such skills. Whether you're heading a team or committee or in charge of a project or a proposal, you'll soon realize the learning opportunities and benefits of teaching skills. Teaching, in this context and taken in its broadest sense, represents one of the most rewarding aspects in professional life. These skills are invaluable to all professionals in the twenty-first century. If you've been employed, in either public or private enterprise, you know how often professionals are called on to teach, whether giving instruction in new software, personnel or policy issues, or safety and health matters.

Mathematics professor Jerry Dwyer speaks about integrating teaching, learning, and service.

Continuing and Lifelong Learning and Professional Development

Well-qualified and effective professionals know how vital continuing and lifelong learning are to professional development. Agencies so value continuing education that they frequently assume the costs of professional development for their employees.

Education and training at its best is guided by a mentor and includes formal education as well as a personalized and integrated plan for lifelong learning.

The concept of mentoring comes from the great Homeric work *The Odyssey*. You might recall that when Odysseus went off to the Trojan wars—a journey that lasted twenty years—he left the responsibility for the personal and intellectual growth of his son, Telemachus, in the hands of his trusted friend, Mentor. The concern for and dedication to the holistic development of others has thus come to be known as mentoring. As a potential twenty-first-century professional, you should seek a mentor who knows your career goals and is dedicated to your success in the context of the goals of a firm, institution, or organization.

A good mentor might begin with "Opulente's prescriptions" set forth by English professor and academic leader Blaise Opulente in 1965: "As an academic diagnostician I would like to prescribe three remedies as a possible corrective to the illnesses of excessive specialization, humanistic isolationism, an enfeebled emotional life, and spiritual starvation. These are (1) continuing education; (2) the reading of seminal books; and (3) the development of an interdisciplinary attitude toward science." This was sage advice in 1965 and is still relevant today.

Continuing education takes place in myriad ways:

- In short courses and workshops: These may be available in your place of employment or through private firms, community colleges, and university-based continuing education operations. Wise professionals make sure to find out if their employers pay for such opportunities.

- Through professional organizations and societies: Professionals should have an opportunity each year to attend and contribute to a regional or national meeting of a professional association or society, through presenting a paper, participating on a panel, or taking part in an equivalent activity. Employers might assume all or some of the cost of these efforts.

- Via retreats or other internal meetings: Supervisors often assign speaking or reporting roles as a prelude to work- or project-oriented retreats and other organized company meetings. These represent good opportunities to reinforce your understanding of the vision, mission, and goals of your place of employment.

• In cross-training: These opportunities broaden your understanding of different segments of an organization by formal and informal training in areas you don't normally deal with on a day-to-day basis. Cross-training benefits employers, who can then count on employees' new skills when they must reassign duties if employees are ill or leave the organization. The individual who is cross-trained is also better positioned for promotion to a job with expanded responsibilities.

• In certificates and advanced degrees: Many colleges and universities offer certificates for the completion of an integrated series of courses, at both undergraduate and graduate levels, in areas such as drug and substance abuse counseling. You should judge the quality of such offerings on a case-by-case basis, keeping in mind the overall reputation of the offering institution. But when considering certificate and degree programs offered through institutions of higher education, keep in mind two caveats: the college or university should be accredited through one of the major regional accreditation agencies such as the Northwest Commission on Colleges and Universities or the Southern Association of Colleges and Schools Commission on Colleges (www.ed.gov/offices/OPE/accreditation/regionalagencies.html), and the specific degree programs should be approved through one of the dozens of agencies or associations (www.chea.org/) that accredit programs—from art and design to business to health services administration to occupational therapy to veterinary medicine.

• In self-directed learning: Various nonprofit corporations, professional societies, and commercial publishers have developed Internet-based courses and multimedia materials that can be useful adjuncts to professional development programs. For example, the American Management Association offers classroom (programs scheduled nine months in advance in cities across America), onsite (programs arranged through an agency, institution, or organization), and live online classes with titles such as "Making the Transition from Staff Member to Supervisor," "Management Skills for New Managers," "Performance Management: Minimizing Stress, Maximizing Effectiveness," and many others.

In addition to formally organized course work, there is a wealth of free digital resources (print, audio, and video, or combinations of these) that you can access and download to your computer, personal digital assistant (PDA), or iPod. The iTunes Store, for example (as of 2010), has partnered with more than two hundred colleges, universities, and affiliated units in the United States, Australia, Canada, New Zealand, and countries throughout Europe to provide access to a host of valuable materials. Many of the offerings are complete courses, lectures that can be downloaded for sequential viewing and study. There are also research and outreach (study abroad) ventures, along with materials that are just plain fun. The opportunities for learning through related digital source material are endless.

I'll address Opulente's second prescription—the reading of seminal books—in the next chapter. But Opulente's third prescription—related to interdisciplinary orientation—merits our attention here.

Professionals educated at the baccalaureate or post-baccalaureate level generally have a degree in a specific disciplinary area. Thus, in software development, for example, you find computer science and software engineering professionals who have focused educational backgrounds. Although a concentration in their particular fields is important, greater success will come to those who have significant interdisciplinary background and understanding. More varied skills and an expanded outlook are required of the computer science or software engineering professional who wishes to enter management. Continuing education may be necessary to make this advance. The computer science major may also realize how important his or her liberal arts background may be. There is, for example, the engineering professional who graduated from a prestigious engineering program in a major research university and then found himself working for a large multinational company in Paris, France. After some time on the job, he called back to one of his former professors asking ruefully: "Everyone here talks about opera. Why didn't you teach me about opera?"

In addition to learning and integrating understanding across disciplines, a concept Edward O. Wilson refers to as "consilience," you will find that Opulente's third prescription involving interdisciplinary interactions supports creative endeavors. You will want to keep Opulente's principles in mind in your other areas of learning such as reading, writing, and communicating.

4

Learning and Reading

Reading keeps me alive.

Enrico Fermi (1901–1954), physicist,
director of the Manhattan Project, University of Chicago

On his hospital deathbed, the great US immigrant physicist Enrico Fermi asked a young but obviously overworked resident, Robert Coles, if he had any time to read. Coles admitted that he was exhausted by his medical duties and didn't have time for general reading. But that would change, in part because of this conversation Coles had with the dying physicist who found solace in reading Tolstoy's novella *The Death of Ivan Ilych*. The lesson of reading for lifelong learning remained with Coles, who has become a well-known author himself.

As we've seen, reading played a pivotal role in Frank Baum's life. From his sickly childhood, during which reading became a surrogate for physically demanding games and group sports, to his adult life as an author, reading was a backdrop and guide to his creative life.

If you were to reinvigorate your intellectual life with a renewed commitment to reading and learning, perhaps as a freshman in college, what might you do? Here are four suggestions that merit consideration:

- Develop effective reading skills

- Attend a college or university that has adopted a campus or campus-community common reading program

- Develop reading strategies that support lifelong learning goals

- Integrate reading with your intellectual, professional, and personal development goals

Effective Reading Skills

Mortimer J. Adler and Charles Van Doren, in their highly effective primer on reading both expository and imaginative writing, *How to Read a Book*, note the following: "The art of reading . . . includes all of the same skills that are involved in unaided discovery: keenness of observation, readily available memory, range of imagination, and, of course, an intellect trained in analysis and reflection." The approaches and skills you should develop to gain the most from reading are based on the premise of your becoming an "analytical reader" who (for expository writing) can effectively articulate the nature of any given work (theoretical or practical) and offer a short description of its content, its organization, and the author's success in posing a problem or problems. As an analytic reader, you should be able to interpret key words, propositions, and arguments, and elaborate solutions. In addition, you should be able to offer a fair and precise critique of the work, assessing whether it is accurate, informed, logical, and complete, with regard to its subject. For the reader of imaginative literature, Adler and Van Doren espouse the importance of classification and summary, and they recommend, especially for novels and plays, total immersion (if possible, a first reading of the work at one sitting), followed by an analysis of the strength and coherence of the work, in addition to "living mentally" through the characters and experiences in the text to determine the work's plausibility.

Beyond their general advice on reading, Adler and Van Doren offer specific insights on reading in disparate fields from the physical sciences and mathematics to the social sciences and the humanities and arts, including history and philosophy.

Reading Programs for Incoming Freshmen

In their quest to enrich social capital and build intellectual community, colleges and universities across America have adopted campus and campus-community common reading programs designed to benefit students, faculty, and staff. Typically, each year a faculty committee is charged with selecting a title that will create intellectual synergy, galvanize ideas, and stimulate conversation among academic community members across the disciplines. The book is assigned to incoming freshmen to read during the summer preceding their enrollment.

Such reading programs have become popular in the United States, with hundreds of programs now in place in four-year colleges and universities. A 2007 survey involving 126 respondent institutions suggests overwhelming satisfaction with campus-community common reading programs.

The choice of a book becomes an interesting question in itself; the selected work should meet important minimal criteria in order to have the intended galvanizing effect. The book should have literary merit; raise significant ethical questions of interest across disciplines; be relevant to contemporary society; broaden students' understanding of matters like diversity, social justice, and tolerance; and have implications for the broader community in order to promote the participation of public libraries, high schools, and other organizations.

Common reading programs offer unique opportunities for students to develop pathways for intellectual growth and community outreach, while providing stimulus for the development of social capital throughout a metropolitan or campus region.

Campus-wide or community-wide reading programs can serve several important functions, such as encouraging the exchange of ideas, fostering new appreciation for advancing reading "across the curriculum," broadening campus and community partnerships, generating informed discussion, and developing intellectual synergy.

There is great variety in the books colleges and universities choose for their common reading programs. In the 2007 survey, 109 of the 200 colleges that participated selected books different from

A dean of students and two undergraduate students comment on participation in a campus common reading program.

those of any other college, and only five books were chosen by more than five colleges. The most popular selections in 2007 were (in order of most chosen): *Mountains Beyond Mountains: The Quest of Dr. Paul Farmer, a Man Who Would Cure the World* by Tracy Kidder (the true story of a Harvard-educated physician who sets out to make a difference in impoverished countries such as Cuba and Haiti), *The Curious Incident of the Dog in the Night-Time* by Mark Haddon (the quest of a fifteen-year-old boy with Asperger syndrome to solve the mystery of the death of a neighbor's pet dog), *The Kite Runner* by Khaled Hosseini (a tale of treachery and redemption set in twenty-first-century Afghanistan), *Long Way Gone: Memoirs of a Boy Soldier* by Ishmael Beah (the autobiographical account of an adolescent boy caught up in civil war in Sierra Leone and Liberia in the mid-1990s), and *The Glass Castle: A Memoir* by Jeannette Walls (the memoir of a successful journalist who grew up in extreme poverty). As these selections suggest, the books chosen for campus common reading programs are often contemporary works of fiction and nonfiction, although some campuses in 2007 were reading older selections like Maya Angelou's *I Know Why the Caged Bird Sings*, Mary Shelley's *Frankenstein*, John Stuart Mill's *On Liberty*, and Truman Capote's *In Cold Blood*.

The same 2007 survey asked respondents, "What qualities do you look for in books for your program?" The top two responses were for books that students might enjoy reading and that stimulate discussion, followed by literary value, works that provide perspectives on diversity, and those that present intellectual challenges.

Many campus common reading programs list selection criteria on their websites and invite students, faculty, and staff to submit suggestions for books to be considered. Another important factor in selecting books for a campus common reading program is the availability of authors to make campus visits.

One of the most important reasons university faculty and administrators cite for establishing a common reading program is that it provides students with a shared intellectual experience or a "center of gravity" for thoughtful conversation that, ideally, will mirror the kind of informed discourse the college or university promotes. For this conversation to take hold, common reading proponents maintain, the program needs to be situated in a particular course or courses and, at the same time, transcend the boundaries of a single course or curriculum. The best common reading programs are integrated throughout different departments of the university, so that various programs, physical spaces, and even virtual spaces can participate in the ongoing conversation about the book.

One university with a particularly successful common reading program is the University of Wisconsin at Oshkosh (UWO), where it is a part of their larger Odyssey Program. At UWO, all incoming students, both first-year and transfer, read the same book, selected by a committee of faculty and academic staff members, during the summer before matriculation. In 2006 the book was *The Mercury 13: The True Story of Thirteen Women and the Dream of Space Flight* by Martha Ackmann; in 2007, it was Beah's *A Long Way Gone*. The book is the subject of the first assignments in freshman composition, which at UWO is taught in writing-based inquiry seminars. The UWO theater department mounts a back-to-school production of a play related thematically to the common text, and first-year students are required to see (and discuss and write about) the play during the second week of the fall semester. About fifty UWO faculty members agree to hold "conversations with faculty" events, fostering discussions not only about the common text but also about their particular fields and university intellectual life in general. UWO students are required to attend a small but specific number of these conversations. Where appropriate, different UWO departments offer panel discussions and public symposia on matters relevant to the common text. For example, during a year when the common reading was Alan Lightman's novel *Einstein's Dreams*, the physics department sponsored a panel discussion on quantum physics for nonscientists.

Reading is an important part of our lifelong learning process, but when it becomes an "event" for communities to engage in meaningful communion, a common reading program becomes something larger, with multilevel implications for building a community's capacity for intellectual growth and expansion.

Campus-wide or community-wide reading programs can serve as an important beginning to reading strategies that you should develop to support your lifelong learning goals.

Reading Strategies That Support Lifelong Learning Goals

Lifelong learning takes place in myriad ways—from self-directed reading and the study of digital materials available on the Internet, to workshops and membership and participation in professional organizations. The reading component should emphasize seminal books, augmented by forays into more modern expository and imaginative works.

Examples of seminal books include the Bible, the *Bhagavad-Gita*, Dante's *Divine Comedy*, Plato's *Republic*, Machiavelli's *The Prince*, Shakespeare's *Hamlet* and *Othello* (to cite just two of his renowned plays), Thoreau's *Walden*, and the *Tao Te Ching*. These are worth reading and rereading. You should also consider reading new works as well. Carl Sagan's Pulitzer Prize–winning *Dragons of Eden*, Joseph Campbell's *The Hero with a Thousand Faces*, Daniel Dennett's *Breaking the Spell: Religion as a Natural Phenomenon*, Jared Diamond's Pulitzer Prize–winning *Guns, Germs, and Steel: The Fates of Human Societies*, and E. O. Wilson's *Consilience* and *The Creation: An Appeal to Save Life on Earth* are among many modern works that help to illuminate the classics in interdisciplinary ways. Reading strategies that include interdisciplinary scholarship represent a key aspect of integrated learning.

Many students underline or highlight phrases in their textbooks as well as other works. These highlighted passages can become a source for quotes and ideas—appropriately attributed, of course. One strategy for the effective use of these reference materials is to capture them in a database that you can mine for future scholarly work. Digital databases available on the Internet are additional sources of material you can abstract or download for future reference, making certain you pay attention to intellectual property rights and avoid the pitfalls of plagiarism.

Integrating Reading Efforts with Intellectual, Professional, and Personal Development Goals and Efforts

Your integrated reading should include the following:

- Books, articles, multimedia, and Internet resources (including blogs) your teachers and colleagues suggest

- Book reviews in professional journals, newsmagazines, public radio or television interviews, and newspaper supplements

- Workshops and continuing education lectures, courses, and institutes offered through local higher education institutions or available online, such as through the iTunes Store and its partnerships with universities worldwide

- Near-term and lifelong career goals and objectives, especially those related to interdisciplinary studies and practices

Your personal and organized reading program can become a platform for your intellectual, cultural, and professional development, in the near and long term, leading to and including baccalaureate, interdisciplinary, and advanced professional or graduate degrees.

When you approach an interview for your first job, you should consider some preliminary reading that will not only enrich the experience for you but also might increase your chances of getting an offer. Few things impress prospective employers more than a job candidate's demonstration of an understanding of the institution and its sociocultural environment. A candidate who interviewed for an administrative post at a university in Amherst, Massachusetts, prepared for the visit by reading more than a hundred poems by Emily Dickinson, who had been a lifelong Amherst resident. You will remember also how Frank Baum made himself more competitive for one of his first jobs in Chicago through preparatory reading and study.

It is also helpful to know about recent financial and organizational changes in a prospective employer's firm or institution. There can be no better preparation for an interview than reading an inaugural or state-of-the-institution address by the organization or firm's chief executive officer, whether he or she is the president of a for-profit or nonprofit corporation or educational institution.

Strategies for reading effectiveness are an important component of your intellectual, personal, and professional development.

5

Learning and Writing

It's the writing, not being read, that excites me.

Virginia Woolf (1882–1941), English novelist, essayist, feminist,
member of the Bloomsbury group, and cofounder of the Hogarth Press

Reading is essential to integrated learning, but writing is its core, whether it is published or not. Writing not only forces a high level of involvement and commitment to learning but also is essential to organization and understanding.

The landmark book *Making the Most of College* by Richard J. Light (based on interviews with sixteen hundred Harvard undergraduates following several years of research in the late twentieth century) revealed that one of the keys to success in college is writing. Light's advice is to take as many courses with writing assignments as you can. Writing is a key to learning, not just in college but also throughout your life of the mind. The message of writing and its importance, however, is not new.

At the time of Frank Baum's move to Chicago, John Stuart Mill in 1891 wrote, "Hardly any original thoughts on mental or social subjects ever make their way among mankind, or assume their proper importance in the minds even of their inventors, until aptly selected words and phrases have, as it were, nailed them down and held them fast." More recently, Hillary Clinton's "understanding through writing" came from her weekly newspaper column in 1995, about which she said, "The exercise of putting my ideas on paper gave me a clearer sense of how to recast my role as an advocate within the [Clinton] Administration as I began to focus on discrete domestic projects that were more achievable than massive undertakings such as health care reform." American essayist Joan Didion said the same thing, more pithily: "I don't know what I think until I write it down." And best-selling novelist Amy Tan noted that "writing is a way of making sense of the world." Virginia Woolf said that for her, writing provided a level of satisfaction nearly unparalleled in the life of the mind.

Taking Notes and Spontaneous Inspiration

You might want to begin jotting down your spontaneous inspiration, ideas, or observations on paper or typing them or dictating them into a PDA or its equivalent and transferring them later to an archival database.

You should recognize that your spontaneous ideas and understanding ("eureka" or "aha" moments) may come to you at odd times, even in moments of clouded consciousness. Stories abound about insight that comes from the interplay of the conscious and subconscious minds. Julian Jaynes referred to the "3 Bs"—the bed, the bath, and the bus—as places where new insights might occur immediately before or after periods of rest and personal hygiene, or when traveling.

Jean-François Champollion's first insight into how to decipher the Rosetta Stone, which unlocked the key to understanding Egyptian hieroglyphics, occurred during a coach trip he took to Paris in 1807. Walt Rostow remembered precisely when he was inspired to write his 1983 book on economics: "At 3:00 on the morning of December 15, 1982, when sleep was light, I got up and outlined this book in just about the form that it now appears." A train trip stimulated Karl Folkers's imagining

the structural formula for penicillin: "On the train from Chicago to Madison, I sat there, looking out the window. . . . As I reviewed the evidence in my mind about the *beta*-lactam formulas, they sounded pretty good. . . . It was on that trip that for the first time in my participation in the penicillin program, that I really took the *beta*-lactam seriously." It was also on a train that J. K. Rowling, the creator of the Harry Potter books, was inspired. As she tells it, she had no pen or pad available, so "rather than try to write it, I had to think it. And I think that was a very good thing. I was besieged by a mass of detail, and if it didn't survive that journey, it probably wasn't worth remembering." Of course, the single mom who was in dire financial straits at the time *did* remember, and the story became *Harry Potter and the Philosopher's Stone* (or *Harry Potter and the Sorcerer's Stone*, its title in the United States).

Many creative people have conjured their best ideas while traveling. Oddly enough, just as the astronauts had to leave the earth to see its grandeur, our ideas for writing projects frequently come to us when we metaphorically abandon them or allow the passage of time for our ideas to emerge and develop.

The effects of the 3 Bs apply to thoughtful people, whether their background is in the arts, humanities, or sciences. An anthropologist noted that his inspiration came while he was bathing. Henry David Thoreau understood the influence of the 3 Bs: "Morning brings back the heroic ages. . . . Then there is least somnolence in us; and for an hour, at least, some part of us awakes which slumbers all the rest of the day and night."

Because of the unusual or unlikely times we are subconsciously receptive to new ideas, integrated learners keep pencil and paper or a PDA handy at all times—on the night table, in the bathroom, and in a travel carry-on bag. You can later mine your notes using the "find" functions of databases you have developed. You can also keep such notes and ideas in diaries or journals.

Writing Diaries and Journals

Diaries are daily accounts of our personal observations, reflections, and inspirational notations. Writing in a diary is an ancient practice of the famous and not-so-famous that can be found in many cultures from the second-century Roman civilization to medieval times and peoples in the Middle and Far East, continuing into nineteenth-century Europe and America, up to the present day in all countries around the world.

Perhaps the most famous modern diarist is Anne Frank, the young Jewish girl who hid from the Nazis with her family in an attic in Amsterdam, Holland, from June 12, 1942, through August 1, 1944. Frank's diary documents her thoughts and experiences while in hiding, ending when the family is captured and taken to a concentration camp (which led to her death); the diary represents a small but significant chapter in the Holocaust. One of the most riveting passages from Anne Frank's writing is this poignant comment: "It's really a wonder that I haven't dropped my ideals because they seem so absurd and impossible to carry out. Yet I keep them, because in spite of everything I still believe that people are good at heart."

Journals are sometimes considered synonymous with diaries, but the journal less often receives daily attention. Rather, it's used as a prelude to more formal writing, in which we save ideas or notes for future reference and use. You may recall that during his off hours as a salesman in the 1890s Frank Baum used a form of journal writing when he jotted down notes for the stories that became the basis for his *Mother* and *Father Goose* books and, of course, for *The Wonderful Wizard of Oz*. George Gershwin kept a "tune book," which served as an important source for his musical compositions in the 1920s and 1930s.

Journals are also commonly used to compile observations and thoughts that occur to travelers. A good example of such a journal is Maud Baum's *Other Lands than Ours*, published after the Baums' trip to Europe and the Middle East in 1906.

With today's technology, it's easy to develop diaries and journals using software templates; you can import graphics, audio and video clips, and links to the Internet in your diary or journal. Internet sites and social networking resources have become increasingly popular since the mid-1990s; they can help you organize, develop, and publish your diaries and journals or blogs. One caution here: intimate or potentially embarrassing online personal revelations or depictions can come back to haunt you, particularly since such information is easily accessible to potential employers.

Formal Writing

Active reading, note taking, and diary and journal writing often lead to formal writing, which Virginia Woolf referred to with excitement. Learning that begins with a "eureka" or "aha" moment often can result in articles, essays, letters, poems, and even book manuscripts.

Imagine, for example, that you have been keeping a diary for some time. You may have integrated your ideas into a journal—perhaps encouraged by a teacher. You might turn your diary or journal into shorter writing assignments for high school or college classes, or you might reach a personal "tipping point" in your journal writing when a theme or idea for a larger work emerges. You might want to begin an outline or other summary of the larger work and see where the effort leads. This commonly used next step is mainly applicable to expository works.

Some writers use topic or sentence outlines, or a combination of both, when they begin an expository work. Some prepare a very rough draft that serves as the basis for their outline, while others prefer to use an annotated outline containing reference notes and topic sentences. There is no right or wrong way. Find the method that works well for you; try different approaches in preparing outlines.

Regardless of the approach, a word processor can be useful in your writing: it allows you to easily make changes, adding and deleting text or transferring material from one section to another, or from one document to another. Word-processing software should contain options for spelling and grammar checks, along with dictionary and thesaurus features, as well as functions for creating tables and diagrams and importing graphics or other visual items.

After your outline is complete, consider having an advisor, mentor, or friend review it. It's a good idea to develop a writing network to review your outlines and manuscripts. Be sure to include in your network friends who write well; make a pact with them to review each other's work honestly. Also, colleges and universities have writing centers with professionals who assist with the art of writing. These arrangements can be immensely helpful.

Red Smith, the Pulitzer Prize–winning sportswriter, once said, "Writing is easy. You just sit at the typewriter, open a vein, and bleed it out a drop at a time." Professionals know that writing is challenging, but the best way to start is to start. Getting some words on your computer screen will encourage further efforts. Follow an outline, begin with a topic sentence (it's better to make it more general than not), and follow it with sentences that outline the paragraphs to come. The physical act of writing, whether by hand or typing on a computer, will help the creative process.

Write simply. Stick to straightforward subject-verb-object sentences. Avoid long-beginning adjectival phrases that the reader is forced to digest before coming to the subject of the sentence.

Keep most sentences under forty words. Produce contiguous sentences of varying lengths. Include summary sentences at the end of major sections. Once you've begun writing, try to get as much as possible composed without stopping. Worry about revision later.

Consider the discipline of a good writer. Writing each day, even if it is just for twenty minutes or so, provides motivation and coherency.

Try using your outline like a to-do list. After you've completed an emotionally exhausting section, reward yourself with a soft drink or fresh cup of coffee or tea, or a walk around the room. This allows you time to reflect on your accomplishment and to encourage your subsequent efforts. Use headings liberally. One accepted format is the following:

MAIN HEADING (usually centered)

Main Subheading

    Text begins here . . .

    Secondary subheading. Text begins here . . .

Use the active voice rather than the passive voice wherever possible. Try to inform, not to impress. Many people around the world, but especially Americans, have a tendency to try to sound important. The main faults in the writing of many Americans are verbosity and the excessive use of jargon. These failings can lead to problems with syntax.

Jargon includes confused, strange, technical, obscure, and often pretentious language. Technical words and acronyms should be used in scientific writing, but they should be properly defined. Avoid using a "word cartridge" instead of a simple word (for example, use "now" instead of "at this point in time"; use "some" instead of "in a number of cases").

Staff members and a student comment on the value of university writing centers.

With practice, your writing style can be improved. Some authors suggest writing as though you are talking to the reader (especially in nonfiction). Your "talk" must be grammatically correct with a minimal use of colloquialisms. This approach works best if you consciously try to speak clearly and well. And you need to choose your words deliberately, finishing each sentence.

Revision is an indispensable part of writing that is greatly facilitated by the use of word processors. Indeed, word processors have made inadequate revision, the bane of several of Frank Baum's Oz works, inexcusable.

The American author James A. Michener said that he retyped everything at least four times and important passages even more. The author and writing teacher Gloria Delamar commented, "Only amateurs don't rewrite. It's in the rewriting that writers bring ALL their knowledge—basic craft, technique, style, organization, attitude, creative inspiration—to the work."

Good writers revise their works many times. The revision process provides you the best opportunity to clarify your thoughts and to correct inconsistencies and contradictions in your work. You should try to develop empathy for the reader. Ask yourself, "Could I understand this material if I were reading it for the first time?" You might also imagine how the work would appear to a reader whose native tongue is not English.

During the revision process, try to eliminate wordiness. You can minimize verbal clutter by avoiding the use of adjectives and adverbs as much as possible. We overuse words such as "very," "quite," "rather," "fairly," "relatively," "several," and "much." In English, nouns can be used to modify nouns. These noun adjectives (art history, gas engine) are useful, but they can become confusing if you string them together (four cylinder internal combustion gas engine).

There are many approaches to the revision process. Many teachers recommend "cooling" or allowing a piece to sit for a day or longer before revising it. Some writers wait a week, others much longer. This helps you see your work as others will see it. It is often surprising how confusing our complex sentences or phrases seem after they have cooled off for a few days.

Another writing stylist suggests this sequence for revising your writing:

1. Write the first section and leave it alone.

2. Revise the first section before writing the second section.

3. Revise the first and second sections before writing the third section. And so on.

This method is most effective if a work has six or fewer sections. Otherwise, you can introduce unnecessary repetition before you write the last section.

A third method for revision involves reading passages aloud. This helps you discover awkward and confusing sentences.

Regardless of the method you use, you should revise slowly, deliberately, and repeatedly until you are satisfied. Ask an advisor or someone in your writing network to review your revised work. Ask for a tough, honest review and respond constructively.

Many of the suggestions noted are applicable to all types of creative writing, which Laurie E. Rozakis, the author of *The Complete Idiot's Guide to Creative Writing*, defines as "writing that uses language in imaginative and bold ways." For many people, creative writing means fiction—short stories, novels, novellas, poetry, and script writing for stage and film. But creative writing also includes essays, memoirs (autobiography), and other nonfiction pieces.

In fiction, story lines (the plot), including the development of conflict, climax, and resolution, are important, along with developing characters and settings, which you should describe vividly and coherently, using allusions employing the five senses.

Whether you are inclined toward fiction or nonfiction writing, consider reading some books on writing to broaden your perspective and to seek additional tips. Throughout your writing, you will need to refresh your understanding of honesty in writing.

Honestly Using and Referencing the Work of Others

If you travel to Paris, you will surely visit the Louvre. In addition to viewing world-famous art at that august institution, you will observe artists in the galleries with their easels, canvases, and painting accoutrements, copying the works of the masters. The city known for art, its appreciation and education, also fosters a tradition of art education in which art teachers encourage their students to copy classic works to build an appreciation and understanding of the styles and techniques of master painters. But teachers and students alike understand that it is unethical to pass off copies of famous Monet or Rousseau paintings as originals.

In educational settings, copying can be a learning exercise. A writing teacher may ask you to copy the style of Ernest Hemingway or Tom Wolfe for a writing assignment. And copying, under many guises, may seem legitimate to Internet users who routinely duplicate the works of others without permission or attribution. However, copying as an exercise and copying with the intent of using the works of others as your own are wholly different matters. The latter is plagiarism, which is one of the most vexing problems in original scholarship as well as in creative writing.

In most parts of the civilized world, taking the words of another and using them as your own, without proper attribution, is a scholarly heist.

Ask English teachers and they will tell you they have heard all the excuses under the sun for plagiarism from their students. But are there conditions or traps in our scholarly environment that trigger plagiarism among students and others?

Plagiarism among Would-Be Scholars

There are numerous roads to plagiarism. Here are some that may sound familiar:

- **Procrastination:** It's easy to put off tasks, to think there will be plenty of time to get a job done, including writing assignments. Then, the due date is tomorrow or the next day and the pressure is on to be original and craft good work without sufficient time. Now there's the temptation to lift material from articles or books, or more commonly these days, from the Internet. The trap has been set and sprung. MIT student Cal Newport offers this sage advice about last-minute writing tasks: "The lure of procrastination is powerful, but you can conquer it by employing one very simple technique: When assigned a long-term project, finish some amount of work toward its completion that very same day. This doesn't have to be a major chunk of work. Thirty minutes is enough. . . . Once you have accomplished something, no matter how small, you realize that starting your project early is not actually all that bad. In fact, it feels good."

- **Feelings of inadequacy as a writer:** How often have you thought while doing background reading for an assignment and coming upon a well-written piece: "I don't know if I will ever be able to write as well as that?" The trap here is, "Why not just pilfer this material?"

- **It's all well-known material:** Word thieves proclaim they weren't plagiarizing, just using material that is well known as fact. This excuse often results from confusion over what is fact and information in the public domain (the date of the Battle of Hastings, the freezing temperature of water, tenets of the First Amendment of the US Constitution, the composer of the music of *The Phantom of the Opera*—all are facts) with the expression of those facts. Plagiarism is not the restatement of fact but the expropriation of another writer's words or the lack of attribution for using another's words.

- **Family and occupational pressures:** Family members may overemphasize achievement or the notion of finishing one's education as a ticket to a good job. An "end justifying the means" mentality might ensue, in which good grades become more important than learning, and plagiarized work becomes the way out of a pressurized situation.

Plagiarists cheat themselves by compromising their own opportunity to develop capabilities and skills that are obligatory in our twenty-first-century world, where innovation and creativity are the keys to successful professional careers. For those who are tempted to think they can get away with plagiarism, I advise you to forget it. With the Internet and software resources for the detection of plagiarism, the risks are too high. Moreover, the professional world of work can be just as harsh on plagiarists as teachers.

Advice to Would-Be and Established Scholars

Historian Peter Hoffer notes that interpretations of what constitutes plagiarism may vary according to the field. In the visual arts, for example, the replication of an artist's style (Cubism in works by Picasso or Braque, for example) is accepted and may be interpreted as a compliment, unless, of course, you are fraudulently trying to pass off your work as an original Picasso or Braque. Similarly, in music composition, the selective reference to passages of others' works (the *Simple Gifts* theme in Aaron Copland's *Appalachian Spring*, for example) is commonly accepted. But, in written works, as

I've emphasized here, the rules of attribution—paraphrasing, quotation, and acknowledgment—clearly obtain.

Here are some tactics to consider:

- **Gain the necessary information and understanding:** Scholars should take the time to learn and fully understand the meaning of plagiarism. Where doubts exist, seek clarification from an English instructor, staff, or faculty member associated with an institutional writing center or library. In the professional work environment, consult a supervisor or his or her designee.

- **Commit yourself to serious scholarship:** Plagiarism, like other lapses in academic integrity, thwarts serious scholarship and threatens lifelong learning. Avoiding plagiarism boosts both professional and personal development.

- **Plan ahead:** Originality and revision are primary preventive measures to plagiarism. But originality and revision take time and can only be assured if you avoid last-minute efforts.

- **Take care in assembling your notes:** Be sure to differentiate material in your notes that you've extracted from other documents or the Internet. Remember that the excuse of "I forgot to use quotation marks" will not impress a teacher or supervisor.

- **Be mindful of plagiarizing literature reviews:** Introductory portions of major papers, theses, and dissertations are off limits, too. As one graduate school administrator, Dennis Brewer, noted, "There seems to be the notion out there that it is okay to plagiarize in this section since it is labeled a 'review' of the work of others." Plagiarism is never proper or acceptable.

- **Cite material in your notes:** Don't depend on your ability to recall the source of a passage or idea when you're writing or revising your work. Properly citing material during the note-taking process may slow your progress in writing, but it will prevent serious problems later on.

- **Be careful about paraphrasing:** Paraphrasing (the rephrasing of the work of others) is tricky. If your rewording is so close as to mimic the words of others, you could be charged with plagiarism. Even if you carefully rephrase the ideas of another, you should still give the author credit for them. For example, you could use the lead-in, "To paraphrase (name of author of work)", and cite the source.

Modern communication, including e-mailing, text messaging, and blogging, tends to encourage sloppiness in writing. How many times, for example, have you received e-mail messages with mistakes in grammar, punctuation, and syntax? The art of writing well is one of the best ways to prevent plagiarism and related temptations. Your careful crafting of all types of communication will pay dividends, and will help you avoid both plagiarism and "writer's block."

6

Learning and Communicating

There is more than a verbal tie between the words common, community, and communication. . . . Try the experiment of communicating, with fullness and accuracy, some experience . . . especially if it be somewhat complicated, and you will find your own attitude toward your experience changing.

John Dewey (1859–1952), professor of philosophy and education,
American proponent of pragmatism

Writing in an academic sense is critical to learning. Turning writing into effective communications—oral and written—requires specially honed talents, beginning with style.

Communicating with Style

Imagine style as a unique signature that is written across your personality and presence. Your approach to others influences the way you are perceived, which includes your personal appearance and presence. All of this is part of your communication signature. When woven together, your appearance and presence make up what in German might be called your personal *gestalt*. The following are elements of your gestalt: formal versus informal approaches, kindliness, the gravitas factor, and your physical appearance.

Formal versus Informal Approaches

Communication begins with a consideration of formality. Among family and friends, informality is the norm in the United States. But in professional life, customs vary. In the United States we generally adopt a less formal approach with our colleagues. Many professionals promote a "first-name basis" in their relationships with colleagues, regardless of the differences in their titles and positions.

A more formal approach is warranted in your first contact with people outside your social sphere and beyond US borders. You will probably find that in today's world your international colleagues and acquaintances will be more comfortable on a first-name basis soon after being formally introduced.

A powerful aspect of an informal style of communication is learning and using others' first names during conversations and meetings. There are many stories like the one of the patient who seeks help from a health care professional who never uses the patient's name during an interview or examination. Exasperated by the health care provider's impersonal approach, the patient challenges him: "If you are so interested in me why don't you address me by my name?" Many people can relate to a story like this one.

Memorizing and using people's names in conversation takes practice, but there are some things you can do to help with this. First, be alert to names during introductions. It's easy to become distracted during the initial exchanges of pleasantries, so it is important to try to register at least a first name in your memory. A trick you can use to fix a person's name in your mind is repeating the person's name during introductions. For example, you are at a reception and you introduce yourself or are introduced to Jane White. You can say, "Hi, Jane. It's very nice to meet you, Jane." This double use of the name looks odd in print, but in an actual situation it doesn't sound strange, and it has a significant reinforcing effect on your memory.

If you forget the newly introduced person's name after a few minutes of conversation, don't be ashamed to apologize and ask the person politely to remind you of his or her name. People generally are not offended by such a request. In any case, try to lock a new acquaintance's name into your memory through a word association or connection to the name of a well-known friend or colleague.

Another thing you can do as a memory aid is to try a little exercise to learn and use people's names. If you're at a meeting as chairperson of a committee or officer of a club or organization and several people are sitting at a table, have a pad of paper and on it draw an outline of the table where you are seated. If you don't know everyone present, suggest that participants introduce themselves sequentially and offer a few words about their responsibilities in their present firm, institution, club, or organization. As they give their names, jot these down at the points on your outline of the table corresponding to their seating positions. This will be of inestimable help when you want to use their names during the meeting.

After the meeting, you can reinforce your memory of participants' names by walking around the table and shaking every participant's hand, as you simultaneously use the first name of each in saying good-bye. This exercise has a powerful impact on participants, in part because many people won't notice that you've used a schematic aid to help learn their names and they'll be impressed with your skill in remembering everyone's name. Others may observe you taking notes but will not necessarily connect it with the details of the exercise. Toward the end of the meeting, you can share information about the purpose and nature of the exercise you've used during the meeting. You'll find that participants appreciate the exercise.

The frequent use of first names is a way to achieve positive results in your oral communication. Just as you like to find your image in a group photo, people delight in hearing their names spoken, especially when the speaker is a respected friend or colleague.

Kindliness

An informal and naturally friendly approach to communicating, especially in face-to-face communications, suggests a kindliness that most people find appealing both in friendships and in professional interactions. People of goodwill are heartened by acts of kindness—hardened people are disarmed by them.

The philosopher Harold Rosen is known for his sage advice to "actively seek what others need," which is at the heart of a kindliness paradigm you will observe among close friends and effective leaders in various fields. In the Dorothy character in most of Frank Baum's Oz books and in particular in the 1900 book, you might remember how readily Dorothy befriends the Scarecrow, the Tin Woodman, and the Cowardly Lion through her personal inquiries and expressions of concern for them. Outward kindliness occurs in real life and is apparent among followers of the Way of Oz.

Others, who don't heed Rosen's advice, are boorish and monopolize conversations with talk about themselves and their interests. A *New Yorker* cartoon some years ago captured such people well. A man is at a cocktail party surrounded by friends and acquaintances. We see by the expressions on some of their faces that he's been boring the company with incessant talk about himself. He's saying: "Well, that's enough about me. What do you think about me?"

People who adopt Rosen's approach actively engage newly introduced acquaintances by asking questions about them: their background, their interests, their reasons for attending the meeting, mutual acquaintances, their interest in participating in activities or projects. The questions indicate sincere interest, particularly if you demonstrate good listening skills, as a collegiate Truman scholar once admonished: "Listen, hear, and be truly present."

An indirect benefit of the Rosen approach is that it can lead the new acquaintance to ask questions about you and your interests. Sometimes, however, the conversation becomes a monologue, diminishing the potential success of a budding relationship. If this happens, the best you can do is to be polite and listen.

The Rosen approach builds mutual trust and interest. If you're successful, you will befriend interesting people and broaden your network.

The kindliness that marks a personal communication style doesn't mean you don't need the courage to face difficult situations and make tough decisions. How often do you hear the comment, "He (she) is too nice a person to be effective"? You need not be disagreeable, but you do need to know when and how to be serious, fair, and just.

Gravitas Factor

According to Lance Morrow, whose short essay titled "The Gravitas Factor" appeared in a 1988 issue of *Time*, gravitas "is a secret of character and grasp and experience, a force of the eye, the voice, and bearing." This powerful combination is reinforced when it is blended with human kindness, pragmatism, and seriousness.

Professionals with gravitas fit well into leadership roles. They are people who have the fortitude and sharpness of wit to weather significant challenges and crises. Gravitas is manifested in the behavior of take-charge people whose voice, stature, and manner inspire confidence. In oral communication, the voice of gravitas is true and resonant, the speaker's posture poised, and the affect strong, straight, and direct.

In the late twentieth and early twenty-first centuries we have witnessed many social and political leaders with gravitas, such as Winston Churchill, Franklin Delano Roosevelt, John F. Kennedy, Martin Luther King, Jr., Gloria Steinem, Barbara Jordan, and Rudy Giuliani. In your personal and professional life you will come to know supervisors, colleagues, and friends who, though typically informal and friendly, are able to assume a seriousness of intent and purpose. These people have an extraordinary ability to focus during challenging times; they inspire commitment and rally groups toward important goals. Their gravitas reflects core values and a sense of confidence that encourages unselfish service in others.

Gravitas is built on democratic beliefs and ideals, motivated by commitment, and fueled by experience, self-confidence, a tolerance of ambiguity, and faith in people and their abilities to contribute to efforts larger than themselves. In other words, the gravitas factor represents a sturdy foundation for the ideal of integrated learning and communicating, one that can enhance professional satisfaction and success.

Appearance

What we have considered about one's personal gestalt, to this point, takes for granted that we are dealing with people of integrity who communicate sincerity. When you couple these attributes with informality, kindliness, and gravitas, you have a dynamite combination for interpersonal communications, which can be enhanced by a striking and dramatic physical appearance.

Keen observers of contemporary America know the effectiveness of professionals whose use of sartorial accessories or certain modes of grooming and dress create a distinctive style. Notable examples include Paul Simon (US representative and senator from Illinois), G. Mennen "Soapy" Williams (governor of Michigan), and Gordon Gee (president of Ohio State University), who all chose bow ties as their trademarks.

Many observers were impressed with Bella Abzug, a women's rights advocate and US representative from New York, who was known for her large and unusual hats. Madeleine Albright, the former United Nations ambassador and secretary of state, is known for her distinctive brooches and lapel pins.

Mark Emmert, president of the National Collegiate Athletic Association (NCAA), wears eye-catching matching suspenders and neckties. Arlene Cash, vice president for enrollment at Spelman College, and Robin Froman, dean and endowed professor in the school of nursing at the University of Texas Health Science Center in San Antonio, use distinctive scarves as a mark of their personal style.

You can use a variety of sartorial accessories, including theme neckties and lapel pins, to attract interest during conversations, speeches, and other presentations. For example, at the beginning or conclusion of a speech you might say something like, "Those who know me know that I like to wear a necktie (scarf) that embodies a theme integral to my overall presentation. Today I am wearing . . ."

The following are two examples of the way your necktie or scarf can make a statement:

- **Using Ouroboros art:** In many cultures, the self-devouring serpent is used to symbolize creation, re-creation, and the interrelatedness of all things. In Egyptian and Greek lore, the term for this creature is Ouroboros; its use is probably most familiar in the art of the Book of Kells, the seventh- to eighth-century illuminated manuscript of the Synoptic Gospels. Ouroboros margin art is often used for neckties and scarves. These accessories can be used effectively to emphasize points about the life-enriching value of scholarly and other creative pursuits.

• **Using paisley art:** Paisley designs originated in sixteenth-century central Asia, India, Persia, and most significantly, Kashmir. Plant forms, especially the shoots of the date palm, inspire the curvilinear teardrop designs. Historians note that the date palm had economic importance (for food, fiber, and shelter) in civilizations going back to the Babylonians, who referred to it as the Tree of Life. In modern times, paisley designs became popular motifs for women's shawls in European salons of the late eighteenth through the late nineteenth centuries. In the twentieth century, paisley designs became popularly incorporated into women's scarves and men's neckties. Paisley neckwear provides a rich source of historic, cultural, and metaphoric symbolism with which you can craft a variety of allusions for conversation and formal presentations.

Besides neckties and scarves, lapel pins make good points of reference during conversations. Consider wearing pins that symbolize institutions where you have studied, worked, lived, or traveled. If you're greeting international visitors, you might consider wearing flag friendship pins, pairing Old Glory with a flag from the visitor's country. Presenting someone with his or her own flag is powerfully symbolic. Wearing lapel pins that commemorate your past personal and professional efforts not only provides a source of conversation but also catalyzes many pleasant memories for you.

Written Communications

For many people, electronic communications—e-mail, text messaging, blogging, social networking, and tweeting—can consume significant portions of every day. For working professionals, 50 percent or more of their time is commonly spent dealing with communication. Electronic communication deserves our attention (including a consideration of relevant etiquette) along with formal memoranda, letters, proposals, reports, and articles for publication.

Electronic communications (or e-communications) have revolutionized our personal and professional lives. It's hard to imagine communication without it. My generation will remember writing memos or letters to friends and supervisors and having to wait several days or even weeks for replies—or no reply at all.

The nearly ubiquitous use of e-communications today has exponentially accelerated written communications in the workplace. Unfortunately, as in many other aspects in life, its strengths are also its weaknesses: spam, chain e-mail, discourteousness, and even bullying are all the "dark side" of e-communications.

Despite these negative aspects, most people, especially younger people all around the world, have enthusiastically embraced e-communications. In the workplace, e-communications have moved us toward the "paperless office," a concept many thought would never come to pass. It's important to organize your e-communications and use them wisely.

Once you've crafted a filing system for your electronic communications and related documents, you can create e-logs that help you save, in chronological order, text and notes on projects or transactions with people. These e-logs provide readily available documents you can access as needed, through the "find" function in word-processing software. You can keep similar logs for casework (transactions and notes related to specific cases or problems you may be assigned to handle in the workplace) in separate e-file folders, which are helpful in reconstructing situations, whether they're part of your school, professional, or private business world.

There's one caveat worth mentioning at this point. In our highly litigious social environment, such log-style files are subject to subpoena in lawsuits. In some states, such files are also subject to Freedom of Information Act (FOIA) requests by litigants, the press, or citizens, in the case of public agencies. You need to be circumspect about what you choose to save.

There are many ways of organizing computer desktop and electronic files. The method is less important than the fact that you create a well-organized plan for codifying your files and minimizing their retrieval times. Any thoughtfully conceived method is better than the lack of such a system. You've probably seen computer screens of friends or colleagues that are cluttered with documents. How often have you heard, "Oh, I can find that for you, but it may take me some time." With a well-planned system, that won't be you.

In addition to having your files well organized, you should review guidelines for e-mail etiquette. How many times have you dashed off a curt or brash response to an e-message and wished later you hadn't? How many times have you copied a person or persons with an abrasive e-communication and wished you hadn't? How many times have you learned about copies of your e-communications being circulated to large numbers of people? These are the nightmares of the e-communication world. But these nightmares can be prevented if you consider these words: stop, think, and respond thoughtfully and congenially. Try to avoid hasty responses to criticism. The advice professional managers have offered for years about allowing forceful memos or letters to "cool" overnight also applies to e-communications.

However, if you are responding to noncontroversial e-communications, correspondents appreciate speedy replies. In fact, the timeliness of replies is an added inducement for friends and colleagues to use e-communications.

Seek brevity and completeness in the content of your e-mail messages and replies. A classic response to a question about your position in any matter can often be framed through a simple "communicator's guide": Here's where I am in this matter, here's why I crafted my position, and here's how that position may affect you.

Regardless of the framework you use for e-communications, a congenial tone is recommended most of the time. Begin with a first name, including a salutation or its equivalent, such as "Hi, Tom," "Dear Marsha," or "Thanks for your note, Don." Avoid sending notes without a salutation. Like the effectiveness of using people's first names in the setting of a business or professional meeting, using personalized salutations in all modes of communication has positive effects. You should also end your e-communications with your first name, preceded usually by a friendly word such as "kindly" or "sincerely." The tone of such a note goes a long way toward engendering goodwill and trust among correspondents.

Be thoughtful about routing electronic communications. If you wish to share the criticism of one person about another, place it in context with your own expression of how you plan to respond to the criticism. For example, if you intend for the person copied merely to be informed, say so in a redirected message. Assume that the person copied may act on the new information before checking with you.

The Dark Side of Electronic Communications

There is a vast dark side to electronic communications. Unseemly and sometimes illegal e-mail practices include spamming, chain e-mailing, lambasting and raging, cyberbullying, and harassment.

Spamming is illegal, despite the apparent impunity with which certain people clutter e-mail channels. Spam, in the world of twenty-first-century information technology, is an annoyance and a curse. Defined by the acronym finder at the University College of Cork (in Ireland), it is "a polite term for unsolicited garbage advertising email sent by ignorant, anti-social, unscrupulous marketing pondscum in the vain hope that someone, somewhere will be interested in their tawdry, second-rate rubbish." Enough said.

A second egregious e-mail practice is the "chain e-mail" request—even if it has a seemingly benevolent purpose. It's not uncommon to receive chain e-mail letters from an official of a sectarian college, university, or organization in which the suggestion is made that if you don't pass along a prayer message to family and friends you will face imminent doom.

A third distasteful e-mail practice relates to messages full of incoherent lambasting and raging against you. These messages have a special place in the e-mail chamber of horrors, and originators of such trash do not deserve the courtesy of reply. Answering the lambasters' and ragers' taunts can lead to worse encounters, such as electronic aggression, or harassment.

There should be a special place in Dante's inferno for people who engage in cyber aggression, such as bullying, or for those who delight in harming others. The best practice—whether you are involved in traditional e-mailing or texting, blogs or social networks—is to avoid the lambasters, ragers, and other demented characters. If you receive direct threats, particularly through e-mail, consider replying with a message such as: "Because of the threat contained in your note, I have shared a copy of this message with the police department."

On balance, e-mail communication has far greater advantages than disadvantages, and when used thoughtfully and congenially, it can be a tremendous help in learning and success in your professional and private lives.

Memos and Letters

It may seem odd to consider this topic separately, but even in the age of e-mail, there remains a need for more formal correspondence, despite the fact that it's being sent electronically.

You will be expected to write formal memos and letters, particularly when such missives pertain to your professional or personal life. You should consider making these letters and memos interesting and effective by adhering to the elements of good writing: thoughtfulness, correctness, appropriateness, and readability.

Well-written correspondence is thoughtful, well organized, and faithful to the stated purpose of the memo or letter. Thoughtfully produced correspondence contains proper assumptions and conclusions. It lacks bias and provides believable justifications. Thoughtful writing reflects your enthusiasm and persuasiveness.

Effectively crafted correspondence is correct in grammar, punctuation, and spelling—all of which are assisted by spell- and grammar-check software available in word-processing packages, along with appropriate use of a trusted dictionary. Correct writing is coherent, marked by proper syntax and appropriate transitions.

Effective correspondence conveys the appropriate tone. The reader is neither patronized nor treated to verbosity and pompousness. You should limit memos and letters to one page whenever possible. Some professionals won't read more than one page of a written communication.

Well-written correspondence is readable. It flows smoothly. It does not require you to reread every other sentence. Readable pieces have a leading topic sentence followed by a summary that outlines the correspondence. The letter or memo adheres to the outline and has clear transitions from paragraph to paragraph.

Writing effectively is like other creative activities—it gets better with practice. Your writing will be enhanced if you are willing to try new approaches. You should apply the elements of good writing in all your writing, from e-mail to text messaging to blogging and social networking. Consistently adopting the discipline of good writing has a positive impact on your thinking and organizational skills.

In your writing consider using a modified version of the communicator's guide noted earlier: Here's where I am, here's how I got here, and here's what I want from you.

Now let's consider the effective use of persuasion. There are many strategies for being persuasive, not those of a huckster like Professor Marvel of Oz. Your assertions must be based on fact, and you should avoid the sensational claims of ragers and lambasters. One author suggests that if you have a sympathetic reader, you should order your arguments with the strongest appearing last. But if your reader is unsympathetic, lead with your strongest argument.

Try appealing to positions you know your reader holds. For example, an educational institution or industrial firm committed to excellence in research and service will be sympathetic to arguments for policy changes that elevate standards.

Well-written and persuasive memos and letters are a point of pride for aspiring professionals. Indeed, establishing trust among colleagues and friends is grounded in well-crafted correspondence, whether it is based on informal e-mail notes or more formal memos and letters. Whatever you do to improve these skills will pay off handsomely—professionally and personally.

Proposals, Reports, and Articles for Publication

Many students and working professionals—from business managers to nonprofit corporation officials to university administrators and faculty members—are expected to write grant or project proposals, reports, and articles for publication.

Preparing a proposal often marks the beginning of a project or new direction for a firm, institution, or organization. A proposal may be strictly an internal document to help direct a new effort or initiative, or it may be intended for transmittal to a foundation, government agency, or other funding source.

Proposals may be structured in many ways, but you should adhere to the format prescribed by a teacher or to a format common to your professional affiliation or the requirements of a funding agency. If no format is defined, you might use the following outline:

1. Cover page

2. Abstract (with key words in bold)

3. Budget

4. Biographical sketches of project participants

5. Project plan

    a. Specific aims

> b. Significance and background
>
> c. Progress report or results of preliminary studies
>
> d. Methods or procedures proposed for the project
>
> e. Collaborative assurance
>
> f. Facilities and equipment available or needed for project
>
> g. Appendices

The cover page should include the title of the proposal, names and addresses of the project managers or principal investigator, in the case of government grant proposals, and the organizational official (president, director, vice president for research) who signs proposals.

The abstract is the most important component of the proposal. It should be written last and with special care. The following elements should be included in an abstract: a one- or two-sentence statement of the project, including its significance; a brief description of methodology and procedures to be used in the project; anticipated findings and results; and the importance of expected results.

The key words of the abstract can be typed in bold, but it is best to limit the treatment to ten words.

In the case of technical work, extramural agencies such as foundations may require a layperson's summary of the proposed work for use in public relations activities. The effectiveness of the abstract cannot be overemphasized because some reviewers may read little else in a proposal other than the budget.

The budget should be a realistic appraisal of all costs. It should include amounts for the following:

1. Salaries and wages plus fringe benefits

2. Supplies

3. Equipment

4. Computer time

5. Special costs

> a. Rental fees

      b. Analysis

      c. Software

6. Travel

7. Indirect cost (in federal government grants and contracts, indirect cost is referred to as facilities and administrative costs)

8. Subcontracts

Guidelines for developing budgets should be available from your institution or firm, in the case of internal projects, or from extramural agencies that you might petition for funding.

Biographical sketches should be included for key people contributing to proposed projects. These should generally be no longer than a page or two (or as may be prescribed by an external agency) and should include background information relevant to the project, including lists of participants' publications. The biographical materials should also indicate the person's relationship to the project.

The impact of a proposal's narrative section depends on how effectively a project director can convey his or her ideas, as well as the ability to state those ideas in objective terms. The proposal writer must be clear and thorough. It is important to develop a "talking style" as we looked at earlier. In the methodology and procedures section, such phrasing as "If this procedure fails to give expected results, a modified process will be designed to . . ." or "We don't divorce the development of software from our modeling work; rather, the two activities are coordinated through . . ." give the reviewer a favorable impression of the proposal writer's maturity—a blend of optimism and reality.

Developing a proposal is one of the best ways of organizing your ideas about a project. And a good proposal offers satisfaction and accomplishment, particularly if the proposal is approved and funded.

Once you have a successfully reviewed proposal in place, you can begin your project with the expectation that you will need to communicate the results in a report or articles for publication.

Report writing is an integral part of project development and pursuit. One author estimated that the preparation of reports and related articles for publication requires as much as a third of the time of research professionals.

Other professionals may spend lesser amounts of time on reports and related activities, but for all professionals, preparing reports is a significant part of their professional endeavors.

Reports should answer the following questions:

• What have you been trying to do?

• How are you accomplishing the work?

• Do the results of the work make sense?

• What is the importance of the work?

Reports are useful at three stages of a project: at the beginning, during difficulties, and at project's end. During the design phase, the report should include a statement of the project and underlying assumptions; analysis of how the project developed; a description of possible results of the project, including problems it might solve; approaches, methodology, and procedures that might be used for the project; and costs—if relevant.

Intermediate reports help you confront apparent anomalies in results, plan new approaches, and challenge assumptions. As W. I. B. Beveridge noted in his seminal work, *The Art of Scientific Investigation*, "The systematic arrangement of the data often discloses flaws in the reasoning, or alternative lines of thought which have been missed. Assumptions and conclusions at first accepted as 'obvious' may even prove indefensible when set down clearly and examined critically." Final reports serve as preludes to manuscripts for publication.

The following is an effective format for interim and final project reports:

• Title

• Table of Contents

• Abstract

• Introduction

• Methodology and Procedures

• Results and Discussion

• Bibliography

• Appendices

The title page contains the full title and name of the author or authors, including department and organization. Titles should indicate the subject and scope of the report. You should avoid unnecessary words in the title, such as: "Studies of . . . ," "Interesting Aspects of . . . ," and "Results of . . .". Factors to consider in crafting a good title include succinctness; using noun adjectives and correct syntax; and avoiding abbreviations, chemical formulae, proprietary names, or jargon. You might also ask yourself: How will it look as a title of a paper? Does it entice the reader into the rest of the report?

Reports should include the effective use of tables and diagrams, which can be easily crafted using modern word-processing software. Be sure to refer, in the text, to any information in tables and figures and create these carefully to enhance conclusions or other assertions you make in results and discussion sections. Also be sure to include source information in the footnotes of tables or captions of figures for any externally derived data or other material.

A well-crafted report is like a work of art. It is coherent and flows smoothly. It is compelling. It reveals thoughtfulness and imagination. In short, it is a pleasure to read. Getting to the point where reports have these qualities takes practice and a willingness to share drafts with colleagues who offer ideas, make suggestions, and provide constructive criticism.

With a well-written report you are on your way to crafting articles and other works that can be considered for publication.

Whether you're preparing an essay, research paper, op-ed piece, or letter to the editor, you should always start by reading the guidelines provided by the venue for which you're writing; usually these are available periodically in magazines, journals, or newspapers or on websites. Length and format requirements—including the use of tables, figures, and photographic or digital imagery—are very important. You need to be sure your subjects and format are acceptable to whatever publication you are approaching.

If you're self-publishing, you can establish your own guidelines. Here are some suggestions to ensure a high-quality piece of writing:

• Ensure your original research paper represents work based on an understanding of previously published work in the field, experiments of sound design, analyses using appropriate instruments, and logical elaborations in results, discussion, and conclusion sections.

- Write essays, articles, and the like using sound and compelling arguments with minimal speculation and conjecture.

- Establish an equivalent to peer review by sharing and seeking comments and suggestions on early drafts of the work.

- Respect copyright law and be aware of fair use provisions of the Copyright Law of the United States.

If you plan to submit your work to journals or other venues, be prepared for rejections. Most professional journals and especially popular media have high rejection rates. The successful author is one who develops a thick skin for critical review, persistence in submitting papers to more than one venue (as necessary but in accord with the venues' policies about simultaneous submissions), and patience to see the process through. Going through the process of peer evaluation may take weeks or months, but it is always worth the effort.

Well-crafted papers, published in high-quality magazines and journals or self-published after much care and review, can become the basis for oral presentations.

Oral Communications

Informative and effective oral communications are critical to success in your personal and professional life.

One-on-One Communications

Imagine a scene in which a friend or colleague is not doing well in a relationship or at work. Imagine, also, a hypothetical conversation in which your friend or colleague is confronted with a series of "you" messages, such as: "You don't understand me," "You seem to be having a problem taking directions," "You are getting this task all wrong," and "You need to improve." If *you* have experienced such a scenario, *you* know how negative and counterproductive it can be.

Now, contrast the *"you*-laced" scenario with one that is more "I" and "we" focused: "I wish we could improve our communications," "Is there something I can do to ensure the performance of this task?," "Why don't we review how the performance of this task could be improved," and "Let's see if we can implement the solution as soon as it is feasible." These sound completely different, don't they? And they sound much more positive to the people you care about or work with.

"I" and "we" messages convey a personal concern for the other and an acknowledgment that lapses are not always one-sided. Through "I" and "we" messages, you give your friend or colleague the benefit of the doubt.

Besides using "I" and "we" messages, effective one-on-one communication benefits from active listening strategies that facilitate understanding. One active listening strategy involves inquisitive feedback in which you frame statements such as, "If I understand you correctly, you are saying . . ." Another strategy involves questioning, "Could you state your position in another way?" A third includes a summary of the discussion, such as, "I believe that we have come to an understanding that . . ."

There's always give and take in such interchanges, but the use of listening strategies helps to clarify understanding, build trust, and direct positive action.

Interacting, working, and communicating with friends and colleagues, particularly those who may report to you in a professional setting, should have an overall tenor of support. Consider being more, rather than less, lavish with praise. Those who do this well say, "I am feeling good about how we are doing with this project" or "I really appreciate your efforts this week" or "You have developed a very effective approach to this challenge" or "Let me know how I can help."

In the world of professional employment, management gurus are fond of reminding us that supervising people is not a popularity contest. But by supporting your colleagues and friends you will become a person who cares about others, a reward in itself.

Group Interactions, Speechmaking, and Other Presentations

Regardless of the size of a group or organization you may be leading or managing, you will undoubtedly be subject to periodic reviews of your performance. A performance review will contain such questions as these: Do you meet regularly with your associates? Do your meetings have an agenda? What mechanisms do you use to engage your associates in the agenda-setting process? How are your meetings used to delegate responsibility and to make progress in projects and initiatives? How do you follow up on matters formally discussed in meetings? If you are able positively and substantively to address these questions, you will have probably created a format and a set of procedures to make meetings successful and receive a good performance review.

Woody Allen once observed that "half of life's success is in showing up. The other half is being on time." There's clearly more to having a successful meeting than that. Meetings should have an agenda, and participants need to play a role in setting agendas. You can appoint a person in your group or organization to be agenda coordinator and ask all the members of the group to work with the coordinator in developing an agenda. You need to make it clear that if someone places an item on an agenda it will be that person's responsibility to address it during the meeting.

Have an understanding about the length of meetings (except under extraordinary circumstances, meetings shouldn't exceed one hour and many can be limited to shorter periods), stick to the agenda, and try to save time for open-ended discussion. The postagenda exercise of "going around the table," asking each participant whether there is something he or she wishes to discuss before the end of the meeting, can be an effective tool to generate new ideas.

Devise measures to include all attendees in discussions and consider the use of treats such as bagels or cookies to encourage attendance and participation at meetings.

You might assign another member of the group to prepare and distribute the minutes of the meeting. The minutes serve not only an archival function but also a mechanism for follow-up. For example, the minutes can be used to create to-do lists.

Meetings are good vehicles for reinforcing the vision, mission, philosophy, goals, and values of your club, organization, institution, or firm. Regular meetings and follow-up work in strategic planning can also serve as a prelude to retreats.

Every six to twelve months, there is value in assembling the leadership of a club, organization, institution, or firm to discuss the unit's strategic plan. Consider a place and setting remote from the workplace or usual meeting place. Create an informal atmosphere, with casual dress and opportunities for socializing (for example, receptions and meals).

Retreats are best organized around a theme or important initiative and are most effective if colleagues are engaged in making group presentations, which encourages participation. The presentations are wonderful opportunities for personal and professional development.

The best kickoff to a retreat is an overview presentation by the group's leader, which also provides the opportunity for the leader to highlight the contributions of individuals and teams within the group. Acknowledging the successes of colleagues has a powerfully positive effect on group morale and esprit de corps.

Besides providing a forum for the review of past accomplishments, retreats facilitate the collective development, brainstorming if you will, of new initiatives, which can serve as the basis for position papers or proposals and public forums. Retreats and public forums represent just two opportunities for oral presentations.

It's often been said that public speaking is the second most frightening thing to Americans. The first is death! But speechmaking needn't cause anxiety, given some guidance.

Presentations can be generally categorized as one of the following:

- **Welcoming (3–10 minutes):** succinct introductory, congratulatory and press conference remarks

- **Short presentations (10–20 minutes):** introductions to projects, luncheon addresses, commencement talks, and professional meeting presentations

- **Substantive presentations (30–50 minutes):** reviewing a project, initiative, strategic plan, or reorganization of an institution, club, or equivalent.

One of the cardinal rules of oral presentations is not to exceed your allotted time, unless you want to risk personal and professional embarrassment.

Some approaches will make presentations informative, dramatic, and intriguing.

Coherence, particularly in the context of public presentations, calls for making certain your message is relevant to the interests of the group addressed. Nothing interests people more than themselves. Psychologists know that when we look at a group photo in which we are included, our image is the first we search for.

When addressing an audience, your most important task is to find out about the group's interests and affiliations, the expectations and occasion for the presentation, and the possible uniqueness of its timing and location. With this information, you can begin identifying what will interest and captivate your audience.

Developing ideas for the content of presentations is akin to other creative processes. Having good ideas, getting them in writing, and allowing time for the ideas to gestate in your mind, you will next want to work on your topic and subtopics. There are several ways to use your topics and subtopics to craft interesting, dramatic, and intriguing content:

- **Use historically linked themes:** Start with important events of the day or year and link them to your topic and subtopics; or, use the three-step approach: here's where we are, here's how we got here, and here's where we are going; or, link timelines and historically important days and events to guide the development of your topic.

- **Use archetypal stories:** A hero's journey, event, or imagery (archetypes of the hearth and the ocean or other bodies of water, for example) can be employed to develop story-based presentations.

- **Use an analytical approach:** Employ a reporter's modus operandi and ask the proverbial "what," "where," "when," "how," and "why" questions about a topic.

- **Use an imaginative approach:** Start with three "what if" questions that help you walk the audience through your subtopics.

As in all approaches, it's important to avoid being overly ambitious. For most talks, you shouldn't try to cover more than three subtopics. These can be divided into major components, but be careful not to try to cover too much. It is axiomatic that "beginning teachers try to tell their students everything they know"; and as Voltaire admonished, "The secret of being a bore is to tell everything." Most audiences can only absorb and remember limited amounts of material. The research you need to flesh out spoken ideas parallels that which you would do to develop a proposal, report, or article for presentation, although it might also incorporate unique and intriguing elements.

As we think back on the life and works of Frank Baum, we find many parallels among the lessons of this chapter and his personal experiences. From his teenage years, we saw his need to communicate, in his production of the *Rose Lawn Journal*. Baum's drive to communicate continued through his myriad pursuits and vocational interests—writing about raising prize chickens, publishing his knowledge of window dressing, communicating the imaginary worlds he created for his children and their friends, not only in books but also in stage productions and unique formats such as in *Fairylogue and Radio-Plays*. Both his character the Scarecrow, with his many attempts to problem-solve and share the fruits of his creativity and learning, and Baum himself became consummate communicators.

7
Learning and Traveling

Frank Baum would discover that there's but one surefire way of finding one's innermost self—and that is to embark when the time comes on a journey. And the more arduous the adventure, the more perilous the path, the steeper the cliffs, the more dangerous the demons, the more choices one is forced to make—all the better for determining one's true character.

Evan I. Schwartz (1964–), American journalist,
editor, author, and film producer

Learning involves a dynamic tension between your inner and outer lives, your thoughts and experiences. Teachers see this tension manifested in their students in various ways. Some are reclusive, consumed by their inner lives, and others are extroverts, who often don't stop to reflect at all. The balance required to bring learning into sharp focus depends on the reflective life, which is reinforced through reading, study, and writing, and the external life, which is dependent on communication but informed through travel. But, not travel for travel's sake—to simply say you have been "someplace." Rather, travel *experience*, where you savor the process of getting there, along with the language, culture, and characteristics of the people encountered during your stay. If done right, even for relatively short stays, you will come away with a valuable set of memories or even a whole new outlook on life.

You might recall how travel influenced the creative life of Frank Baum. The archetypal quest of going forth, having adventures along the way, and returning home as a changed, more effective and loving person, permeates the original *Wizard of Oz* and most of its thirteen sequels. Many of Baum's other published works have travel as a major component as well.

Here are a few of the ways travel changed Baum's life:

- His visit to a printing shop in Syracuse as a young boy influenced him to become a writer and a publisher.

- His job as a traveling salesman, particularly during his years in Chicago, stimulated many ideas that influenced his early works of fantasy.

- His travels to Southern California influenced the themes in several of his books, in particular, the earthquake in *Dorothy and the Wizard of Oz*.

- His son Frank Josyln's travels to the Far East and his subsequent portrayals of these experiences in slide presentations influenced Baum's development of *Fairylogue and Radio-Plays*.

- His travel to the Middle East and Europe in 1906 shaped the development of at least two works, including *The Last Egyptian: A Romance of the Nile*.

Even in the context of life more than a hundred years ago—without modern telecommunications and the Internet—travel had a great impact on Frank Baum's creative endeavors. Today, through the use of modern technology, particularly distance learning, special learning software, and the Internet, most everyone can reap the benefits of travel to real and virtual worlds.

Travel: Start in the Home Environment

Travel typically begins close to home. US demographers learned years ago that a third of Americans live and die in their hometowns. Another third live and die in their home states, and the last third live some part of their lives in many different states or countries. From personal experiences and interactions with your colleagues you can relate to all three types of individuals. And you probably have come to realize that there are varying degrees of geographic awareness among your friends and colleagues. It's not uncommon to meet people who have little knowledge of other communities or states, not to mention awareness of different countries. Such parochialism is a detriment to learning and its place in the Way of Oz. Just as Dorothy and the other characters in the Oz sequels had to travel the Yellow Brick Road or its equivalent to learn about Oz and beyond, you gain immensely, in learning and other aspects of the Way of Oz, through travel.

A yearning for travel often begins with a fascination for different places, cultures, and peoples, including their customs, beliefs, historical roots, rituals, and traditions. Even within the United States, such differences continue to exist—in Amish communities or on Native American reservations or in small enclaves in Appalachia, for example. Fewer such differences exist today than in Frank Baum's day. Nevertheless, developing an understanding and appreciation for cultural differences, including those among your fellow citizens, sets the stage for an international perspective that is critical to life as an educated citizen and leader in the twenty-first century.

For some students, the opportunity for international travel may occur before attending college. But for many, if not most, Americans, international trips and study abroad do not occur until their college years. Let's add some perspective to this discussion: Among adult Americans in 2009, only about 25 percent had earned a baccalaureate degree or higher; 46 percent of Americans hadn't attended college at all. Of those who had earned a degree, generally fewer than 20 percent had studied abroad, even though it's probably a truism that such experiences promote the development of leadership skills and change lives profoundly.

Travel: Studying Abroad

If you survey the mission statements of US colleges and universities, you'll find a variety of assertions espousing their commitments to global understanding. The vision statement of Texas Tech University states clearly that the future of the university and its academic community is tied integrally to "student success and engaging the world." Middlebury College in Vermont says its mission is as follows:

> At Middlebury College we challenge students to participate fully in a vibrant and diverse academic community. The College's Vermont location offers an inspirational setting for learning and reflection, reinforcing our commitment to integrating environmental stewardship into both our curriculum and our practices on campus. Yet the College also reaches far beyond the Green

Mountains, offering a rich array of undergraduate and graduate programs that connect our community to other places, countries, and cultures. We strive to engage students' capacity for rigorous analysis and independent thought within a wide range of disciplines and endeavors, and to cultivate the intellectual, creative, physical, ethical, and social qualities essential for leadership in a rapidly changing global community. Through the pursuit of knowledge unconstrained by national or disciplinary boundaries, students who come to Middlebury learn to engage the world. (Adopted in 2006)

These examples are hardly unique. You will find a commitment to internationally based or study-abroad educational programs in nearly all US colleges and universities. But such programs vary considerably. The college-bound student interested in pursuing a study-abroad program should investigate the strengths of various schools.

Different institutions committed to study-abroad programs have one or more of the following characteristics:

- Centers or campuses in selected countries, with varying numbers of home campus faculty members participating in the program

- Contractual agreements with internationally based universities for exchange students or the support of students from the US-based institutions

- Arrangements with larger interinstitutional consortia

The size and scope of institutions with centers or campuses abroad range from full-fledged campuses served by faculty and staff members employed by the home institution to physical centers owned or leased by the college or university with varying arrangements for the institutional involvement of faculty and staff members. For example, a US college or university may partner with an institution in another country; instruction and student services are a joint responsibility. If you are interested in study abroad, here are some questions to ask:

- Is the non-US-based campus or center and its programs fully accredited by the institution's regional accrediting agency as certified by the US Department of Education, as well as program-accrediting bodies where applicable?

- How are internationally based living arrangements handled? Must students find their own accommodations or does the institution own or lease residential facilities, or maintain well-developed relationships with host families?

- For programs in countries where English is not the first language, what arrangements are offered for foreign-language instruction either before or during a study-abroad period?

- Given differing options for study-abroad stays (typically one month, six weeks, or one- or two-semester terms), what opportunities are provided (paid or otherwise) for travel to neighboring cities or regions? Are extended stays (involving instruction in areas such as art, architecture, culture, and history) an integral part of the study-abroad program?

- What systems are in place to ensure the health and welfare of student participants?

Investigating such matters in advance will be immensely helpful in deciding whether an institutionally run campus or center is preferable to an institution with a contractual arrangement with the home college or university.

When discussing study abroad, you frequently hear about "exchange programs." These require students to trade places at US-based and non-US universities. In theory, there should be no cost to the cooperating institutions, with the savings passed on to the participating students. But these programs require administrative attention (and therefore funding) to make them work. The cooperating institutions are frequently challenged to find matches for students, and for this reason alone, exchange programs are less common than you might imagine.

Instead of exchange programs you'll more commonly find contractual relationships between US colleges and universities and their international counterparts in which institutional and student services are the responsibility of the international institution. Such arrangements entail greater potential risk than operations run exclusively through an American college- or university-managed campus or center. However, there are ways to mitigate the risks. For instance, Americans can choose study-abroad options involving one or more American-style colleges and universities in host countries that are members of the Association of American International Colleges and Universities (AAICU). These institutions, based in such countries as Bulgaria, France, Ireland, and Greece, are accredited by US regional accrediting bodies and are administered like similar institutions in America. They have the "feel" of a US-based college or university despite being located in a foreign country. Learning systems are in place, along with personnel, including faculty and staff members, who are often citizens of the United States. Nevertheless, the day-to-day experiences in these institutions will involve many of the cultural advantages of living and learning in another country.

In addition to institutions coming under the AAICU umbrella, a college or university may have specific contractual relationships with internationally based institutions in which instructional and student services more closely reflect the norms and culture of the host country. This arrangement will involve some risk, although the relationship between the college or university may have been built over many years and may be reinforced by regular faculty exchanges or visits by family members from the US-based institution. The point is this: As you move away from home-institutional control, you will want to exercise caution and ask questions about what study and life will be like at the foreign host institution. Such preliminary exploration will be especially important if you take part in study-abroad experiences arranged through large educational consortia.

Many US colleges and universities partner with regional and national consortia that provide organizational and logistical help in arranging study-abroad services. The consortia vary from specific interinstitutional arrangements, such as the Committee on Institutional Cooperation (CIC) of the Big Ten (Indiana University, Ohio State University, and the University of Michigan, among others) and the Southeastern Conference Academic Consortium (SECAC) of the Southeastern Athletic Conference (Auburn University, the University of Georgia, and up to twelve others) to large consortia bodies, such as the Institute for Study Abroad, involving many opportunities in countries around the world. Although the interinstitutional consortia such as the CIC and SECAC and some of the other, larger multi-institutional consortia will provide reliable and high-quality services, others may not. The difference is often based on the profit status of the organization.

Not many people think about the profit status of colleges and universities, and although many Americans have an understanding of public versus private universities, fewer people know the differences between nonprofit private colleges and universities (Dartmouth and Yale, for instance) and those run for profit (the University of Phoenix, among some fourteen hundred others). Many for-profit institutions—in the United States at least—are fully accredited (by regional accrediting organizations) and are creditable, though many are not, and when you look internationally, the picture involving for-profit higher education becomes murky. Former American College of Thessaloniki president Richard Jackson recently highlighted some of the risks involved, while at the same time pointing to the exceptional status of the American International College and University system that operates nonprofit institutions with full accreditations.

College students will want to avoid the nightmare of arriving in a foreign country, being handed an envelope with instructions for getting settled and beginning study, and then, in effect, being abandoned. Students in a foreign environment need and deserve thoughtful and continuing services, especially if they are embarking on their first study-abroad experience. All prospective study-abroad candidates should seek help through a US college- or university-based study-abroad (or international studies) office. Professionals who staff these offices are generally well versed in the opportunities, advantages, and potential pitfalls of the myriad study-abroad options.

Learning through Travel and Study-Abroad Experiences

In our complex and information-saturated world you can use almost everything you learn, at one time or another, in your career. Traveling (near or far) and studying abroad can be broadening and enriching experiences. Here are some suggestions for maximizing the value of these opportunities:

- Do your homework about your destination. What museums and other cultural attractions there might help you to understand the area or nation? What indigenous authors might help to illuminate the scene? For example, a trip to Amherst, Massachusetts, would not be the same if you had not

learned about the life and work of Emily Dickinson. Similarly, an awareness and understanding of Michelangelo's life and work would add immensely to a trip to Rome or Florence.

- Consider keeping a journal during your trip. You will remember that Maud Baum did this and that her husband later published her journal.

- Try to "go native" whatever your destination (although, of course, avoid the use of the word *native* in African nations where it has a pejorative connotation). Try new foods, experience local customs, and seek an understanding of the local culture.

- If you travel or study in a country where English is not the first language, try to learn as much as you can of the local language. You may not become fluent, but some proficiency will take you a long way. You'll be surprised at how appreciative people will be even if you can only muster morning or evening greetings along with a few courteous expressions. If you are committed to an extended stay in a non-English-speaking culture, make arrangements, preferably ahead of time, for formal language training. This is especially important in study-abroad programs in which students board with host families.

- Seek opportunities to get to know people who live in your host country.

- Look for study-abroad opportunities that feature service-learning courses, in which directed volunteer work, often with the participation of local citizens, becomes part of the formal learning.

- Consider how international service might lead to special postgraduate opportunities. Some universities have partnerships with the US Peace Corps, which requires coordinated foreign service and study and leads to master's degrees in fields such as agriculture, education, and public administration.

Two college students reflect on their study-abroad experiences.

- Think of extending the benefits of travel and study abroad through speaking and writing projects at home.

Imagine how travel and study abroad can round out the learning component of the Way of Oz, and consider your personal stakes in enriching your career opportunities as you head down the Yellow Brick Road.

Distance Education and Life in Virtual Worlds

Distance education or learning through correspondence, telecommunicated classes, and self-paced Internet-based offerings are options for people who are place-bound or who desire learning opportunities not available at a home campus or home community. In recent years, relatively inexpensive technology has become available for audiovisual interactions through Internet linkages, such as Skype-type technology. A combination of self-paced learning and live interactions are now possible and likely to become more commonplace via Internet hookups. When combined with international partnerships with institutions abroad, a surrogate to study abroad results that offers experiences previously possible only through actual travel.

East Carolina University (ECU), for example, has taken advantage of inexpensive Internet audiovisual linkages to bring experiences from twenty-three institutions in seventeen nations on five continents to students based on the campus in Greenville, North Carolina. ECU students, only 1 percent of whom in the past studied abroad, now are able to expand their horizons through the university's Global Understanding Program. Options such as those at ECU are likely to be adopted more widely, and although they now represent only a modest substitute for study abroad, the cross-cultural and cross-national interactions provide many benefits to people who are unable to travel internationally.

Other institutions, encouraged by creative faculty members, are supporting efforts to bring virtual worlds into learning environments. New Mexico State University geography professor Michael DeMers uses Second Life game technology to teach his students about worldviews—in a virtual environment. Second Life electronically creates people and places that resemble counterparts in the real world. Players create their own identity-characters, called avatars, that function for them in the virtual world. Using avatars, in DeMers's experience, allows his students to express themselves more freely and thereby learn more readily in the world he and his students create.

For decades the US military has used software for virtual reality simulations to teach, for example, fighter jet piloting and combat tactics. Second Life and other such Internet-supported virtual reality programs offer opportunities to create international simulations that will likely become powerful teaching and learning tools in the future. Perhaps technology will someday allow for the three-dimensional projection of real people across distances to allow interactions that many *Star Wars* fans witnessed beginning with Episode IV, first released in 1977.

Opportunities for study-abroad experiences, real and virtual, will become increasingly prevalent in the future. The Senator Paul Simon Study Abroad Act of 2009, in which Congress authorized funding to support one million Americans each year in study-abroad programs, was a positive step for the United States to become part of the world's community.

III

The Way of Oz and Loving

8

Loving: An Integrated Perspective

I believe in kindness and love. . . . I love—love and kindness. . . . I wish the churches would emphasize kindness—kindness to everybody.

Rowan LeCompte (1925–), American artist, creator of fifty stained-glass windows and several mosaics for the National Cathedral in Washington, DC, commenting in a National Public Radio broadcast about his belief system

Frank Baum would undoubtedly have appreciated Rowan LeCompte's words about kindness as well as his life and work. As we have seen in his articles for *The Aberdeen Saturday Pioneer*, Baum was critical of institutions that send contradictory messages about love and kindness. Even though they lived in different times and generations, Baum and LeCompte would probably have agreed that love in its broadest sense includes the love of others, love of place, love of learning, and love of self (particularly as a portal to service). All these variations of love play a role in the Way of Oz.

Love is what binds us to people, places, times, and events. Imagine a time in your life when everything seems to come together. You have completed a college education and have found a job in an attractive and supportive setting. You have an intimate relationship with another, and perhaps a family. You are able to extend affection to others, and you have neighbors, colleagues, and friends who reciprocate your friendship and affection. You feel empathy and even love for other creatures in the natural world, and perhaps you have a beloved pet. You have learned as much as you can about where you live and work and are beginning to contribute to this place toward which you feel a sense of obligation, wanting now to safeguard its sustainability. Your love of place also gives you perspective on how you fit into your state, nation, and beyond.

Idyllic? Perhaps. But the coming together of loving relationships, times, places, and events happens for many people—at least during some periods of their lives. It seems to have happened to Frank Baum at times in his life: in his early teens at Rose Lawn in upstate New York; in his years in Chicago around the turn of the twentieth century when he published *The Wonderful Wizard of Oz* and successfully mounted the theatrical production of the book; in the years when he and his family shuttled among Chicago, their summer home at Macatawa Park in Michigan, and the Hotel del Coronado in San Diego; and in the final years at Ozcot in Los Angeles.

Just as it did for Baum, love, of all types, can sustain us through good times and bad. Love has powerful effects on your creativity, motivation, feelings of self-worth, and ability to contribute to society. The beneficent effects of love are synergistic and self-reinforcing. There is good reason to seek and cultivate love in all we do.

9

Loving and Others

To have pleased you, to have interested you, to have won your friendship, and perhaps your love, through my stories, is to my mind as great an achievement as to become President of the United States.

L. Frank Baum (1856–1919),
"To My Readers" in *Dorothy and the Wizard of Oz* (1908)

There is a continuum of affections, attachments, romantic relationships, and devotions when we think about the love of others. Different people, or some of the same people at different times in their lives, will develop bonds with deities, other people, and nature, including creatures in the animal world.

Bringing Others into Your Heart and Mind

Years ago, when I was an undergraduate student at St. John's University in New York, I had several teachers, mainly in theology and philosophy classes, who were priests. One of them recommended reading the Jesuit priest Raoul Plus's book *God within Us*. The thesis of the work is that special supernatural benefit is derived from continual and sustained internal dialogue with God. Father Plus referred to it this way: "The end of piety, its object and reward, is *intimacy with God* [italics in original]. Comparatively few souls attain it. Many imagine it to be an impossibility."

I was intrigued and moved by Father Plus's advice, but when I grew older, I came to see that sustained internal devotion to a deity (or perhaps *the love within us*) is true for people of various belief systems, even nontraditional believers (as for example Frank Baum and his espousal of theosophical beliefs). Our challenge is to avoid exclusivity, thinking ours is the only true path to God (understood differently according to various traditional religious or other beliefs), which leaves worthy others outside our sphere of love.

In his 2009 landmark address to a multicultural audience in Cairo, Egypt, President Barack Obama said, "There's one rule that lies at the heart of every religion—that we do unto others as we would have them do unto us. This truth transcends nations and peoples—a belief that isn't new; that isn't black or white or brown; that isn't Christian or Muslim or Jew. It's a belief that pulsed in the cradle of civilization, and that still beats in the hearts of billions around the world." This "golden creed" permeates the hearts and minds of all people—Christians, Muslims, or Jews, as well as Buddhists and Hindus, the followers of Confucius, secular humanists, and others. In short, the Golden Rule should extend to all humanity.

From Plato and Aristotle to Freud and Jung to Modern Behavioral Researchers

For many in our contemporary society where entertainment and media offerings are permeated with sexual innuendo and vulgar expressions, the word *love* conjures up only images of erotic love. Conversely, the prudish fear of romantic expression and physical love inhibits understanding, not only of the importance of sexuality to human emotional and physical well-being but also of the broader concept of love. To appreciate the concept of love in all its forms, it is helpful to look back at its historical and philosophical roots.

The ancient Greek philosopher Plato (ca. 427–347 BCE), who was inspired by Socrates (ca. 469–399 BCE) and taught Aristotle (384–322 BCE), organized his understanding of love into three aspects: *eros*, *philia*, and *agape*.

Eros is the love of beauty in all its manifestations—from art to ideas to human beings, pursued with passion and a sense of merging or possession. In the context of human relationships, the word *eroticism* applies. *Eros* that doesn't necessarily involve sexual interactions is called platonic love.

Philia is the love of others woven into family affections, friendships, and business or professional relationships. Love as *philia* may or may not be reciprocal, but should be shared. *Philia* also includes love of work or scholarship, loyalty to one's institution of employment and love of self, but not (according to the Greek ideal) egocentric, self-glorifying, or hedonistic love.

Agape is universal love, or the love of others as oneself, sometimes called "brotherly love." The concept of *agape* includes the love of God for his creatures and implies passionate reciprocal devotion. For Christians, *agape* may include self-sacrificial love—as in martyrdom—for their Messiah.

There is obvious overlap among the concepts embodied in *eros, philia,* and *agape,* but the distinctions provide some understanding of the different aspects of love that can be embraced as a part of the Way of Oz. Many notable thinkers after the great Greek philosophers—the Roman poet Ovid, the medieval troubadours and poets (including Eleanor of Aquitaine and her uncle William) and their Arabic counterparts, eighteenth- and nineteenth-century novelists (such as Jane Austen and Henry James), twentieth-century psychologists and psychiatrists (such as Sigmund Freud and Carl Jung), human behavioral researchers (chief among them Alfred Kinsey and the team of William H. Masters and Virginia E. Johnson), and biological and cognitive psychological researchers also illuminate for us the variations of love. The composite picture of humanity and the human need for love that emerges from their writings includes the love of God; affection for other people, including friends, colleagues, and family members; romantic love; and the love of nature and nature's creatures.

Love of God

You may be surprised that two-thirds of the world's people embrace other faiths than those in the Judeo-Christian tradition. America's founding fathers, many of whom were Freemasons, understood that an acceptance of beliefs from all the world's religions was preferable to dogmatism and intolerance. As members of a democratic and pluralistic society we need to adhere to our beliefs, God-centered or not, and approach relationships with others based on kindness and a respect for their beliefs even if we cannot fully embrace them.

Kindness, or what LeCompte calls a love of "love and kindness," has guided most enlightened people throughout their lives. But, we might ask, how does a love of "love and kindness" manifest itself in a typical social or work setting?

Affection for Others, including Colleagues, Friends, and Family Members

The tone of a home or workplace says a lot about whether it is a pleasant environment in which to live and work. Are colleagues, friends, and family members supportive of one another? Are criticisms of others rarely heard? Are interactions marked by gratitude, kindness, and concern? Are compliments on good work commonly extended? If the answers to such questions are positive, you have undoubtedly found an environment where kindness is a way of being.

Frank Baum found such places where he lived and worked. Recall his amicable relationships with collaborators in his creative work, including the illustrator W. W. Denslow (at least during the early years of their work together) and other creative geniuses, such as Paul Tietjens, with whom he worked on the *Wizard of Oz* stage production, and Louis Gottschalk, who contributed to Baum's later stage and film productions. Baum's positive interactions with children in settings from Aberdeen to Chicago to California were central to the development of many of his stories that became *The Wonderful Wizard of Oz* and other works.

Unfortunately, in our personal lives and at work, all of us at times experience unkindness or meanness. What can we do?

With friends and acquaintances—and even family members—a direct, though gentle approach is best. It's always preferable to use kindness and extend the benefit of the doubt to others, using questions rather than accusations. You can counter a mean-spirited remark with something like: "Would you mind explaining that comment?" or "Your comment seemed unkind and hurtful. Did you mean it that way?" Questions like these sometimes help prevent an unnecessary confrontation, for often a seemingly hostile comment is merely the result of an unintentional, poorly phrased, or mistaken expression. If, on the other hand, you discern true meanness, an assertion such as "I can't believe what I have just heard, given our prior friendship" may be followed by attempts at remediation and reconciliation. The subsequent healing process may take time, but whether the conflict is resolved or not, it is important for you to move on.

You should focus on meaningful friendships with colleagues, friends, and family members, reinforced by frequent (large and small) acts of kindness. Probably you've seen sign-offs such as "Thanks for bringing this matter to my attention. Kindly, _____" or "You've handled this situation well. Kindly, _____." The "power of kindness"—so expressed— can be significant in forming new friendships or cementing old ones. And the expression of kindness can be reinforced by small acts of kindness. In Seattle, Washington, some companies use special coffee treats at breaks as perks. In Athens, Georgia, the president of a small biotechnology company buys specialty chocolates for her staff when she returns from business or pleasure trips. One university's chief academic officer designed a lapel pin with the institutional logo and unit designation, signifying the camaraderie he promoted among all who worked for him. He gave these to all his associates and employees. Most wore the pins proudly because of his affection, support, and communication style.

For supervisors, hosting periodic luncheons or other outings does much to boost morale and signal gratitude and kindness toward members of a unit or organization. The value of such events is enhanced when the supervisor offers remarks to highlight the accomplishments of everyone present. One supervisor of a forty-member unit takes the opportunity, following year-end retreats, to point out at least one contribution each member of the unit had made.

In another work setting, a supervisor sponsors a birthday fund for everyone in his office. Such celebrations occur throughout the year, providing frequent reminders of his caring for staff members.

It is important to point out that relationships in the workplace must be platonic and that supervisors need to avoid any situation that could be construed as sexual harassment. Sexual harassment is sexual discrimination, a violation of Title VII of the Civil Rights Act of 1964. The act's provisions are enforced through the office of the US Equal Employment Opportunity Commission (EEOC). According to the EEOC, sexual harassment involves "unwelcome sexual advances, requests for sexual favors, and other verbal or physical conduct of a sexual nature . . . when submission to or rejection of this conduct explicitly or implicitly affects an individual's employment, unreasonably interferes with an individual's work performance, or creates an intimidating, hostile, or offensive work environment." Language on the EEOC website indicates that the victim may be of either gender; the victim may be a supervisor or any other agent of the firm, institution, or organization, or a nonemployee permitted into the workplace; harassment does not have to cause economic or bodily harm; and the conduct of the harasser must be unwelcome.

According to the EEOC, sexual harassment can be a quid pro quo arrangement (where exchange of favors is proposed either implicitly or explicitly) or as a result of a hostile or abusive environment. Harassment is a serious offense if it is pervasive and severe. It can include sexual innuendos, sexually suggestive or offensive signs, graffiti, or pictures, discriminatory intimidation, insults, or ridicule.

You've perhaps witnessed the painful results of sexual harassment. Perpetrators of sexual harassment are often, but not always, men. In sexual harassment cases where there is a power differential (the harassing of a female student by a male faculty member, for instance), victims often require professional counseling.

Avoiding the appearance and substance of sexual harassment is an inviolable principle of the Way of Oz.

Romantic Love

There are relatively few references to romantic love in the Oz stories, but it is clear from his biography that Frank Baum was himself a romantic. One story stands out. When Baum met his future wife, Maud Gage, at a Christmas celebration on the evening of December 25, 1881, at his sister Harriet's party, his romantic boldness was apparent. In introducing the young people, his aunt Josephine said, "Frank Baum, I want you to know Maud Gage. I'm sure you will love her." His immediate response was "Consider yourself loved, Miss Gage." To which Maud is purported to have replied, "Thank you, Mr. Baum. That's a promise. Please see that you live up to it." They were married less than a year later.

Sigmund Freud (1856–1939), who coincidentally shares Baum's birth year, began studying sexual behavior around 1900 when he published *The Interpretation of Dreams*, the same year as the publication of *The Wonderful Wizard of Oz*. In this seminal work and others that would follow, Freud categorized the normal developmental sexual urges of babies and children as the Oedipus complex (the love of a male child for his mother and jealousy of his father) or Electra complex (the love of a female child for her father and jealousy of her mother). He described the importance of erogenous zones in human development and preteen latency periods that end with puberty. He was among the first to codify normal sexual drives and desires. The picture, of course, is much more complex, but any understanding of mature human intimacy must take into account normal sexual behaviors.

Not long after the publication of *The Psychopathology of Everyday Life* in 1901, Freud was contacted by another twentieth-century giant in psychology and psychiatry, Carl Gustav Jung (1875–1961), who presented him with a copy of his own book, *Studies in Word Association*. They had a close personal relationship that lasted for several years until the two had a falling out, in part because of a perceived snub of Jung by Freud in 1913. The two had drifted apart because of their differing views: Freud believed in a personalized psychosexual unconscious, and Jung developed the idea of a collective unconscious of the human psyche. Jung believed in the spiritual underpinnings of human longings, including the desire for human intimacy. In the end, the Freud-Jung feud energized the emerging field of psychology that informed studies of human sexuality that took place in the decades after Freud and Jung's fractured relationship.

Human sexuality is complex and cannot be adequately covered here; however, Freud's pioneering studies during Frank Baum's lifetime and those of other sexuality experts up to and including the first decade of the twenty-first century have come to the following generally accepted conclusions:

• Sex is a healthy and natural component of humanity and human intimacy.

• Sexual intimacy is an important, though complex phenomenon—emotionally, physically, and neurologically—and should be pursued primarily in mature relationships.

- • Casual or coerced physical intimacy is hurtful and, in most instances, illegal and is certainly unethical and immoral.

- • Romance interlaced with intellectual, emotional, and physical intimacy profoundly reinforces mature relationships.

Romance should be accompanied, of course, with due consideration of modern contraceptive and safe sex practices. The freedom in our contemporary society to engage in sexual relationships does not absolve anyone from taking responsibility for preventing unwanted pregnancy and sexually transmitted diseases. Although incidences of both diminished during the 1990s, they are on the rise again in the early twenty-first century, according to studies by the Centers for Disease Control and Prevention. You should be aware of the necessity for safe sex but also, and perhaps even more importantly, that sexual intimacy should be guided by respect for one's partner and oneself. This careful approach requires you to integrate scientific and ethical understanding, along with religious beliefs, which should guide your behavior, consistent with the love and kindness imperatives of the Way of Oz.

The Toto Perspective

Many of us think of the Cowardly Lion in the 1939 Oz film as more human than animal, in part because of Bert Lahr's brilliant portrayal of the character. Readers of the original Oz book know that Baum treated other animals anthropomorphically, giving them the ability to speak. Later, as Baum spun the tales that became his thirteen Oz sequels, animals beyond those native to Oz take on the human power of speech as well. In fact, all animals that come to Oz, including Toto, acquire the gift of human speech. With few exceptions, the animals in Oz are endearingly human. Baum's Cowardly Lion and other animals are the fantasy element of the Way of Oz, but they are part of the continuing spectrum of life and are worthy of love, too.

In the past century biologists have found evidence of communication and reasoning among animals at several levels of the phylogenetic tree. Most people of Baum's generation could not have imagined such capacities in animals. Contemporary science suggests that there is not a distinct dividing line between animals and human beings; instead, there is a continuum of consciousness and communication skills that demands our attention and should foster our love for our fellow creatures. We should condemn cruelty toward animals and punish offenders—though, unfortunately, this is not what happens in some US states and in many nations around the world. If we honor the "Toto perspective," we should be dedicated to respect for and humane treatment of animals along with our obligation to teach the same to members of the younger generation.

Recent US polls indicate that 80 percent or more of American households have dogs or cats. Dog owners make up 60 percent of the total number of pet owners. Other surveys and studies suggest that pet ownership and interactions with animals have several benefits for their human owners, among them improved physical and emotional health (reduced blood pressure and stress); greater understanding of the contributions of animals to our natural and cultural environment; and special help to those with developmental and physical disabilities (such as guide or seeing-eye dogs, and in therapeutic horsemanship programs).

Frank Baum would be proud of our contemporary understanding of animals in the United States. The consciousness of the sustainability of our environment should include protections and concern for animals—both domesticated and wild.

10
Loving and Place

Home is the place where, when you have to go there, they have to take you in.

Robert Frost (1874–1963), American poet

You might recall Dorothy's famous final words at the end of the 1939 *Wizard of Oz* film, "Oh, Auntie Em—there's no place like home!" At the end of Baum's 1900 book, she says: "Aunt Em! I'm so glad to be home again."

Baum's sentiment comes through: a sense of home and the love therein are seminally important to us. Place is a metaphor for an epicenter of love.

Place for you may be your parents' home, the home you've created for yourself as an adult, your home away from home, your workplace, or a virtual home, where you retreat to seek comfort and familiarity.

Love of Birthplace and Family Home Place

There's an old joke about human origins and home: A preteen boy comes to his father with the age-old question: "Dad, where did I come from?" The dad pauses, gulps, but proceeds with a careful description of human reproduction in the context of marriage. The explanation takes several minutes. After listening intently through the end of the explanation, the boy says, with a tinge of irony in his voice: "That's funny; Bobby said he's from Indiana."

One of the most frequently asked questions at social events is "Where are you from?" The questioner wants to know where you were born and grew up. An answer from the son or daughter of a career military mother or father says a lot about place. This answer goes something like this: "Well, I'm a military brat. I've lived many places, but I was born in _____." Thus, military service often has the unintended consequence of depriving career military progeny of a solid identification with their birthplace. There are undoubtedly many advantages of being the child of a career military parent, but forging a strong identity with one's birthplace is usually not one of them.

Your identification with your place of birth (or where you grew up) can have a powerful influence on who you are and what you become. Take, for example, the five-term US senator from Arkansas, J. William Fulbright. He was born in Missouri, but his family moved when he was a year old to Fayetteville, Arkansas, where he attended school from first grade through college (he went to the University of Arkansas, where he earned his bachelor's degree in history). For all his life, he thought of himself as a native of Fayetteville and Arkansas. He became a faculty member and president of the University of Arkansas at Fayetteville and later served as a member of the US House of Representatives (for one term) and Senate (for five terms) from Arkansas. Clearly, Fulbright's caring for his adopted hometown and home state helped seal a career that might well have gone differently without such affection.

Guy Bailey, who has served as chancellor of the University of Missouri–Kansas City and president of Texas Tech University, is fond of saying he's from L.A.—not the city in Southern California but Lower Alabama! He frequently uses this humorous comment as an introduction to a folksy story from his rural Southern past. His listeners are hooked, and he's able to go on with his speech assured of their attention.

Your birthplace and the place where you grew up help to define you and can provide a source of stories that will entertain and endear you to colleagues, family, and friends. You should develop and nurture these stories; they will serve you well in your private and public lives. You can wear (and offer as gifts) sartorial accessories like state flag lapel pins, neckties, or scarves that relate to your birthplace or those of others. You can use aesthetically pleasing neckties or scarves that depict maps of famous cities to suggest metaphorically (in an oral presentation or in introducing out-of-town guests)

Honors college professor
Susan Tomlinson
comments on the
love of an adopted
place.

that one's life can be seen as a map to be filled in with accomplishments that are of value to society. If you are like the majority of Americans, who are born, live, and die in the same town or state, your stories and allusions to place can serve as meaningful references in your speeches or presentations.

If, however, you are like Frank Baum (or the child of a career military parent) and life takes you to many places, you will find that it is of great value to relate to each of these places as your home place.

Love of an Adopted Place

Attaining success in a new place of study or work has a lot to do with your ability to fit in with the customs and way of life of the natives in your new setting.

Before Taylor Eighmy, vice president for research at Texas Tech, took his new administrative post in the Southwest, he'd always lived in New England. In taking this new job, he anticipated new experiences, both culturally and geographically. And since he was an adherent of the Way of Oz, within the first month of his new job he began taking weekend trips to local sites of interest, and he soon began to understand the local and regional culture. He quickly became familiar with local legend and lore, collecting stories he heard from longtime residents of his new home.

If you relocate, learn as much as you can about your new environment. Use this knowledge to help you make the transition from your former setting to the new one. Try to become a "naturalized citizen" in your new setting as quickly as possible.

Love of Special and Virtual Places

Thomas Jefferson suggested that if well-educated Americans could choose a home other than the United States, most would choose France. Jefferson had a great fondness for the French Republic because he knew it well, having served as ambassador there from the young United States, and because it was a place where his relationship with his slave, Sally Hemings, wasn't hampered by societal prejudice.

Jefferson's love for an adopted home is far from unique. Winston Churchill, whose mother was a US citizen, was awarded honorary US citizenship because of his love for and service to the United States by President John F. Kennedy in 1963. Think about the influence on Frank Baum's creative and personal life of such places as Aberdeen, South Dakota; Chicago; western Michigan; and Southern California. Many other prominent and not-so-prominent people have had special places in their hearts for an adopted homeland.

Junot Díaz, a Massachusetts Institute of Technology professor and Pulitzer Prize–winning author (for his novel *The Brief Wondrous Life of Oscar Wao*), was born in the Dominican Republic and lived there until he was six, when his family immigrated to New Jersey. He attributes his success to two things: his great love of reading, which served as a refuge from prejudice, and his love for his homeland. In an aside, however, Díaz has said, "I don't think that I would have thought so fondly of Santo Domingo had I stayed there my whole life."

Many artists, writers, and scholars have immortalized places special to them—both near and far from where they were born. Here's a sampling:

- The French Impressionist painter Pierre-Auguste Renoir (1841–1919) loved to paint scenes of his friends in and around Paris. In later life he moved to Provence in southern France, which he came to love and where he continued to paint, producing some of his most famous works. Vincent Van Gogh (1853–1890) and many other late-nineteenth-century artists joined Renoir in Provence, which they loved because of the luminosity of the light there.

- The Chilean poet Pablo Neruda (1914–1973) was influenced greatly by the time he spent in Burma (now Myanmar), Colombo (now Sri Lanka), and Indonesia.

- Nikos Kazantzakis (1883–1957), best known for his novel *Zorba the Greek*, was deeply influenced by the culture of his native Crete, even though he spent much of his life in France, Germany, and the Soviet Union (now Russia).

Some home places can be virtual places. As we have seen, faculty members in some universities are using telecommunications in various courses to give their students virtual access to foreign countries. For these students, another country can come to seem as familiar as their own. For Frank Baum, the Land of Oz became as real as the many physical places where he lived.

11

Love of Learning and Self

"The best thing for being sad," replied Merlyn, beginning to puff and blow, "is to learn something. That is the only thing that never fails. You may grow old and trembling in your anatomies, you may lie awake at night listening to the disorder of your veins, you may miss your only love, you may see the world about you devastated by evil lunatics, or know your honor trampled in the sewers of baser minds. There is only one thing for it then—to learn. Learn why the world wags and what wags it. That is the only thing which the mind can never exhaust, never alienate, never be tortured by, never fear or distrust, and never dream of regretting."

T. H. White (1906–1964), English author,
creator of the quartet of novels *The Once and Future King*

If you ask friends and relatives about people who have had the most influence in their lives, they will typically name teachers. If you ask what it was that made these teachers so influential, you are likely to hear such things as "enthusiasm" and "passion for their field of study." Such comments are common, reflecting not only good teachers' love of learning but also their apparent love of self. There are countless examples of people who have been profoundly influenced by a gifted teacher. Edward R. Murrow (1908–1965), arguably the best broadcast journalist of the twentieth century, was influenced greatly by Ida Louise Anderson (1921–1970), a diminutive and frail Washington State University English professor, who inculcated in him a love of words. Known for his investigative reporting, Murrow infused his love of scholarship and learning into the production of touchstone programs such as *See It Now* and *Person to Person*.

For Griffin Smith, Jr. (1941–), executive editor of the *Arkansas Democrat-Gazette*, one of his most inspirational teachers was Charles Alan Wright (1927–2000), the notable US constitutional scholar, who taught for many years at the law school at the University of Texas at Austin. Smith even changed his name (to Smith Griffin) for a year during law school to improve his odds for taking one of Wright's courses. (Because of Wright's popularity, students were admitted to his courses through a type of lottery, based on the first letter of their last names; the year of Smith's quest, the *S* names were disallowed.) Griffin Smith, who has changed career emphases at least twice, says his experience in Charles Alan Wright's class has been profoundly influential throughout his life.

But love of learning and self aren't exclusive to good teachers. Many other dedicated and successful professionals exhibit these qualities.

All for the Love of Learning

As we saw earlier, learning involves reading, writing, communicating, and traveling. It also requires critical thinking, curiosity, dedication, and creativity. When you combine the *process* of learning (reading and the like) with the *scholarship* of learning (critical thinking and complex reasoning) in unique ways, you will begin to experience the love of learning that good teachers know well.

Let's take, for example, Stephanie, a junior premed student at a major university. She has enjoyed several general education and upper-division courses, particularly those in the biological and chemical sciences containing material vital to her future professional studies. But she's also required to take electives, and she chooses to enroll in a classics course on ancient Greece. The instructor of this course—we'll call him David—is an enthusiastic and engaging teacher. He's charismatic, but he displays gravitas when it comes to the serious application of learning he expects of his students and himself.

While taking David's course, Stephanie learns how the works of the ancient Greeks have extraordinarily influenced our modern concepts of culture and science. As the semester proceeds, she is impressed by David's lectures on how Western literature is infused with allusions to Greek literary work, especially from Greek epic poetry. She studies Greek art and architecture and the impact these have had on artists and architects throughout the centuries. When David tells the class he'll be leading a study group to Greece during the upcoming summer, Stephanie signs up. David's three-week Greek study tour takes the students to London, where they visit the British Museum to view the Greek artifacts there, including the famous Elgin Marbles (monumental sculptures from the pediments of the Parthenon on the Acropolis in Athens). The group then flies to Athens, where they tour the Acropolis, the Agora (the ancient Greek market and meeting place), and archaeological museums. From Athens, the tour continues through the Peloponnese, with stops at Mycenae and Olympia and other sites on the Greek mainland, including Delphi and Marathon, followed by trips to the Aegean islands, including Crete, Naxos, and Santorini. The trip is magnificent, enhanced by the scholarly exercises David builds into the tour. He assigns each student a project related to some classic feature or site the group visits. The assignment requires each participant to write a paper and give an oral presentation at a site relevant to the paper. Stephanie is assigned a paper on the Erechtheum (a temple dedicated to Athena and Poseidon) and its caryatids (columns crafted in the form of female figures that hold up the roof of the "Porch of the Maidens") on the Acropolis.

Imagine this scene: David and his students are gathered on the Acropolis on a bright sunny day, positioned in front of Erechtheum. David asks Stephanie to make her presentation, and as she begins, she feels the extraordinary gestalt of the situation: she's here, prepared to speak knowledgeably about the significance of this major Greek temple right on the spot where it stands.

Undergraduates augment lifelong learning through research.

A sense of intellectual wonder and emotional satisfaction wells up in her—a phenomenon she's not felt before. She is at this moment experiencing a profound love of learning that will leave an imprint on her inner being that will help guide her through her successive years of study and in her profession. The intellectual, psychological, and emotional satisfaction she feels now will more than likely continue throughout her life of learning.

Teachers and Teacher Types

A teacher can be one of three types: instructor, mentor, or peer, and certainly these categories overlap. The categories have varying potential for having an impact on learning and ultimately a love of learning.

Instructor

Everyone has had instructors; these are expert and authoritative teachers, in a tradition that has rich historic roots. Moses Maimonides (1135–1204), the great twelfth-century Talmudic scholar, wrote in his *Guide for the Perplexed*: "A man who has instructed another in any subject, and has improved his knowledge, may in like manner be regarded as the parent of the person taught, because he is the author of that knowledge." Teachers who may be involved only marginally in their students' lives may nevertheless have a powerful influence on them when they are charismatic and gifted in their craft. The hypothetical premed student, Stephanie, was positively influenced by the instructor aspect of her classics teacher David. If her contact with him increased, a student-mentor relationship might have emerged.

Mentor

Anyone who has successfully completed a graduate degree, particularly a doctorate, understands the importance of good mentors. Mentoring has become increasingly important in undergraduate programs as well, especially for students in programs requiring internships and clerkships and for students engaged in scholarly and research projects, such as those enrolled in honors programs.

Good mentors serve as advocates and career advisors; your relationship with your mentor can become a lifelong association and friendship.

Peer

Teachers can also be peers, especially if you are involved in collaborative or interdisciplinary scholarship or research. You may be part of a team of researchers whose members have complementary skills and backgrounds. In the course of your interdisciplinary research, which will involve synergistic interactions, various team members might emerge as teachers.

The Teacher in You

Teachers, of all types, are important, but there is *no one* more important in the lifelong learning paradigm than you. Like Stephanie, you may have a watershed moment or experience that anchors your commitment to lifelong learning. What lifelong learners realize, even early in their journey, is that learning is self-reflective or self-reinforcing. As you learn and experience the thrill of learning, whether such experiences result in journal entries or an article, book, invention, painting, or some other accomplishment, you will be inspired to learn more, to achieve more, to serve more.

You should reinforce your journey with a plan for professional and personal development. You can pursue continuing education and advanced degree programs. But the most important ingredient is your commitment to lifelong learning.

Love of Self

When we talk about a love of self, we are not talking about egoism or narcissism. It's true, however, that some degree of egoism can be healthy since it can serve as motivation, and combined with a service ethic, it can be of great benefit to society. Humility modulates the negative effects of egoism. The next time you think you know it all, take a walk through the stacks of any public or university library. Observe the thousands of books on topics you've never heard of. In such a setting you will begin to see that in

your lifetime your ability to achieve a mastery of the world's collective knowledge is impossible.

A large part of loving yourself is having faith in yourself and welcoming challenges in life. Compare the person who has self-esteem with one who has great doubts or fears, such as those who suffer from post-traumatic stress disorder (PTSD). PTSD became acutely apparent in the United States among surviving victims of the tragic events of 9/11. In addition, many military personnel returning from conflicts such as those in Iraq and Afghanistan have been diagnosed with PTSD. For people suffering from PTSD, life can be miserable because of their seeming inability to meet the challenges they face, which they may eventually interpret and internalize as failure. What is most damaging is that these perceived failures compound the stress of PTSD.

Even people who do not suffer from PTSD can fall into the "stress-challenge" trap. Among students, this trap may decrease motivation, contribute to procrastination, and paralyze their efforts. This is most unfortunate because some challenges and stresses (particularly of the moderate type or "eustress") can actually energize life. In his bestselling book *The Road Less Traveled*, the American psychiatrist M. Scott Peck (1935–2005) said, "Once we truly know that life is difficult—once we truly understand and accept it—then life is no longer difficult. Because once it is accepted, the fact that life is difficult no longer matters." Self-assured and successful professionals—those who make a difference in all areas of life—understand Peck's message.

IV

The Way of Oz and Serving

12

Serving: An Integrated Perspective

> To be fulfilled we need to recognize, all of us, that the world doesn't owe us a living—rather we owe the world a living. And in the brief time that is given to us, we must somehow learn to give ourselves away.
>
> F. Forrester Church (1948–2009), American author,
> senior minister of All Soul's Unitarian Church, New York City

Let's think about people who adopt the principles of the Way of Oz. Imagine the hero who balances his commitments to learning, loving, and serving—Baum's wisdom, heart, and courage—and the heroine who has a similar balance but also brings together the three components into an integrated whole: she learns new ways to serve through unselfish giving to noble causes; she develops a love for the recipients of her service; and she realizes the need for greater understanding as she continues serving others.

When our heroine and hero realize the extraordinary interactions of learning, loving, and service, they come to see how these can be integrated through the heart, mind, and resolve.

Now, if the integration of our hero and heroine's efforts sounds so ideal as to be impossible, think about another real example of the way the integrated elements of learning, loving, and serving came together in a great American institution, the land-grant university. America's land-grant institutions were the brainchild of

Jonathan Baldwin Turner (1805–1899), who, in the 1850s, tried to convince the Illinois legislature to develop a university for the working classes. Turner's ideas were adopted by a Vermont storekeeper, Justin Smith Morrill (1810–1898), who served in the US House of Representatives (1855–1867) and the US Senate (1867–1898). He embraced Turner's altruistic idea and crafted the language that became the Morrill Land-Grant Colleges Act of 1862, which was signed into law by President Abraham Lincoln on July 2, 1862, at the height of the Civil War. It provided federal land subsidies for establishing universities that would offer liberal and practical education for the working classes. As President Lincoln said at the bill's signing, "The land-grant university system is being built on behalf of the people, who have invested in these public universities their hopes, their support, and their confidence." The legislation emphasized agriculture, mechanical arts (engineering), and military tactics. The land-grant university, as it evolved, not only blended liberal and practical studies but also had at its core extension (also referred to commonly as cooperative extension) efforts that would help identify community problems that could be addressed through research. The research and extension efforts were codified and received funding through two congressional acts, the Hatch Act of 1887 and the Smith-Lever Act of 1914.

Driven by problems in the real world, other universities emulated what became land-grant universities. Problems in food production, for example, were brought to universities for problem-solving research, the results of which were incorporated into course syllabi and curricula that would guide the teaching mission of land-grant programs. The land-grant model is directly analogous to the learning-loving-serving paradigm of the Way of Oz, in which learning is the equivalent of research, loving is equivalent to teaching, and serving is equivalent to extension under the land-grant system. What is needed is to emphasize the blending of the interactive components, which, if done well, results in a synergy that positively influences creativity and productivity.

Consider, for example, the case of Juan Muñoz of Lubbock, Texas. Muñoz was born of Mexican immigrant parents in Southern California. After an English teacher encouraged him to go to college, he enrolled at the University of California–Santa Barbara, where he earned a baccalaureate degree. He went on to California State University at Los Angeles and UCLA, where he earned master's and PhD degrees, respectively, following a stint in the US Marine Corps. Subsequently, he pursued a life in higher education, becoming vice president for diversity and community outreach at Texas Tech University in 2008.

What has defined Muñoz's vocational dedication is service to his community; he's had a gubernatorial appointment to the board of directors of the Texas Department of Housing and Community Affairs; he's held board membership on the Covenant Health System of Lubbock, on the Lubbock Civic Service Commission, and on the editorial advisory board of *The Lubbock Avalanche-Journal*. Muñoz is a past president of the Lubbock Boys & Girls Clubs. His extraordinary dedication to service is an outgrowth of his early years. He says, "I grew up poor in a family of immigrants, but I was helped by many people—people of all backgrounds and persuasions. I have a fierce sense of obligation to give back." His service experiences have guided his teaching and research in Texas Tech's College of Education, where he is an associate professor. His administrative responsibilities are energized by the synergy that has evolved from his teaching, research, and service, with service always leading the way.

The links of teaching and research to service may seem obvious, but they are not always affected easily. For Muñoz there were undoubtedly challenges in assuming roles and responsibilities where there was little precedent or example in his family's background. Thus, Muñoz or anyone else in his set of circumstances must draw upon courage to act. We recall Baum's Cowardly Lion mustering up the courage to help fight the Kalidahs, jumping into the river to help ferry the Tin Woodman, Dorothy, and Toto to shore on their way to the Emerald City, and most impressively, killing the giant spiderlike creature to free the animals of the forest. Courage is the activating force for service and it has supported Juan Muñoz and countless others who have found ways to blend learning, loving, and serving for the good of society and our planet, making them Way of Oz practitioners whether they know it or not.

13
Serving Others

In Matthew 20, the mother of two of Jesus' twelve disciples basically pulls an "end run." She goes behind the backs of the other disciples and goes to Jesus with a little request. She wants her two sons to be able to sit at Jesus' right and left when he comes into His Kingdom. . . . She wants the best seats in the house for her boys for eternity. After all, it's just a small favor. . . . Jesus doesn't say yes or no. He basically tells her: you've got the wrong perspective. That's not the way to look at things. "Whoever wishes to be great among you, must be a servant."

Karen Hughes (1948–), global vice chair at Burson-Marsteller, former under-secretary of state for public diplomacy and public affairs in the US Department of State

Altruism. It's a word for a profound idea, an ethic promoted in most if not all of the world's religions and a principle many people embrace, including the traditionally religious and humanists alike. The great French philosopher Auguste Compte (1798–1857) coined the word and defined it as the deliberate and morally compelling pursuit of the welfare of others. People who meet Compte's criterion are said to be altruistic.

The notion of altruism permeates the Oz tales, from the original 1900 story through nearly every sequel, and is exemplified in many of the characters—the Cowardly Lion, Dorothy, Princess Ozma, and Glinda. In the context of the Way of Oz, altruism is tied to service to others.

Serving Others—One at a Time

For the adult, the path to the Way of Oz may be service, but adolescents are more likely to enter the Way of Oz through the love they receive from their parents and other relatives and friends—love that, as adolescents grow older, is reciprocally exchanged. Ambassador Karen Hughes has said, "Many of us act and work as if fame or power or money and all the stuff we collect are our true loves, yet if we drag ourselves away from that list that keeps us busy and focus on what is truly important, most of us would say that our family and friends and the people we care about are what we truly love."

Adolescents should move on with a "loving heart" through high school and college, pursuing at minimum a baccalaureate degree, which is vital for success in the twenty-first century. Many budding professionals will need to go on to graduate or professional school to qualify for entrance into their chosen profession, and along the way there will be opportunities for service through volunteer efforts, internships, and service-learning courses. The combination of loving and learning, with its companions, competence, and courage, puts you in a powerful position to serve. If you develop an ethical framework within a beneficent milieu, altruism is likely to emerge. You will begin to see that the loving-learning-competence triad joined with courage bolsters your ability to discern and deliver genuine service. Without such an understanding, a shallow "do-goodism" may result, in which good intentions can do more harm than good. With the loving-learning-competence triad in place and motivation through altruism or a passion for service, re-markable things can happen that help change the world—one person at a time.

Scott Pelley, a correspondent for CBS's *60 Minutes*, offers an interesting perspective on serving others. He recently challenged a group of college graduates to think about taking a test sixty years hence. The test, on the worth of your life, poses questions with no easy answers and is timed but may come to fruition at any time given the differences in our personal life clocks. Pelley cites two examples of those who will pass his sixty years test with flying colors.

The first is Paulette Schank, a US Air Force nurse who served in battle zones in Iraq. Pelley describes Schank's behavior during an incident in a tent hospital at Balad Air Force Base, about forty miles north of Baghdad. She was on duty in a trauma center when a badly wounded marine arrived who needed a lot of blood while surgeons attempted to repair his three arterial lacerations. At a critical moment, the blood supply ran out, and Schank volunteered to get more. She ran to the blood blank to donate her own blood. Word spread of the young marine's plight, and many fellow service personnel heeded the call. The marine's life was saved, and Schank reveled in the altruistic joy of the young man's extended life. Paulette Schank answered her sixty-year test question—"how to serve"—with compassion, daring, and courage.

The second of Pelley's examples is Marcy Van Dyke, whom he met when Van Dyke was the public health program manager for the International Rescue Committee Refugee Camp in Chad. Pelley describes Van Dyke's tireless efforts to take care of the nutritional needs of thousands of undernourished children, many of whom are from other developing countries that are all too commonly seen on television news programs. For Van Dyke's life test, the question was about intolerance and injustice, and she answered with compassion and mercy.

There are countless other examples of the unselfish service Americans provide. As a people, Americans are among the most caring, compassionate, and service-oriented in the world. If you couple these laudable characteristics with the tenets of the Way of Oz (service as critical to converting learning into wisdom; intermingling of heart and mind to reinforce loving; linking courage to service) and a commitment to lifelong learning, you should be poised to make significant contributions to our national and world communities.

14

Serving the Nation and the World

Young Americans have a growing interest in service: In 2008, more than a quarter of Americans over the age of sixteen volunteered. Research shows that youth who engage in service and volunteerism are more likely to be altruistic adults, and more likely to say they'll pursue college.

Betsy Miller Kittredge (1972–), research and outreach director,
US House Committee on Education and Labor

Seasoned university academic officers will tell you that the most compelling and successful candidates for faculty tenure are those with demonstrable records of service, including prior commitments to programs such as the Peace Corps, AmeriCorps, and Teach for America. For confirmation of the link between service and professional accomplishments, take a look at the short profiles of the twenty-one young professionals who are affiliated with the nonprofit corporation Americans for a National Service Act. These young people have their baccalaureate degrees; often have graduate degrees, military service, or service in federal or other nonprofit agencies (AmeriCorps, Teach for America, for example); and have an ethos for service—to America and the world. They are the forerunners of the many who will follow as a result of the passage in 2009 of the Edward O. Kennedy Serve America Act, which creates or expands a range of programs that provide support for nationally critical areas such as alternative energy (Clean Energy Service Corps), education (Education Corps), health (Healthy Future Corps), and social services (Opportunity Corps).

Although service to America, and by extension, to the world, is not new in our national consciousness, there's been a resurgence of interest in public service since 9/11.

A National Service Model

Service should be a part of all you do. It is integrated into the psyche and lifelong efforts of all who subscribe to the Way of Oz. Indeed, America's founders, including Thomas Jefferson and Benjamin Franklin, believed in the value of service to the emerging Republic; they knew that the nation's strength came from an involved and participatory citizenry.

American journalist Richard Stengel has proposed a model for national service based on volunteerism, which can be supported by such programs as those authorized through the Serve America Act and its precursors, the National and Community Service Act of 1990 and the Domestic Volunteer Service Act of 1973. Young people should have instilled in them a model for national service early in childhood, which should extend through adolescence and adulthood. It is important for youthful volunteers to understand the larger purpose of service to their fellow citizens, to the country, to the world, and to themselves. The leadership of America's armed forces has inculcated this service ethic in their recruits for years.

Since 1973, when the draft was eliminated and the all-volunteer force was instituted, the military has emphasized a constellation of patriotism, service, and leadership in recruiting and training. This combination of attributes has helped the United States develop and strengthen its armed forces that are now the envy of the world. Indeed, the American model of voluntary military service is being emulated in developing nations across Eastern Europe, the Middle East, and Asia.

The armed services, however, have no monopoly on the use of service and the development of leadership skills as inducements to engagement. Analogous approaches to recruitment and re-tention occur in federally sponsored agencies such as AmeriCorps and in NGOs or organizations such as Boys & Girls Clubs of America, the League of Women Voters, the National Urban League, and a host of other well-known service organizations such as Kiwanis, Lions, Rotary, and their youth affiliates.

College-level service-learning courses have become common on many campuses, and students testify to the value of such offerings, not only in facilitating learning but also in instilling the motivation to serve. Many college-level programs from areas as diverse as fashion design, nursing, nu-trition, retail, and social work incorporate internships with core service ele-ments.

Professor of law Vaughn James and professor of management Claudia Cogliser speak about their use of service-learning in teaching.

Service Is Their Mark of Honor

Millions of Americans can claim service as a mark of honor. Here are a few outstanding examples:

Norman Borlaug (1914–2009): A native of Cresco, Iowa, Borlaug was trained in forestry and plant pathology at the University of Minnesota (where he received his BS, master's, and PhD degrees). In 1944 he assumed a leadership role in a project sponsored by the Mexican government and the Rockefeller Foundation to improve grain production in Mexico. The project led to his career in what became known as the Green Revolution, in which he developed wheat varietals that transformed countries like India, Mexico, and Pakistan from net importers to net exporters of grain. The Green Revo-lution is credited with preventing the starvation of more than a billion peo-ple worldwide; it brought many accolades for Borlaug's work, including the Nobel Peace Prize in 1970. Those who knew Borlaug testify to his breadth of interests and his passion for service. His commitments were literally to the world. Up until his nineties, Borlaug spent time in Africa, trying to im-prove life in sub-Saharan countries as he done earlier in Latin America and Asia.

Nancy Goodman Brinker (1946–): Best known for founding the Susan G. Komen Race for the Cure, Brinker has led an effort that has raised more than $1 billion for breast cancer research. Her foundation, named in honor of her sister, who died of breast cancer, is responsible for the formation of cancer support groups throughout the world. In addition to her work with the Komen Foundation, Brinker served as US ambassador to Hungary and chief of protocol of the United States during the George W. Bush administration. She was awarded the Presidential Medal of Freedom by President Obama in 2009.

William Cahir (1969–2009): Motivated by the catastrophe of 9/11, Bill Cahir enlisted in the Marines in 2003 when he was thirty-four years old. Marine recruits older than twenty-nine are rare, but Cahir was committed and completed boot camp at Parris Island, notorious for its tough training. He had a degree from Penn State University and was a successful journalist and a Democratic primary candidate for Congress, but he chose to serve his country as a private first class with a ticket to service in Iraq. His goal was to help make the world safer for democracy. After two tours of duty in Iraq and an assignment in Helmand Province in Afghanistan, where he earned the rank of sergeant major, Bill Cahir was killed by an insurgent's bullet to the head. He left behind a wife pregnant with twins. Friends and relatives remember his passion for service to his country and the world.

Pedro José Greer, Jr. (1956–): Born to immigrant parents from Cuba, Greer has most recently served as professor and chair of the Department of Humanities, Health, and Society and as assistant dean in the School of Medicine at Florida International University. Perhaps his most notable contribution has been to the homeless and indigent communities in Miami. With the help of his father, who is also a physician, Dr. Greer founded the Camillus Health Concern and the St. John Bosco Clinic. He was awarded the Presidential Medal of Freedom by President Obama in 2009.

Brennan LaBrie (1999–): As a ten-year-old resident of Port Townsend, Washington, LaBrie began publishing the *Spruce Street Weekly* in 2009. He seems to be a born journalist who believes that "everyone has a good story in them." His weekly paper focuses on "good news" pieces about local notables (a juggler or a café owner known as the local "latte king," for example). LaBrie has begun what promises to be an illustrious creative career like that of Frank Baum, who got his start at age fourteen, writing and publishing articles for the *Rose Lawn Journal*. LaBrie's motto is, "I am always ready for an assignment," and among his increasingly ambitious assignments, he covered the 2010 Winter Olympics in Vancouver, Canada.

Sharon Christa Corrigan McAuliffe (1948–1986): The first teacher to fly on a space shuttle, through NASA's Teacher in Space, which began in 1984, McAuliffe was one of seven members of the crew of the *Challenger* space shuttle that exploded seventy-three seconds after blastoff from the Kennedy Space Center in Florida on January 28, 1986. Born in Boston, McAuliffe grew up in Framingham, Massachusetts, where she attended high school and went on to earn her BA in history and education from Framingham State College. She later moved to Maryland, where she became a middle school teacher while earning a master's in education supervision and administration at Bowie State University. In 1978 she returned to New England, taking a job teaching history, law, and economics at Concord High School in New Hampshire. There she developed and taught "The American Woman," an American history course focused on American women who contributed to our nation's greatness. She applied and eventually was chosen to be the first teacher in space by NASA from a field of more than eleven thousand applicants. McAuliffe was selected because of her extraordinary communication skills and infectious enthusiasm, which stemmed from her dedication to teaching and the array of service and volunteer work she had engaged in during her adult life. Though destiny cut short her opportunities to contribute to humanity, her spirit lives on in her achievements, her vision, and her commitment, which she expressed so well just months before she died: "You have to dream. We all have to dream. . . . Imagine me teaching from space, all over the world, touching so many people's lives. That's a teacher's dream! I have a vision of the world as a global village, a world without boundaries."

Michael T. Sullivan (1992–): Recognized in 2009 with a national Youth Achievement Award from the NGO Smart Kids with Learning Disabilities, Sullivan has overcome years of his own learning handicaps to serve his local community's homeless citizens as well as youth in Haiti and Iraq. This young man from Wantagh, New York, distributes leftover food from New York Dragons arena football matches to the homeless through the Sports Wrap Program of the Nassau Coliseum. Sullivan has also collected surplus soccer equipment and donated it to children in Haiti and Iraq, for which the Nassau County Soccer Coaches Association presented him the Unsung Hero award. Sullivan was a semifinalist in the Intel Talent search pre-science competition, which honored him for an evaluative study he conducted about antiracism in the English Football Association. Sullivan intends to pursue economics in college and is well on his way to becoming an exemplar of the Way of Oz.

Andrew Young (1932–): Civil rights leader; former US Congressman; mayor of Atlanta, Georgia; United States Ambassador to the United Nations; and confidant of Martin Luther King, Jr.; Young has had a fifty-year career of national and world service. He was born in New Orleans to a mom who was a K–12 teacher and a dad who was a dentist. He completed a baccalaureate degree in predentistry at Howard University, but because of his passion for public service, beginning with his participation in the civil rights movement of the 1960s, he chose instead to go into the ministry. He received his bachelor of divinity degree in 1955 from Hartford Seminary, based in Connecticut. During a subsequent posting as minister in Marion, Georgia, Young became interested in the philosophy and writings of Mohandas Gandhi, especially his message of nonviolent protest. Following service to the National Council of Churches in New York, Young returned to Atlanta, where he joined the Southern Christian Leadership Conference (SCLC), becoming executive director in 1964. The combination of his philosophy of nonviolence and his association with Martin Luther King, Jr., and the SCLC gave Young opportunities to contribute to the developing US civil rights movement, at times to his peril. These early civil rights experiences set the stage for his later service in the US Congress, as UN ambassador (1976–80), and as mayor of Atlanta (1982–1990). Young's mayoral service, with the help of Maynard Jackson, was of pivotal importance in the extraordinary economic and cultural development of the city. He and Jackson worked to put aside the racism of the past so that Atlanta could become a hub for Georgia and the nation. With Atlanta's designation as host of the 1996 Summer Olympic Games, Young's early contributions to the broader goal were clearly apparent.

V

The Way of Oz and a Focus on the Future

15

Focus on the Future: An Integrated Perspective

Imagination has given us the steam engine, the telephone, the talking-machine, and the automobile, for these things had to be dreamed of before they became realities. So I believe that dreams—daydreams, you know, with your eyes wide open and your brain-machinery whizzing—are likely to lead to the betterment of the world. The imaginative child will become the imaginative man or woman most apt to create, to invent, and therefore to foster civilization.

L. Frank Baum, from *The Lost Princess of Oz* (1917)

Think about the Dorothy figure of the Way of Oz. Like the storied character in Baum's tales, she is focused, strong-willed, caring, and concerned for the people and other creatures around her. As Evan Schwartz notes, "Dorothy becomes a new kind of hero, a feminine one, sharing her duties with three traveling companions, who do indeed put themselves in danger and sacrifice themselves again and again." She has a vision of where she is going and an idea of what her surroundings should look like well into the future.

In a modern context, the Dorothy of the Way of Oz is not only informed by the sciences and arts, but she also knows how powerful the sciences, in their broadest sense, can be in guiding policy and decision making. She sees that the social sciences have led clear thinkers to conclude that democracy

Professor of biology Lou Densmore speaks about the importance of science and diversity, even for the youngest students.

and democratic principles are critical to the cultural and economic development of the world's peoples. She knows she must take personal responsibility for our collective future in her pursuit of the integration of the learning-loving-serving constellation of the Way of Oz. This modern Dorothy should be a model for all adolescents, as well as for people of all backgrounds, origins, and beliefs, because she understands the elements necessary to shaping a better environment for the world and all its creatures.

Highlighting the Focus-on-the-Future Elements

Although our modern Dorothy is armed with the learning-loving-serving skills and ethos of the Way of Oz, she also needs context and a focus on the future to help shape her actions. The context, vision, and commitments to action will come from an integrated understanding and adoption of personal and institutional planning; a commitment to diversity, sustainability, and understanding of science; democracy and its power to serve the planet's peoples; and a sense of personal responsibility.

Personal and Institutional Planning

The key to success (in its broadest terms, not merely as a measure of financial success) is planning. For the individual, planning involves a vision of what he or she would like to achieve in life, recognizing that goals may change many times during a forty- to sixty-year span of working. For firms, institutions, and organizations, effective planning and execution determine whether they will survive and thrive.

Diversity, Sustainability, and Understanding of Science

We need to consider these topics broadly. If we don't understand and embrace the positive concept of diversity in American society and in the natural world, the planet is doomed to an unhealthy and unproductive future. The principles of diversity, particularly of the natural world, are critical to the sustainability of the United States and the world. A commitment to sustainability should cause us to think holistically about the world's climate and energy and food production, using science, technology, and mathematics.

Democracy and Serving the Planet's Peoples

The twenty-first-century Dorothy knows that dictatorships and repressive political systems have failed because they deprive people of life, liberty, and equality. It remains to be seen whether the people of Tunisia, Egypt, Libya, and other African and Middle Eastern countries will be able to create viable democracies following the dramatic overthrows of dictators during 2011. But it is clear that the people of this volatile region of our globe are eager to embrace democracy that is common in the Western world.

Personal Responsibilities

The modern Dorothy knows that self-determination, persistence, priority consciousness, critical thinking, time management, and a devotion to the service—all elements of the Way of Oz—help to make the world a better place.

16

Personal and Institutional Planning

The future ain't what it used to be.

Yogi Berra (1925–), former New York Yankees catcher,
"king of malapropisms"

The characters of Oz, especially Dorothy, frequently started down the Yellow Brick Road or its equivalent not knowing what the future would bring. In your life you will find yourself in analogous situations but will have opportunities both personally and professionally to hedge your bets through planning.

You need to keep in mind one major caveat: many things happen without any discernible link to the past. In other words, you can't predict what will happen in the future by merely looking at the past—or the present. There are "wild cards" in life—human developments, technologies, and other systems or events that sometimes seem to come from nowhere. Who in the 1950s, for example, could have predicted the US civil rights movement beginning with the federal legislation of 1964, the environmental movement starting with the first Earth Day in 1970, the collapse of the Soviet Union in 1992, or the development of the Internet in the late 1990s?

Personal Planning

There wasn't much need for personal planning in America's industrial past. Most people would either follow their parents' vocations or, after completing high school (or not), would go to work in a manufacturing plant or become a tradesperson (a plumber or electrician, for example) after apprenticeship training. Events of the twenty-first century and the two decades leading up to it have changed this picture. Now, much of the country's manufacturing base is gone, and employment opportunities have changed, shifting toward jobs for which a baccalaureate degree is necessary. Career development of the future will require continuing education and graduate degrees. Lifelong learning and personal planning will be essential.

According to geriatrician Thomas Perls and neuropsychologist Margery Hutter Silver, teenagers in the early twenty-first century have significantly improved chances of reaching one hundred years old given favorable genetics and adoption of healthy lifestyles. Even if you only make it to eighty, there is the prospect of working five to six decades, especially given the fact that retirement ages are increasing and may reach seventy soon. How many significant career changes are you likely to experience in those fifty to sixty years? There will certainly be more than five and perhaps as many as ten. Moreover, your career will involve not only new jobs but also new fields that don't currently exist or fields that have fundamentally changed by scientific or technological advances. Consider four examples of profound changes that have influenced the work of certain professions:

- Prospective geosciences faculty members earning PhD degrees in the late 1960s would have begun careers when the concept of plate tectonics had only recently been adopted as a fundamental feature of geological study. Syllabi and entire approaches to the understanding of the geosciences had to be changed in the 1970s when theory and experimentation revealed new ways of looking at the geological world.

- Musicians, composers, and performers educated and practicing before 1980 were astonished in the decades that followed by the software and computerized instruments that revolutionized their art.

- Pharmacists practicing today cannot rely on information from their course work in degree programs ten or twenty years ago since thousands of new drugs (with their side effects, contraindications, and drug-drug interactions) and drug products have come onto the market.

- Business professionals today have to adjust to major changes in information systems software and federal regulations (such as the accountability provisions of the Sarbanes-Oxley Act) that have facilitated operations but have also made professional life much more complicated. These same professionals know that business life will become even more complex, particularly with new federal and state regulations in the aftermath of the ethical lapses and bad financial practices leading up to the recession of 2008–2012.

These professionals have had to reinvent themselves during their careers. If you're in your twenties, or soon to be, you will inevitably find yourself having to adapt to new situations. The question becomes "How can I be successful given the certainty of change?" The answer is personal planning, which needs to begin when there's a change in your field or area of study, typically when you're in college. Your need for personal planning, however, will extend throughout your career.

Begin with Disciplinary and Career Counseling

Earning a baccalaureate degree is the first step in developing a career. Seek advice from others already established in your chosen area. A good place to start is with college advisors and mentors. But seek advice broadly. In his book *Making the Most of College*, Richard Light recommends that undergraduate students befriend at least one new professor a year. You'll gain different perspectives on career development from them, and you'll be building a network of professionals who can be of vital importance to you when you seek reference letters for internships or graduate or postgraduate professional schools.

Faculty advisors can help guide you in developing independent research or scholarly projects. The skills you gain through independent research and scholarship are becoming increasingly important for all professionals. Faculty advisors can also help you develop study-abroad plans.

Having advisors and mentors is especially crucial in graduate school, where student–faculty one-on-one relationships are a significant part of postgraduate research and scholarly efforts.

You should make an appointment with professional advisors (especially during your pre-professional years of study); most colleges and universities have such advisors on staff in career development centers. These advisors can help you assess your interests and strengths, particularly if you have not declared your major or are thinking of changing it.

Continue with Planning as Careers Begin and Develop

Planning shouldn't end with your baccalaureate (or higher) degree. On-the-job mentors and advisors will be especially helpful to you when you begin your career. Many firms, institutions, and organizations designate a formal advisor or mentor when you begin your job. If not, ask your supervisor to help in finding a mentor, and then carefully consider the mentor's advice. With seasoning, you will be able to plan for your own career development, but you will still find the advice of others useful, even through the last decade or two of your career.

Many people understand the popular metaphor of "parachuting into a new position," which is like the military use of parachutes, when suddenly you're in new territory and need advisors to interpret the maze of new policies, procedures, and organizational constructs you face. Sometimes your new position will put you in a supervisory role and you will need to seek the advice of your new colleagues who report to you. If you seek their advice and delegate appropriate responsibility and accountability, you'll be empowering them, and you'll find these colleagues expressing their gratitude for being brought into the management decisions of the unit.

Here are some suggestions for formulating your own career development plans:

- Consider pursing a graduate degree, perhaps with the help of your employer. In 2006, a survey of 226 US private and public sector companies revealed that more than 90 percent offered educational assistance to employees.

- Become active in an association or society affiliated with your field. Attend meetings regularly, even though they may only be offered once a year. Some national associations have regional affiliates that make it easier to attend professional development meetings and seminars close by. Expositions attached to professional meetings will provide opportunities to review the latest technical and professional developments in a given field.

• Take advantage of continuing education programs offered through local educational institutions to keep up to date. If there are no such institutions in your locale, consider online instruction.

• Join and become active in service clubs (such as Kiwanis, Lions, Rotary) that give you a professional network and provide opportunities to contribute to community projects.

• Publish the results of your scholarly pursuits in professional journals or magazines. Many of these are now facilitated online.

• Create your own web page, blog, or online journal to share information on professional interests and developments, particularly if you are serving in a leadership role.

Strategic Planning in Firms, Institutions, and Organizations

If you serve in a leadership role in any organization, you will become involved in strategic planning.

Strategic planning involves the development of a vision statement; a mission statement; an environmental context or an assessment of strengths, weaknesses, opportunities, and threats; overarching goals or strategic priorities; and specific goals and objectives.

Vision

Where are you headed? What will your unit look like when you get there? When you put these questions into the context of a firm, institution, or organization, you know what President George Herbert Walker Bush meant by "the vision thing." A vision is a statement, at best a single sentence that describes the destiny of an organization, or a subunit thereof. Crafting a vision statement can take many months, if not longer, if it is to achieve the status of a shared vision.

Academic administrators are painfully aware of the difficulty of crafting a vision statement that represents the institution's constituent faculty, students, and staff. It took several months for the Texas Tech University academic community to develop a clear and well-articulated vision statement (in 2010). Here is the result: *Texas Tech is a great public research university where students succeed, knowledge is advanced, and global engagement is championed.*

We can dissect this statement to find elements that have universal application. First, consider the phrase "great public research university." Texas Tech did not always think of itself as such. From the time of its founding in 1923, Tech has had great undergraduate programs, but research and graduate education weren't emphasized until the last half of the twentieth century. Recently the state of Texas encouraged the formation of new public national research universities to enhance economic and cultural development in the state. In 2009 House Bill 51 passed, providing extraordinary funding opportunities for seven "emerging national research universities"— if they met certain criteria. The race was on for Texas Tech and many of its sister institutions for the special resources and designation, now codified in Tech's vision statement.

Consider next the phrase "where students succeed." The term "research university" defines a comprehensive research-intensive institution with a variety of programs from baccalaureate through professional to master's and doctoral degrees. The formidable size of Texas Tech (with an enrollment of approximately 31,600 in 2010, typical of research universities, thus implying an impersonal atmosphere) needed to be offset by making the institution "student-centered." The new emphasis on research could not leave undergraduate education behind.

The next phrase, "where knowledge is advanced," includes research and scholarship (the interpretation and reinterpretation of knowledge) as well as study in the creative and performing arts.

And, finally let's look at the phrase "where global engagement is championed." This signifies the importance of giving back to the state, nation, and world. Texas Tech is committed to service-learning and study-abroad programs, engaging students, faculty, and staff in efforts that change people's lives.

Texas Tech University crafted a highly successful vision statement true to the shared commitments of faculty, students, and staff. This statement could be adapted by many other organizations. For example, "nationally prominent" or "world-class" could be substituted for "great." "Student success" could be replaced by references to community orientation or other phrases, such as "putting clients first." The phrase "global engagement" could be changed by referring to specific cities, regions, or nations. The following are hypothetical examples of such adaptations:

- **Software firm:** "Trans Ware is a niche software firm that serves transportation industries worldwide."

- **Regional planned-parenthood organization:** "Patience Foundation is a client-oriented planned-parenthood organization serving the Dallas–Fort Worth Metroplex."

- **Quasi-government statewide economic development agency:** "AriSTA is the primary agency for advancing science- and technology-based industrial development in Arizona."

- **Metropolitan arts education organization:** "Popular Arts is a community-managed nonprofit organization that promotes the arts and art understanding in the greater Northampton area of Massachusetts."

Sometimes people confuse a vision statement with a mission statement. When we look closely we see the two are clearly different.

Mission

What do you do? How do you do it? These questions, when answered properly, help to define the mission of a firm, institution, or organization. The components of a mission statement are quality, scope, responsiveness to needs, and effectiveness.

In most places of business, quality is the sine qua non of operations. Quality sets organizations apart and gives them their competitive edge.

Scope is a critical consideration in defining a mission, in part because no organization can be all things to all people without sacrificing quality.

Responsiveness to needs helps define a niche, and defines, as well, the economic, social or cultural importance of a firm, institution, or organization.

Effectiveness can be defined in terms of costs, a product or service's success rate, as well as its impact on society. Articulating a company's effectiveness might also be posed as cost-benefit or risk-benefit ratios.

Consider, then, how these elements can be used to craft mission statements for two of the hypothetical organizations.

For Trans Ware: "Trans Ware is a high-quality developer of software to manage transportation systems worldwide. The software supports systems that run the gamut from traffic control of interstate highway systems in highly developed countries to railway systems in developing nations. The need for Trans Ware has been demonstrated in countries on five continents around the world. When used effectively, Trans Ware software offers significant reductions in costs, accidents, and other transportation failures."

For Popular Arts: "Popular Arts provides Northampton's citizens entrée to the arts and art understanding. The organization promotes art events by working collaboratively with school systems and other community organizations. Popular Arts develops and produces art workshops and other offerings ranging from film festivals to hands-on arts and crafts events. Through its grant development work, Popular Arts brings value to art events and art education in the greater Northampton area."

With an understanding of a destination (vision) and the means of getting there (mission), you have an opportunity to consider the environment (commonly referred to as "environmental scanning") for your organization's growth and development.

Environmental Context

Strategic planners know that their future and effectiveness are not entirely in their hands, but are dependent on successes in achieving the organization's goals and objectives. The context for strategic planning is thus defined by organizational strengths and weaknesses as well as external opportunities and threats (or SWOT).

The strengths of firms, institutions, and organizations can be defined in terms of the quality and numbers of people, programs, resources, and products (when applicable) associated with them. Weaknesses can be assessed over the same range of factors. For nonprofit organizations in particular, strength may not necessarily be related to overall size. Successful organizations know that there is power in being selective, in seeking excellence in a few areas, rather than achieving mediocrity over a wider range of activities.

Opportunities and threats require a bit of prognostication and a broad understanding of the milieu of operations. What, for example, would grants and contracts potentially available through the US Department of Homeland Security bring to a firm such as Trans Ware? How might changes in abortion legislation challenge the operations of the Patience Foundation? How would new state legislation for public-private partnerships enhance opportunities for an agency such as AriSTA? What opportunities might be afforded by a formal partnership between Popular Arts and the University of Massachusetts at Amherst? A parallel set of questions could be crafted to assess threats to the model organizations. For example: How might severe federal budget reductions affect the grant-getting potential of Trans Ware? Are increasing environmental protection regulations going to inhibit the location of certain high-tech firms in Arizona? What will happen to Popular Arts if local government eliminates its funding? Posing such questions may help lead to the environmental scans that are critical to firms, institutions, and organizations. These scans can include developing benchmark data, such as critical comparisons of your organization's strengths with those of peer or competitor organizations.

In higher education, for example, we commonly find offices of institutional research, which gather comparison data—of the quality of students (entering grade-point averages, high school class rankings), faculty (percentages of faculty with doctorates), programs (student-faculty ratios, success of students in state licensing examinations), and the institution as a whole (research funding, size of endowments)—relative to a set of peers. The comparisons help elaborate the institution's strengths and weaknesses, which inform discussions of opportunities and threats.

If you have a carefully crafted environmental scan, you can create goals and objectives to support the mission and achieve the vision of your organization.

Goals and Objectives

To realize a vision, to serve a mission, and to achieve success, firms, institutions, and organizations need goals and objectives. While occasionally the terms are used interchangeably, goals are generally long term, what I like to think of as overarching end points, whereas objectives deal with shorter-term results.

Think of goals and objectives that might be drafted for the hypothetical organization Popular Arts.

Overarching Goals—Popular Arts

I. Seek excellence in all programs.

II. Increase the number of programs.

III. Enhance the diversity of programs.

IV. Develop a mix of public and private funding to ensure infrastructure support and program viability.

Following are sample objectives corresponding to each of these goals:

I. Seek excellence in all programs.

1. Engage two to three nationally or internationally recognized artists a year in programming.

2. Prepare three op-ed pieces a year that describe the importance of the arts to the greater Northampton area.

II. Increase numbers of programs.

1. Increase the numbers of programs from 12 to 18 per year.

III. Enhance diversity of programs.

1. Plan expansion of programs to include visual arts as well as performing arts offerings.

IV. Develop a mix of public and private funding to ensure infrastructure support and program viability.

1. Seek local tax revenue to support art education offerings.

2. Submit at least one proposal to the National Endowment for the Arts and six additional proposals to private foundations.

With an established set of goals and objectives, you have a basic strategic plan, but now you need to ask questions about implementation to move from planning to action.

Regardless of the approach and scope, it's best to have teams or groups of colleagues conduct planning efforts. Team efforts not only ensure a diversity of views but also help build common understanding within firms, institutions, and organizations. Well-developed planning and implementation have a positive influence on the workplace. A good vision statement can become a mantra. As one colleague of mine put it, "A leader's frequent use of a vision statement, indeed even overusing it, fixes it in the minds of internal and external constituents, who, during public presentations, will revel in finishing the statement once the leader begins it." And, if it is shared, a cogent vision statement can have a positive effect on motivation, as well as on employees' understanding of the institution's mission and commitment to goals and objectives. With a well-crafted strategic plan, the chances for success of a firm, institution, or organization are significantly increased. A positive assessment of such an organization, through an external program review, accreditation, or other certification, often depends on how well plans are developed and implemented. A good performance evaluation of a supervisor or manager often depends on how well he or she is able to develop and follow through with plans, and how well these plans mesh with the organization's goals and objectives.

17

Commitments to Diversity, Sustainability, and Understanding Science

The skills students need to form better understandings are very similar to those they need to become engaged citizens in a pluralistic democracy: written and oral communication, teamwork, inquiry and analysis, intercultural competence, and critical thinking.

John "Jack" Meacham (1952–), State University of New York–Buffalo, distinguished teaching professor emeritus

Informed and contributing citizens of democracies in the twenty-first century face a daunting task: how to keep up with societal developments in the context of diversity, sustainability, and science and technology. With prescience, Thomas Jefferson said, "If a nation expects to be ignorant and free, in a state of civilization, it expects what never was and never will be." The defeat of ignorance has never been more challenging than in the twenty-first century. But we have tools to fight ignorance that could not have been imagined by the nation's third president. These include enlightened understanding and civil rights legislation that have helped us make great strides in freeing us from past prejudices and inspired in us the realization that diversity is a source of strength, not weakness, in society. Americans now have an evolving understanding of global climate change, clean energy alternatives, disease prevention, new approaches to food and fiber production, and environmental cleanup and sustainability; and we are learning to use the sciences and technology in new global cooperative ventures—all of which means that we might begin to see the insights and skills of the Way of Oz addressing many of the planet's ills.

Diversity: A Mosaic

Imagine standing in front of a mosaic, whether of ancient or recent origin. Note how it appears different depending on your vantage point. Up close, you will be struck by differences among individual pieces: colors, textures, and shapes. But if you step back, these differences recede and you observe new patterns and new levels of coherence. The strength and beauty of the work come from individual differences incorporated and blended effectively in diverse and artistically effective ways. In short, the mosaic offers a metaphor for diversity.

In the Way of Oz, diversity is a philosophic commitment to the value of variety in people, places, and ideas—people of different genders, ethnicities, backgrounds, beliefs, sexual orientation, and physical abilities; places that ensure a welcoming environment for different people; and ideas developed creatively and expressed freely in a manner that respects the rights and dignity of all members of a community.

People

Those who speak about diversity tend to begin with themselves—their gender, race, ethnicity, background, beliefs, sexual orientation, disability, or some combination thereof. The logical extension is to friends and colleagues. Broader thinkers extend their perspective to the greater civic community, state, and nation. The most cosmopolitan thinkers imagine a global community. For these people, parochial thinking is counterintuitive and irrelevant. Consider, for example, professionals who have traveled and worked in different parts of the world. Having experienced myriad languages, literature, and religions, these people are uncomfortable associating with colleagues who think the world is made up of people just like themselves.

Less traveled but well-educated professionals begin to think in diverse terms after study, reflection, and scholarly work, particularly in the liberal arts. The biological and cultural diversity of the peoples of the world become not a threat but a reason to celebrate. Wise people know that racial differences are far less important than humanity's biological and cultural commonalities. The study of the biological and social sciences leads enlightened people to the conclusion that a narrow definition of gender and sexual orientation is inconsistent with biological reality, which supports much greater diversity than a simple two-gender model.

The arts and humanities provide an appreciation for and understanding of the benefit of association with diverse peoples. In the arts you learn that diversity cannot be too narrowly defined or you miss the mosaic qualities that grace and enhance modern social and work environments. Or, as American studies theorist Richard Florida would add, you miss "the creativity in all of us."

Places

A supportive climate must exist for a societal unit—a school, social club, firm, institution, or organization—to grow as a diverse community. Only in such a supportive climate will people continue to develop positively. And it is only within a supportive climate that a community will benefit from the dedicated and creative work of its diverse members. The supportive climate is the mortar that holds the mosaic's diverse pieces together in beautiful and coherent patterns.

A favorable climate means that colleagues and friends are not uncomfortable in a diverse community. A positive and supportive climate affirms that you are looking at character rather than appearance, as Abraham Lincoln and Martin Luther King, Jr., admonished. Our constitutionally guaranteed principles of life, liberty, and the pursuit of happiness are a powerful rationale for creating the climate that supports diversity. As importantly, the strength, effectiveness, and attractiveness of societal units are directly related to the variety of ideas that come from a diverse community.

Ideas

The gestalt, or total effect, of a mosaic as an objet d'art is ultimately its effect on viewers. The gestalt of a diverse community includes the creativity and ideas that result when diverse people contribute in an environment that welcomes creative or innovative work. Although you may not agree with all that a diverse group of colleagues or friends may propose, you recognize that it is important for them to have the opportunity to speak out and for you and other colleagues or friends to listen. Likewise, when you participate in a diverse group and your ideas are challenged, you should not be offended, because you realize that you are not being personally challenged; rather that your ideas are being considered on their merits.

The well-developed diverse community understands how diversity ensures future creativity and the richness of ideas. In short, a diverse community, combined with a welcoming climate, provides a fertile environment for creativity and inventiveness.

Reflections on America's Past

In 1999, Everett Carll Ladd, Jr. (1937–1999), a political scientist and long-term director of the Roper Survey Research Center at the University of Connecticut, was asked: "What has profoundly changed in America during the second half of the twentieth century?" His answer was "attitudes toward race and the environment." These changes demonstrate a major shift in American attitudes since Frank Baum's times.

In his derogatory allusions to African Americans in some of his stories and other works, Baum displayed the racial stereotyping that was prevalent in his day. Yet the trio of allies Dorothy befriended in the original Oz story, and the variety of characters in the Oz sequels, from the Patchwork Girl to the Shaggy-Man to the Frogman, suggest Baum's attraction to diversity.

It would be interesting to see how Frank Baum would react to twenty-first-century America, particularly to the country's civil, economic, legal, and social structures that have helped to diminish the prejudices of the past. I think he'd be proud of our acceptance of differences, despite the fact that there is still some lingering prejudice in our times. The modern Dorothys of the world inherit a much more positive framework for encouraging diversity in personal and professional associations. Assuming a modern Dorothy serves in a leadership position, she doesn't have to break new ground with regard to the interactions among racially and ethnically diverse populations in her workplace. She knows there are other groups—gays, lesbians, bisexuals, and transsexuals—deserving of special sensitivity regarding civil rights, along with religious minorities and immigrants who will come to America in this new century. Our opportunities to benefit from diversity—to enjoy the living mosaic of American life—would impress both Frank Baum and Everett Carll Ladd.

Sustainability—A Modern Necessity

In 1999 Everett Carll Ladd reflected on growing up in Saco, Maine, in the 1940s and early 1950s. He had vivid memories of walking across a foot-bridge spanning the Saco River and inhaling the malodorous emissions of the nearby pulp and paper mill, and thinking of the experience as "totally normal." His experience, though stunning in retrospect, was not unique to Saco or Maine. People from all over the country can tell similar stories from their childhood when their towns were adversely influenced by industrial pollution (by steel production, for example, and strip mining).

When we think about the environmental advances that have occurred in the United States since the first Earth Day—in places such as Pittsburgh and the Lake Erie region—we can revel in these improvements. However, there is much more to be done to achieve sustainability, especially in terms of a global perspective. The peoples of the world must continue to strive for progress in finding alternative forms of energy and new ways to deal with climate change, food and fiber production, disease prevention and human health, renewable resources, and the use of water. Here are some twenty-first-century concerns facing us:

- In many places, nonrenewable energy reserves—oil and natural gas—will be depleted in fifty years. We need to escalate our clean energy production, through wind, solar, and nuclear systems.

- Despite some naysayers, our global climate is changing; the earth is warming, and we are seeing more melting of the Arctic and Antarctic ice caps. We need to stem the production of greenhouse gases that are causing our oceans to expand, which could literally eliminate whole countries (such as the Maldives) and change the coastlines of the United States and many other countries.

- By 2050, the world's population will have

grown from seven billion in 2011 to more than 8.5 billion. The need for new and enhanced food and fiber production is critically important.

- We need to do more in developing renewable resources. We need to develop plants that can be cultivated without stripping the earth of its nutrients.

- We need to address the health and welfare of the earth's people to mitigate epidemics and starvation, in addition to making at least modest improvements in the quality of life of all the people of the planet.

- What about the countries or regions that run out of potable water supplies in the coming decades? This isn't a Frank Baum fairytale, but a reality for countries in the Middle East and Africa and even in regions of the southwestern United States. We need to invest our resources in addressing the availability of water for people around the globe.

A modern Dorothy might be daunted by all these challenges, but she knows that through a devotion to the loving-learning-serving constellation, we can make progress, but only through the lens of a focus on the future that includes an understanding of science and technology, informed by interdisciplinary approaches to scholarship and research.

The Need for Science and Technology—Broadly Conceived

Carl Sagan (1934–1996), the award-winning astronomer and science advocate of the twentieth century, said, "Many of the problems facing us may be soluble, but only if we are willing to embrace brilliant, daring, and complex solutions. Such solutions require brilliant, daring, and complex people." This sage observation is as true in the twenty-first century as it was when he made it.

We have witnessed long and sometimes contentious discussions about climate change. And as we seek innovative interventions, including modeling and other research approaches to solve climate change, we see that a battery of sciences and technologies will be necessary. These will include the integration of natural sciences, social sciences, and applied sciences and technologies. Here are some of the fields we will need to further develop to meet our new challenges:

- **Climate and climate change:** atmospheric sciences; computer sciences; earth sciences, including geology and geography; mathematics; and statistics

- **Energy, particularly alternative energy:** atmospheric and earth sciences; engineering, particularly the subdisciplines of computer, electrical, mechanical, and petroleum engineering; environmental sciences, including environmental toxicology; natural sciences, especially biology, chemistry, and physics; and natural resource sciences

- **Food and fiber:** plant and soil sciences, especially agronomy, food sciences, and horticulture; developmental and evolutionary biology; genetics and microbiology

- **Health:** biological sciences, biomedical sciences, chemistry, pharmaceutical and public health sciences

- **Water:** civil engineering; geosciences, especially hydrology; and natural resource sciences

Civil and environmental engineering professor Andrew Jackson describes the importance of a future focus, priority setting, and interdisciplinary approaches in studies of water conservation in space missions.

For the undergraduate, study in one or more of these disciplinary areas will provide career options that address the challenge of our planet's sustainability. However, two further points are necessary: First, no single discipline or even two or three disciplines will be adequate to deal with climate change or inadequate water supply. Developing alternative forms of energy, food, and fiber will require the interdisciplinary efforts of specialists in the social sciences, including demography, public administration, and the law. Humanities specialists with backgrounds in areas such as creative or technical writing and history can also make valuable contributions in addressing these challenging issues.

The second point relates to relevant professionals' responsibility to reach out through community action to help improve public understanding of science and technology. In their recent book *Unscientific America: How Scientific Illiteracy Threatens Our Future*, Chris Mooney and Sheril Kirshenbaum say, "We need a nation in which science has far more *prominence* in politics and the media, far more *relevance* to the life of every American, far more *intersections* with other walks of life, and ultimately, far more *influence* where it truly matters—namely, in setting the agenda for the future as far out as we can possibly glimpse it."

The college student or professional needs to think carefully about the education and training required to position himself or herself to contribute to the world's great sustainability challenges. Even if a professional is employed in areas far removed from sustainability efforts, he or she should have sufficient understanding of science to be a responsible citizen. And, of course, these challenges cannot be successful without a political infrastructure that empowers democratic approaches to change. Even though our Constitution guarantees this country's democracy, we need to understand how democratic principles can have a positive impact on the engagement of other countries in meeting the challenge of the sustainability of our planet.

18

Democracy and Serving the Planet's Peoples

It has been said that democracy is the worst form of government except all the others that have been tried.

Winston Churchill (1874–1965), British statesman, author, artist

The Land of Oz was hardly a democracy as Frank Baum portrayed it in his original book and as it appeared in the 1939 film. In Baum's thirteen Oz sequels, Ozma is a benevolent dictator, one who honors diversity and cares deeply about her subjects. She ensures life (every creature is immortal) and happiness (all worthy subjects are guaranteed freedom from want). But of the three defining principles of our American democracy, the central element of liberty is missing in Oz. In France, the three defining democratic principles are liberty, equality, and fraternity. The Canadian constitution guarantees the rights of life, liberty, and security of person. The defining objectives of the European Union are freedom, security, and justice. Collectively, these elements are intended to ensure equal treatment and protection from discrimination and caring for one's neighbor in the spirit of fraternity and brotherhood. Baum's Ozma might not explicitly grant freedom to her subjects, but she assures their happiness, albeit in a fairyland construct. The principles of democracy should serve as touchstones to all who embrace the Way of Oz.

A View from the World's Stage

Many of the Western world's former leaders do not spend their retirement playing golf and discussing their scores. Most of them contribute to democratically oriented organizations and causes. Consider the Club of Madrid, for example. Founded in October 2001 following the 9/11 catastrophe, the organization brings together nearly ninety national leaders from more than fifty countries, leaders who are dedicated to "democratic leadership, governance, human rights, and the rule of law." Its members meet yearly, usually in Madrid, Spain, where they hear reports and discuss action plans developed under the group's major initiatives, such as democracy, security, and terrorism; energy and democracy; shared societies: democratic leadership for dialogue, diversity, and cohesion; and women's leadership for peace and security.

The Club of Madrid members and sitting governmental leaders around the world pursue these initiatives through their personal interactions. They help to shape planning and policy making globally, especially in the developing world.

The Club of Madrid is a wonderful example of how many world leaders

value democracies and globally recognized democratic principles, but it is not the only organization pursuing such initiatives. Many other organizations do beneficent work consistent with democratic principles, including unstinting devotion to human rights, the rule of law, justice, and economic development: the United Nations and its affiliate agencies, including the United Nations Educational, Scientific and Cultural Organization, or UNESCO; a host of nongovernmental organizations, such as *Médecins Sans Frontières*, or Doctors Without Borders, the recipient of the 1999 Nobel Peace Prize; the Grameen Bank, winner of the 2006

Nobel Peace Prize, along with its founder Muhammad Yunus, for promoting credit as a human right and establishing financial microlending programs in the developing world; the International Red Cross and Red Crescent; and the Rockefeller Foundation, in its work to alleviate world hunger and poverty. So we can say that many of the world's leaders devote great portions of their lives and energies to the components of the Way of Oz.

Reaching Out to the Developing World

Recall how traveling, especially through study-abroad programs, can spark special learning opportunities that can lead to changed perspectives and insights. Consider how travel and outreach influence human and economic development in America and abroad. When these ideas are directed toward democratic and economic reforms in the developing world, they take on new dimensions.

If you have not traveled in developing countries in Africa, Asia, Latin America, and certain nations in southern and eastern Europe, or studied the human and institutional conditions in these lands, your knowledge of the majority of the world's citizens is deficient. Here is a statement from UNESCO: "Working to create conditions of genuine dialog based on respect for shared values and the dignity of each civilization and culture. This role is critical, particularly in the face of terrorism, which constitutes an attack against humanity. The world urgently requires global visions of sustainable development based on the observance of human rights, mutual respect, and the alleviation of poverty, all of which lie at the heart of UNESCO's mission and activities."

How can an emerging leader who is a proponent of the Way of Oz contribute to a more sustainable, just, and economically viable world that ensures the dignity and basic necessities of the planet's citizens? The answers are not easy, but there are opportunities for even the youngest devotee of the Way of Oz to contribute to what UNESCO calls "sustainable development based on the observance of human rights, mutual respect, and the alleviation of poverty." These opportunities begin with understanding through study and travel; volunteer efforts through religious, social, or benevolent nongovernmental organizations; study-abroad and service-learning programs; along with a sense of personal responsibility.

19
Personal Responsibilities

All of us share this world for but a brief moment in time. The question is whether we spend that time focused on what pushes us apart, or whether we commit ourselves to an effort—a sustained effort—to find common ground, to focus on the future we seek for our children, and to respect the dignity of all human beings.

Barack Obama (1961–), forty-fourth president of the United States, Nobel Peace Prize laureate, from his 2009 address in Cairo, Egypt

For Dorothy and the Wizard, Glinda's insight was twofold: the power for change lies within us, and we can make a difference in the world. Both admonitions are central to the theme of personal responsibility in the Way of Oz. Adopting such principles requires determination and persistence, critical thinking, time management, and the ability to set priorities.

Determination and Persistence

There are countless examples of people who have had to overcome self-doubt, difficult financial situations, negative peer pressure, the bad advice of family members, and the temptation of short-term gratifications. Consider, for example, Governor Mike Beebe of Arkansas, whose family was too poor to send him to law school; he worked night shifts processing chickens so he could earn his law degree. The key to Governor Beebe's success, and that of so many others, is self-determination and persistence. You can develop these attributes, but you can also often benefit from the help of others.

The Advancement Via Individual Determination (AVID) program is designed for underachieving but capable high school and college students. In a supportive environment, the program encourages students to take on a rigorous curriculum and provides them with mentors to help with organizational, time management, and critical thinking skills. The program promotes writing, inquiry, collaboration, and reading (WICR) and emphasizes the importance of persistence in reaching one's goals.

The AVID principles and practices support self-determination, which is critically important to developing personal responsibility and integrating the learning-loving-serving triad of the Way of Oz. Experienced teachers will attest to the fact that "success leads to success." There's no greater motivation for self-determination and persistence than a job well done, which becomes self-reinforcing. You can create your own positive reinforcement if you begin each day with the thought, "Even if everything goes wrong today, I accomplished something yesterday, and I know that I can accomplish something again." This feeling of confidence that can come from even modest accomplishments enables students and scholars to apply themselves effectively, and, inevitably, other successful efforts will follow. The eminent geneticist Barbara McClintock (1902–1990) noted aptly, "I was just so interested in what I was doing I could hardly wait to get up in the morning and get at it. One of my friends, a geneticist, said I was a child, because only children can't wait to get up in the morning and get at it."

Priority Consciousness and Critical Thinking

Crafting a vision for the future, having a sense of mission, and setting goals all contribute mightily to achievements in life. The important thing, however, is to stay on track and to focus on the future, through priority consciousness and critical thinking.

Developing priorities and adhering to them are keys to success for people and institutions. Your priorities should be based on the following principles, offered with cogent examples:

- **Quality:** The sine qua non of all that is done. In choosing a college or university, for example, you should consider the reputations of its successful alumni as well as the quality of its faculty and staff members.

- **Consistency with goals:** Your efforts should support your goals. Consider whether an internship or study-abroad option might help you reach a goal such as skill development or language proficiency.

- **Coherence with strengths:** Build on strengths. You should try to maximize your strengths as you bring together accomplished specialists in the pursuit of interdisciplinary research.

- **Contributions to noble causes:** Pursue ideals. Try to ensure that your volunteer efforts will make a difference in the lives of disadvantaged people or in the sustainability of the planet.

- **Cost-benefit assessments:** Be practical. You need to balance your efforts to create sustainable energy with a consideration of potential losses in environmental quality.

Maintaining priority consciousness will require you to develop hypotheses, collect data, analyze and elaborate results, and draw conclusions. Here is where critical thinking comes into play.

Critical thinking involves the purposeful and organized assessment of

thoughts, observations, perceptions, analyses, judgments, and conclusions. Critical thinkers apply rational, logical, and scientific modes of thinking to personal and societal challenges in order to devise solutions that are intellectually honest and make the best use of resources. The dealings of critical thinkers are characterized by empathy, fairness, and service to others. Through critical thinking, you can defeat falsehood, prejudice, and dishonor if you remain humble, open to the views of others and critical of your own faults and biases.

With personal determination and persistence, with priority consciousness and critical thinking, you are ready to use these principles and practices to your advantage.

Managing Your Life's Time

Time is asymmetric. It moves inexorably forward—it waits for no one. The effective use of time requires planning and organization.

Time management is not rocket science. It's a straightforward approach for using time effectively to meet your goals. Managing your time can involve the creation of simple to-do lists that serve as a daily reminder of what needs to be done. You should make it a practice to assign A, B, and C priorities to your tasks. A-priority items must be done today. B-priority items are important, but can wait a day or two. C-priority items have some future importance but should not take precedence over A- or B-priority items. Daily to-do lists, simply jotted down or more systematically formulated through the use of a planner, Day-timer, or computer software systems, are a good way to keep your time and your life on track toward important goals. Many colleges offer first-year courses with study units on time management.

Managing your time will work, and if you integrate it into the learning, loving, and serving components of the Way of Oz, it can lead you to notable accomplishments.

VI

The Way of Oz and Humility

20

Humility: An Integrated Perspective

After half a lifetime stumbling through the Gilded Age and half the vocations a man could try, [Baum] had found his fortune within himself, in the humble gift of storytelling. Perhaps he even thought of himself as the Wizard, for as the saga of Oz extended itself through book after book, the Wizard who began as a Prince of Humbug became a genuine wizard.

Frank Joslyn Baum and Russell P. MacFall, from *To Please a Child: A Biography of L. Frank Baum, Royal Historian of Oz* (1961)

Think about the dynamics of Frank Baum's relationship with producer Frederick Hamlin and director Julian Mitchell, during the revision of the stage play of *The Wizard of Oz*. As author Michael O. Riley said, "Little was left of the original plot [which] became like a thin thread holding various disparate and shifting elements together." Although we might imagine how Baum would have been humiliated by such radical changes to his work, he probably realized that the play wouldn't have become the smash success it was without the Hamlin/Mitchell metamorphosis. It's tempting to speculate that this major transformation of his play might have caused Baum to recall the embarrassing time he was duped by the theater troupe that ran off

with his expensive costumes under the guise of borrowing them. We can only imagine how deflating this was to the naive eighteen-year-old Baum.

But what we know of Frank Baum's temperament suggests that he rarely lost his sense of optimism. We have seen that he never let his failures deter him from renewed creative efforts, from the love of his family and friends, and from service to others.

His biographers have documented many other humbling experiences in Frank Baum's life:

- The loss of his dry-goods store (Baum's Bazaar) and his newspaper publishing enterprise in Aberdeen, South Dakota, between 1888 and 1891

- Harsh critical reviews of several of his works

- The demise of the baseball team (Hub City Nine) he started with several other business leaders in Aberdeen

- The failure of his business ventures in the theater and film industries, particularly the abject failure of his second theater production—*The Woggle-Bug*

- His lifelong coronary heart disease

Although some of Baum's failures were due to other people or fate, these were undoubtedly humbling experiences to someone who has been characterized as a thoughtful and reflective individual. But he seems to have made use of his failures and humbling experiences to strengthen his resolve to succeed, which in turn led him to renewed creativity and happiness.

Humility Defined and Enlarged

Humility can be defined as "a self-reflected modest appraisal and expression of one's skills, accomplishments or contributions, and place in the world." In many religions, humility requires an acknowledgment of a divine being. Outside any particular creed, humility is part of our universal experience because of these considerations:

- Human beings' finite and short lives are mere nanoseconds relative to the age of the universe.

- All human beings have frailties and foibles.

- Earth is relatively insignificant—a small planet in a small galaxy in a remote place in the universe.

- Most human accomplishments are relatively insignificant—such as publishing a book among the more than 100 million published to date.

- No one can know even a tiny fraction of the world's knowledge, as we are reminded in a stroll through the stacks of any university or major public library, or by imagining the millions of hits of Google or other Internet searches.

- Most people will never travel to more than a few of the 195 countries of the world (as of 2010).

Characterizing Humility

The humble person

- is self-effacing, demonstrating a reluctance to draw attention to himself or herself;

- is self-deprecating, using humor to criticize his or her personal frailities and foibles;

- turns humiliations into positive learning opportunities—sometimes after hitting bottom, as observed among many recovering addicts;

- feels compassion for others;

- acknowledges the roles of others in his or her successes; and

- takes life's insults and turns them into kindness to others.

Humility is an important virtue for those who are members of a team or are charged with supervising others. The successful team leader will be the person who is able to identify and promote the strengths of all members of the group.

The humble supervisor knows that a unit's success relies on others and that the recognition of such contributions is vital to the continuing success of the unit and the supervisor. Perhaps you've attended a public presentation where a team leader, receiving an award on behalf of the group, fails to acknowledge the contributions of the team's members. The embarrassment among the team members (and even among members of the audience) is palpable.

The humble leader, one who fairly acknowledges the work of others, becomes revered among colleagues and friends. As a result, such units and teams are poised for success after success. Not only is humility important to the individual, but it serves as a portal to other virtues that round out one's citizenship in the Way of Oz.

21

Humility among Other Virtues

Humility is the solid foundation of all virtues.

Confucius (551–479 BCE), Chinese philosopher and social critic

Genuine humility guides us to the development of other virtues and character traits that have profound effects on our ability to lead. Integrity, a devotion to ethical principles, empathy, and beneficence are all vital to personal and professional growth.

Integrity Leads to Honesty

The word *integrity* has different meanings in the material, intellectual, and ethical worlds. The material integrity of the skin of an aircraft's fuselage displays strength, flexibility, and resiliency, protecting the plane from fissures and cracks, and ultimately, catastrophic failure.

Intellectual integrity is the consistency of an individual's beliefs with scientific and other scholarly evidence and proofs. People whose religious or political belief systems contradict well-established scientific findings have potential conflicts with intellectual integrity. Consider the following examples:

- Christoph Luxenberg, a linguistic scholar, in studying the literary and philological origins of the Koran, offers insights on the so-called Muslim martyrs who commit homicidal acts against innocent victims around the world. The radical jihadists who enlist these suicide bombers promise them a heavenly reward for their diabolic acts: seventy-two virgins to enjoy in heaven. Luxenberg says this promise is based on a misinterpretation of the Syriac (a dialect of Aramaic) in the seminal texts, in which the word *hur*, rather than meaning "sultry virgins," refers to refreshing beverages or chilled white raisins. This knowledge adds to our understanding of how intellectually dishonest jihadist recruiters can be in justifying their egregious missions.

• Despite one hundred fifty years of scrutiny and relevant scientific advances, about 40 percent of Americans reject evolution as the best explanation for natural selection and diversity in biological systems. Some say evolution is just a theory, misled by the term *theory* as it is used in science. Scientific theories are *never* fully proven. They become accepted as proofs develop. In the case of evolution, the proofs are so overwhelming as to make its rejection an affront to intellectual integrity.

• Rampant commercial self-interest or political ideology may challenge intellectual integrity when claims are made for cause-and-effect relationships. The tobacco industry, for example, hoodwinked the American public for decades, challenging the overwhelming proof of the link between smoking and cancer and cardiovascular disease. Consider also the case of Heinrich Himmler (1900–1945), propaganda and SS Nazi leader, who created a cult around his claim that he was the reincarnation of the first king of Germany, Heinrich I (who ruled from 919 to 936 CE). The bizarre claim helped to advance Nazi influence in Germany before and during World War II.

Intellectual integrity, guided by informed skepticism and critical thinking, helps to uncover disparities between outmoded beliefs that have hardened into fact and new knowledge that is the product of objective scholarship and research.

In addition to intellectual congruence, integrity calls for consistency of beliefs, values, and actions. For the student of the Way of Oz, the moral compass of integrity will direct you toward an appreciation for diversity, democracy, sustainability, personal responsibility, and accountability. Embracing these concepts calls for action, which links integrity and honesty. We need honorable men and women to speak up for their convictions, and sometimes integrity comes at a personal cost. When people of integrity encounter situations where their values and beliefs are challenged, they must express their views, modulated through humility. Why? Because humble people know they can be wrong and know as well that the likelihood of persuading others to their positions is furthered by a temperate approach.

Leading with a Devotion to Ethics

In an age of transparency, responsibility, and accountability, ethics and a devotion to ethical principles become enabling factors. Whether you're in school or working as a professional, you need to become acquainted with the codes of ethics and conduct relevant to your situation. Look at the codes of ethics and conduct of various firms, institutions, and organizations—for example, those of the Hewlett-Packard Company, the University of California, the Council of International Schools, the Forum on Education Abroad, the International Red Cross and Red Crescent, and the Institute of Internal Auditors. Reading through the codes of these organizations will offer insight into what leaders consider to be ethical principles and practices. Codes of conduct generally include these principles:

- Respecting different cultures and customs and the dignity of others, regardless of gender, race, ethnicity or national origin, color, creed, ancestry, age, disability, marital status, sexual orientation, social class, political affiliation, or economic condition

- Treating others fairly

- Protecting free speech, privacy, and the practice of one's religion

- Holding employees, volunteers, and organizational entities responsible and accountable for behavior and actions, both individually and collectively

- Honoring individual employees' or volunteers' rights to fair and proper performance reviews, with a guarantee of due process, including the opportunity for appeals

- Ensuring truthfulness and transparency in individual and collective actions

- Abiding by federal, state, and local law and regulations

- Promoting sustainability

- Defending individual intellectual property rights

- Avoiding or managing conflicts of interest and commitment

- Ensuring consistency among ethical principles and organizational policies and practices

- Striving for honor and excellence in individual and collective efforts

These principles are taken seriously in most organizations of democratic countries, and the principles are energized by empathy and beneficence.

Cultivating Empathy and Beneficence

The mathematician, philosopher, and Nobel Peace Prize recipient Bertrand Russell (1872–1970) once remarked, "Three passions, simple but overwhelming, have governed my life, the longing for love, the search for knowledge, and the unbearable pity for the suffering of mankind. The world of loneliness, poverty, and pain make a mockery of what human life should be." When you are empathetic, you try to understand the plight of others, putting yourself in their proverbial shoes. In doing so, you are also experiencing one of the highest values of the Way of Oz.

The last value we'll consider is beneficence. The concept of beneficence goes beyond being benevolent, beyond seeking good for others, to ensuring the future welfare of others. You will find beneficence among International Red Cross and Red Crescent professionals and volunteers, who deal with human distress and natural disasters all over the world in places like Darfur in Sudan and East Timor in Indonesia, not only attending to an immediate need but also trying to secure a better future for the millions of people who live in these places. Empathy and beneficence are the actionable aspects of the humility and ethics components of the Way of Oz.

Beware of Wicked Witches

The "wicked witches" that challenge your commitment to the Way of Oz can bedevil you internally as well as externally. Internal "wicked witches" manifest themselves as self-doubt, which is a lack of self-confidence and feelings of being an impostor. Someone who begins to think he or she is inadequate is handicapped at best and crippled at worst if the self-doubt inhibits learning, loving, serving, and growth in leadership development. Similarly, someone who has been a successful leader but is stunted by feelings of having undeservedly achieved success may be a victim of the impostor syndrome—a psychological disorder that manifests itself when the person discounts his or her success as a "mistake"; thinks of himself or herself as a fake or fraud; or becomes inordinately upset by criticism, including constructive criticism.

The negative results of the impostor syndrome include persistent self-doubt, perfectionism, and procrastination. These internal "wicked witches" can be thwarted by positive self-talk or self-mentoring, the knowledge that such doubts have plagued some of the most famous people in the world, learning to love one's self, and serving others. In sum, we need to recognize that life, as F. Forrester Church notes, is a process where "we must somehow learn to give ourselves away."

External "wicked witches" are people who cause failures in the academic, personal, and professional development of others, through malevolent intent and behavior. These "wicked witches" can be hostile acquaintances, coworkers, or even members of your family or people counted among your friends, who may injure you through aggression, arrogance, envy, manipulation, narcissism, and prejudice. You can thwart the malign influences of many of these external "witches" by cultivating the qualities and values inherent in the Way of Oz.

Epilogue

It's all on the inside
To say you can find it elsewhere
Would be wrong.
It's all on the inside
Each soul has its song.

Michael Franks (1944–), composer, jazz singer,
and guitarist; from his song "On the Inside"

At this point in your study of the Way of Oz, you are empowered in special ways, not only in enhancing your personal and professional development, but also in using a "Way of Oz telescope" to look at the world in new ways. In your life's journey you'll meet many people like the Scarecrow, who are seemingly not very intelligent but often have wisdom and good ideas. Listen to them; encourage their next stage of learning and intellectual development.

You will also encounter many people like the Tin Woodman, whose hearts seem to be locked in a box in their chests. Be kind to them, for kindness and concern will often bring out heartfelt expressions from them. Encourage their love of life and others.

You will also meet many Cowardly Lions in society, people who are almost paralyzed to the point that they are unable to extend themselves to others. Yet among these emotionally crippled people are core elements of goodness and caring that can be directed toward service to others, the nation, and the world. Sometimes a participatory experience, such as a volunteer effort or service-learning course, will help Cowardly Lions envision what they can do to help others while they journey through life.

Then there are the Dorothy figures of the world. Dorothy is an apt model for leadership because in today's world women are outnumbering and outperforming men in colleges and universities. With women's expanded opportunities, we might even envision a century for women not far into the future. The Dorothy figures of the world understand leadership, and Dorothy's focus on the future offers a model we can all emulate—men and women alike.

Finally, there are the Wizards of the world, people who exhibit prideful behavior but whose life experiences help move them toward humility. You'll meet many arrogant and self-centered characters in life. Be patient with these people as long as their failings are not harming others. But, like the reformed Wizard, we need to speak up when arrogance and pride harm people or an organization. Your modeling of humility and its associated ethical values and virtues will go a long way in encouraging prideful Wizards to adopt desirable traits.

You now have the Way of Oz within your grasp. May it serve you well as you travel down life's yellow brick road.

Summaries of the Second through Thirteenth Baum Oz Sequels

Sequel 2: *Ozma of Oz: A Record of Her Adventures with Dorothy Gale of Kansas, the Yellow Hen, the Scarecrow, the Tin Woodman, Tiktok, the Cowardly Lion and the Hungry Tiger; Besides Other Good People Too Numerous to Mention Faithfully Recorded Herein,* 1907

Dorothy is swept off the deck of a ship she and Uncle Henry are taking to Australia. She clings to a bobbing chicken coop from the ship and winds up on the shore of Ev, a new land Baum has created. Here she meets Ozma, the Scarecrow, the Tin Woodman, the Cowardly Lion, and a new character, the Hungry Tiger, all from the Land of Oz. Baum introduces Tiktok, the copper-clad robot man who is only mobile when he is wound up; Billina, a feisty yellow hen; and Roquat, the evil Nome King. Dorothy and her friends, including Ozma and her comic-opera army, manage to defeat him and restore the rightful rulers of Ev. Dorothy and crew return triumphantly to Oz, and through the use of a Magic Belt seized from the Nome King, Dorothy rejoins Uncle Henry, who has made it to Australia after the storm.

Sequel 3: *Dorothy and the Wizard of Oz,* 1908

Dorothy, her second cousin Zeb, her carriage horse Jim, and her pet cat Eureka are swallowed up in a hole created by an earthquake. While they're underground, Dorothy and her crew meet up with the Wizard of Oz. The entourage has a series of life-threatening adventures, involving nasty characters like the merciless potato Mangaboos, invisible ferocious bears, evil wooden gargoyles, and people-eating baby dragons. This book has been criticized because it lacks a quest theme and because the Dorothy character neither learns from her adverse experiences nor is able to suggest solutions to the many difficulties she and her team face. In contrast, the Wizard—in his first appearance in an Oz sequel—is the consistent problem solver, perhaps as redemption for his chicanery in the original Oz book. The book ends with an odd scene in which Dorothy remembers that Ozma of Oz looks in on her at four o'clock each afternoon using the sorcerer's Magic Picture. On this crucial day in her present difficulty, Dorothy gives Ozma the distress signal that causes her to transport the underground captives to the Emerald City.

Sequel 4: *The Road to Oz: In which is related how Dorothy Gale of Kansas, The Shaggy-Man, Button-Bright, and Polychrome the Rainbow's Daughter met on an Enchanted Road and followed it all the way to the Marvelous Land of Oz,* 1909

In contrast to its dark predecessor (*Dorothy and the Wizard of Oz*), *The Road to Oz* is a picturesque book without a plot. Dorothy and Toto set out to find Butterfield, Kansas, wishing to help a new Oz character, Shaggy-Man, a nonconformist wanderer, perhaps patterned after the many vagabonds wandering around America after the Civil War. As they proceed on their journey they stumble onto a road that leads to Oz. Along this road the trio meets Button-Bright, a lost little boy wearing a sailor's outfit whose wealthy family believes him to be "bright as a button," and Polychrome, the rainbow's daughter, who is also lost. The group has a series of adventures, including one with the infamous Scoodlers, who threaten to make soup of several members of Dorothy's troupe, but they eventually arrive in Oz where they do some touring. Baum now describes the utopian conditions in Oz, which is a harmonious place where money is of no value and all its inhabitants derive satisfaction from helping one another. At the end of the book, the traveling crew arrives in the Emerald City just in time to celebrate Ozma's birthday. Baum uses this occasion to reintroduce most of the characters that populated the four Oz books preceding this one.

Sequel 5: *The Emerald City of Oz,* 1910

In *The Emerald City of Oz*, all citizens work for the general good, and all wealth is shared. Nonviolence is an inviolable principle, and most inhabitants are immortal. Ozma maintains order through the power of the Magic Belt (captured from the Nome King in *The Road to Oz*) and her Magic Picture, which gives her constant surveillance of the citizens of Oz. Glinda's Magic Record Book, with its twenty-four-hour coverage of events, also plays a role in keeping the population in line.

Some critics think the late-nineteenth-century utopian novels by Edward Bellamy and William Morris helped shape Baum's ideas. World events just prior to World War I also markedly shaped Baum's conception of a need for order to ensure a civilized society.

In this work Baum closes out the Oz series by having Dorothy, Toto, Aunt Em, and Uncle Henry teleported to Oz by its ruler, Ozma. Aunt Em and Uncle Henry agree to join Dorothy because the bank has foreclosed on their drought-plagued farm. Subsequently, the foursome plus a contingent of Oz citizens tour Oz, where they encounter many strange characters and places, such as Bunbury, populated by living baked breads and cakes; Cuttenclips, a town with cut-out paper people; Flutterbudget Center, a place where its people are always anxious about unlikely events that haven't occurred; and Rigmarole Town, where people can't say what they mean because they are pedantic and boring.

Sequel 6: *The Patchwork Girl of Oz*, 1913

Some critics consider this sequel to be one of Baum's best; he thought so, too. The main character—a life-sized doll also known as Scraps—is the creation of Margolotte, who is married to the magician Dr. Pipt. Baum introduces the boy Ojo the Unlucky, and his uncle, Uncle (or "Unc") Nunkie, poor and underfed residents of the Blue Forest in Munchkin Country. Ojo and Uncle Nunkie seek the help of the disreputable magician, Dr. Pipt, who has developed the Powder of Life. During Ojo and Uncle Nunkie's visit, Dr. Pipt uses the life-giving powder to animate Scraps. Unbeknownst to Pipt, Ojo adds small amounts of "Brain Furniture" potions to the powdery mix to imbue cleverness, courage, ingenuity, judgment, learning, poetic abilities, and self-reliance. But during the encounter, the magician's bottle of the Liquid of Petrification spills and Uncle Nunkie and Margolotte are turned into marble. Ojo teams up with the odd-looking but talented Scraps and an animated Glass Cat brought to life by Dr. Pipt. The trio sets out to find exotic ingredients (a single clover with six leaves, three Woozy tail hairs, four ounces of water from a dark well, one drop of oil from a live human being, and a yellow butterfly's left wing) so the magician can formulate an antidote to the Liquid of Petrification. Along the way, they meet another new character—the Woozy, a four-legged, nearly hairless creature (it has three short, thick hairs on its tail), whose body is composed of cube and rectangular parts. The team resolves to travel to the Emerald City to seek Ozma's help. During their quest they encounter the Shaggy-Man, who helps extricate them from a run-in with leaf-wrapping plants. When they reach the Emerald City, the group enlists the help of Ozma, the Scarecrow (who instantly becomes smitten with Scraps and she with him), Dorothy, and Jack Pumpkinhead.

After some trouble when Ojo unlawfully picks a six-leaf clover, Ozma admonishes the group not to conduct unauthorized acts of magic, and she encourages them to make a second trip. Ojo, Scraps, Dorothy, and the Scarecrow set out once again to find the missing ingredients for the antidote. The journey takes them to a mountain community in Quadling Country, where they find the dark well water, and Winkie Country, where they visit the Tin Woodman, who supplies the necessary drop of oil. But the group is stymied because they don't want to have to kill a butterfly to obtain its left wing. Disheartened, they return to the Emerald City with the Tin Woodman. Ozma reports that Glinda has told the Wizard about a spell that will bring the statues back to life. Ozma says she'll escort the frozen pair, along with Dr. Pipt, to the Emerald City.

At the story's end, Ozma allows Scraps, the Glass Cat, and the Woozy to live in the Emerald City. She gives Ojo and Uncle Nunkie a home just outside the city's boundaries. Happy futures are assured for all.

Sequel 7: *Tik-Tok of Oz*, 1914

Based on the modestly successful play of the same name, the seventh sequel is a complex set of interwoven tales, involving the threat of an attack on Oz by Queen Ann Soforth and her all-officer army (with the exception of Private Files); the shipwreck saga of Betsy Bobbin, a little girl from Oklahoma and her companion mule, Hank; a quest to find the Shaggy-Man's brother who has been kidnapped by the Nome King (whose name has been changed from Roquat to Roggedo because he drank from the Waters of Oblivion and forgot his name); and a trip by a newly formed group, including Betsy, Hank, the Shaggy-Man, Polychrome, and Tik-Tok, through the Nome King's Hollow Tube to the opposite side of the earth. Here they encounter a society of royal fairies (the King of the Animals, the Queen of Light) and their only Private Citizen, the Great Jinjin or Tititi-Hoochoo, who, like the Tin Woodman, does not have a heart. A series of adventures on the originating side of the earth take place, including the freeing of the Shaggy-Man's brother and the defeat of the Nome King (with the help of the dragon Quox, commissioned by the Great Jinjin), and the introduction of Ozga (the Rose Princess, Ozma's cousin), who falls in love with Private Files. Betsy and Hank are transported to Ozma's castle in the Emerald City, where they meet and befriend Dorothy, Ozma, and the Wizard. Hank becomes acquainted with the other animals, and Toto begins talking, as is common for all the animals in Oz. The newcomers become residents of Oz.

In *Tik-Tok of Oz*, Baum borrows not only from his play of a similar name but also from the third Oz book, *Ozma of Oz*. It's important for Oz devotees to read the whole series of Baum's Oz books in order to gain a coherent picture of Oz, even though it's well known that the author himself occasionally created geographic and other inconsistencies in his works. Notable in *Tik-Tok of Oz* is the inclusion of a set of detailed maps of Oz, including a delineation of the dreaded deserts: the Impassable Desert (north of Gilligan Country), the Deadly Desert (west of Winkie Country), the Great Sandy Waste (south of Quadling Country), and the Shifting Sands (east of Munchkin Country). One of the maps contains details of the lands outside Oz (beyond the deserts) whose location and inhabitants have played important roles in prior sequels. It is important to note that the Oz maps—portrayed as the work of Professor Woggle-Bug—were reversed, the western Winkie Country appearing on the right side of each map, as opposed to the convention of depicting western features on the left side and eastern areas on the right. Apparently this mistake was rectified in part by the publisher's addition of reversed east-west markers on the maps—but Baum's presentation of the maps has created confusion about the locations of his fantasy lands.

Sequel 8: *The Scarecrow of Oz*, 1915

In his many sequels, Baum recycled characters, places, and plot lines, and in some instances, he used characters, scenarios, and story ideas from his non-Oz books, as is the case with his eighth sequel, *Scarecrow of Oz*. The book begins with a young girl, Trot, and an older salty sailor, Cap'n Bill—both from *Sea Fairies* and *Sky Island* fame. The adventures take place in the Valley of Mo (from *The Surprising Adventures of the Magical Monarch of Mo and His People*), and parts of the story line are similar to the earlier Trot books. The book follows Baum's typical pattern, in which characters, old and new, have frightening adventures and narrow escapes but end up in quest of Oz. In this tale, while they're out in a rowboat, Trot and Cap'n Bill get caught in a whirlpool and end up in an underground cavern (like the earthquake adventure in *Dorothy and the Wizard of Oz*), where they meet Ork—a four-legged storklike creature with a propeller tail (for skyward and water-bound journeys). They journey for some time in the dark, but then Ork flies them to an island beyond Oz and on to the land of Mo, where they are joined by Button-Bright. Eventually they cross the Great Sandy Waste to arrive in Jinxland in the southeast corner of Oz (within Quadling Country). In Jinxland, they assist Princess Gloria in pursuing her love for a commoner, Pons, the son of a gardener. They are joined by the Scarecrow, whom Glinda has sent to help depose the wicked ruler, King Krewl. When they topple the evil king, Queen Gloria reigns with her Royal Consort Pons. This is only the second time Baum introduces romantic love into an Oz tale. At the story's end, the travelers are transported to the Emerald City where they meet Ozma and many of the characters from earlier books, who are all now residents of Oz.

Sequel 9: *Rinkitink in Oz: Wherein is recorded the Perilous Quest of Prince Inga of Pingaree and King Rinkitink in the Magical Isles that lie beyond the Borderland of Oz,* 1916

With its medieval setting and the fact that most of the action takes place outside Oz, *Rinkitink in Oz* is an oddity. King Rinkitink, a bulbous and jolly character from the land of Rinkitink (which is northwest of Oz on the coastline of the Nonestic Ocean), decides to travel to the Isle of Pingaree, taking his ill-tempered goat Bilbil with him. The plot revolves around the question of the royalty of Pingaree, King Kitticut, Queen Garee, and their son, Prince Inga. During Rinkitink's visit, Pingaree is invaded by armies from Regos and Coregos, who ravage the island and carry off its citizens, along with their king and queen. Strangely, Inga, Rinkitink, and Bilbil are left unscathed and have at their disposal three magic pearls—a blue one that gives infinite strength, a pink one that provides invulnerability, and a white one that ensures wisdom. With these jewels they are successful in releasing the Pingaree citizens. Glinda, who had dispatched Dorothy and the Wizard to help the Nome Empire, has watched the action through her Magic Record Book. Inge frees the royal parents, and Pingaree is filled with celebrations. Meanwhile, Rinkitink returns to his home country to become king for "three hours a day," and Glinda transforms Bilbil back into Prince Bobo of Boboland. His metamorphosis takes place in stages, in which he first assumes animal forms, then human ones, including tottenhot and mifket. In this instance Baum displays the racism typical of his day, assigning inferior intellect and abilities to Africans.

Critics consider *Rinkitink of Oz* one of Baum's weakest Oz books because of its lack of coherence, its unusual moralistic tone, and its racist allusions and imagery.

Sequel 10: *The Lost Princess of Oz*, 1917

The idea for *The Lost Princess* apparently came from a young reader who wondered what Oz citizens might do if Ozma were somehow lost or kidnapped. The book begins in the Emerald City with Dorothy and the others waking up to learn that Ozma is nowhere to be found. The Magic Picture is missing, the Wizard's magic tools are gone, and so is Glinda's Magic Record Book. Dorothy proceeds to organize a team to look for Ozma.

In the southwestern corner of Winkie Country in the country of Yips, Cayke the Cookie Cook also discovers the loss of her diamond-studded gold Magic Dishpan that produces perfect cookies and allows instant travel from one end of Oz to the other. As she prepares to set off in search of Ozma, Dorothy hears about Cayke's loss and agrees to help her search for the Magic Dishpan. She enlists the aid of Betsy, Button-Bright, the Cowardly Lion, Hank, the Patchwork Girl, the Saw-Horse, Toto, and the Woozy. The Wizard joins them, along with nine piglets, and the search party heads west into the far reaches of Winkie Country. There they encounter new places and characters—the Merry-Go-Round Mountain; the City of Thi, which is populated by Thists who eat thistles; and the city of Herku, where they first learn about Ugu the Shoemaker. Ugu had been a resident of Herku, where he is well known for his magic arts. The Oz group learns that he has recently left for parts unknown to build a wicker castle. Meantime, Cayke has paired up with Frogman, a spiffily dressed frog the size of a man. Frogman has been known as a dandy and an arrogant know-it-all for years. On his journey with Cayke, after a swim in the Truth Pond just north of the country of Yips, he becomes a modest and reasonable fellow. After a few adventures in the forest known as Bear Center, where they meet the King Lavender Bear and his wind-up Little Pink Bear (who can answer correctly any question posed save those about the future), Cayke and Frogman learn that Ugu the Shoemaker has stolen the Magic Dishpan. They head north, where they meet up with Dorothy and company. The groups join forces to look for Ugu, whose castle is nearby.

Ugu turns the room with the adventurers in it upside down, and they are then captives. Fortunately, Dorothy has with her the Nome King's Magic Belt, and she uses it to turn the room right side up and to turn Ugu into a dove. Using his own magical powers Ugu turns himself into a giant Dove of War. When the giant dove threatens Dorothy, the Frogman, not knowing of Dorothy's immunity from harm (because of the Magic Belt), begins to struggle with Ugu, which causes Dorothy to use the Magic Belt to turn Ugu into a canary-sized dove. In his new form but with his old magic, Ugu disappears with the Magic Dishpan. Shortly thereafter, with the help of the Little Pink Bear, the group learns that Ozma is locked in a golden peach pit in Button-Bright's pocket, and with some magic from the Wizard, Ozma is released. She and her friends return to the Emerald City to celebrate their reunion. In the meantime, the Scarecrow and the Tin Woodman, who have been off on their own searching for Ozma, discover the Magic Dishpan. They return to the Emerald City with the magic pan and learn of Ozma's release. They witness her giving the jewel-studded pan to Cayke. Ugu returns to the Emerald City, where he receives Dorothy's forgiveness after he confesses his sorrow for his past transgressions and offers a pledge of humility.

Although *The Lost Princess of Oz* follows Baum's formula of "exciting adventures, unexpected difficulties . . . and marvelous escapes," it has a philosophical bent that permeates many of his later works.

Sequel 11: *The Tin Woodman of Oz: A Faithful Story of an Astonishing Adventure Undertaken by the Tin Woodman, assisted by Woot the Wanderer, the Scarecrow of Oz, and Polychrome, the Rainbow's Daughter,* 1918

The action begins with the Scarecrow meeting the Tin Woodman in the Woodman's castle in Winkie Country. During the visit, a new character—a young Gilligan boy, Woot the Wanderer—drops in to ask for food and engages the two in conversation about themselves. After hearing their life stories, Woot inquires about the Tin Woodman's love for Nimmie Amee, the young Munchkin woman, and the Tin Woodman remembers his words from the original Oz story: "While I was in love I was the happiest man on earth; but no one can love who has not a heart, and so I am resolved to ask Oz to give me one. If he does, I will go back to the Munchkin maiden and marry her." They discuss the fact that the Tin Woodman's new heart is a "Kind Heart instead of a Loving Heart," one that won't let him love Nimmie Amee any more now than he could when he had no heart. Woot finds this hard to believe, so the trio resolves to travel to Munchkin Country to find Nimmie Amee to see if her affections have changed since she and the Tin Woodman parted. Baum hints that the Tin Woodman will marry Nimmie Amee to make her the Empress of the Winkies.

In an aside, we learn that Nimmie Amee was actually a ward of the Wicked Witch of the East rather than the unnamed "unsavory woman" as she was described in the original 1900 book. Readers understand now that Nimmie Amee could have escaped her involuntary servitude after the Wicked Witch of the East was killed by the descent of Dorothy's tornado-propelled Kansas house. The Scarecrow, the Tin Woodman, and Woot begin their trip east to Munchkin Country, passing through Gilligan Country, where they encounter a land of threatening balloons, or Loons, from Loonville. The three travelers puncture the Loons, defeating them easily, and then pass through Yoop Valley, where they encounter the beautiful but gigantic and insidious Mrs. Yoop, who wishes to capture them for her own delight. She turns the Tin Woodman into a tin owl, the Scarecrow into a straw-stuffed bear, and Woot into a green monkey. Mrs. Yoop has also transformed Polychrome into a caged canary. With the cleverness of a monkey, Woot steals Mrs. Yoop's magic apron, which provides the means for them to escape with Polychrome in their changed forms. Heading south into Munchkin Country, they arrive at Jinjur's farm, where they are encouraged to go to the Emerald City to seek Ozma's help in transforming them back to their original forms. Arriving in the Emerald City, the group visits Ozma and Dorothy. Ozma immediately restores the Scarecrow and the Tin Woodman to their original forms; Polychrome is transformed back to her beautiful and sweet self through a series of metamorphoses. Woot's transformation takes a bit more ingenuity. Ozma first transforms Mrs. Yoop into Woot and then exchanges the Woot's and the green monkey's forms to restore Woot's original form as a boy.

The quartet is now free to continue their journey, first through the same woods where the Tin Woodman was found in the 1900 book. Here they come upon a rusted Tin Soldier (Captain Fyter), whose fate seems to parallel that of the Tin Woodman. After some judicious oiling, the Tin Soldier describes how a spell the Wicked Witch of the East cast on him caused his tinny transformation and caused him to cut off his body parts with his enchanted sword. The Tin Soldier says he had had a relationship with Nimmie Amee, who once expressed love for him. The Tin Soldier now pledges to join the quartet to find Nimmie Amee—both tin men seeking her hand in marriage. Presumably she will accept the proposal of the better of the two tin men.

The quintet continues the journey, coming upon the workshop of Ku-Klip—the tinsmith—who had worked on both the Tin Woodman and the Tin Soldier. Ku-Klip admits that—using a special glue obtained from the Wicked Witch of the East's hideaway—he took human parts from the Tin Woodman and the Tin Soldier to make a humanoid being, Chopfyt, a creature reminiscent of Mary Shelley's *Frankenstein*. Apparently, the Tin Soldier's head was used in constructing Chopfyt, leaving the Tin Woodman's head as a "spare" and in an odd scene inside Ku-Klip's shop, the Tin Woodman finds and strikes up a conversation with his own head—made possible because the immortality of creatures in Oz extends to body parts as well.

Having learned Nimmie Amee lives near the flat-topped Mount Munch, the seekers now head in that direction. Along the way, they have a series of adventures: first traveling through an invisible country that is home to a monstrous Hip-po-gy-raf that wishes to consume the Scarecrow's straw, then meeting Professor and Mrs. Swyne, a smug bovine couple whose nine progeny live with the Wizard in the Emerald City. They arrive finally at the base of Mount Munch, in the easternmost part of Munchkin Country. Here they befriend a rabbit that points them toward Nimmie Amee's cottage at the summit. However, an impenetrable wall of "hardened air" surrounds the cottage. Fortunately, the rabbit has burrowed under the wall, and with a little magic, Polychrome shrinks her friends so they will fit through the rabbit hole. After being "right-sized" on the opposite side of the "hardened air wall," the Tin Woodman and Tin Soldier go up to the cottage where they have a fateful encounter with Nimmie Amee. They are surprised to learn that she has married Chopfyt, who is neither a great brain nor a caring person, though he does cater to her needs. She bids the pair of tin characters farewell, saying, "Go back to your homes and forget me as I have forgotten you." And so they leave, returning to the Emerald City where they report to Ozma, who allows Woot to continue his wandering through Oz. Polychrome becomes Woot's new ward. Ozma sends Captain Fyter to Gilligan Country to serve on guard duty, and the Scarecrow and the Tin Woodman return to the Tin Woodman's castle to continue their earlier interrupted visit.

In *The Tin Woodman of Oz*, Baum amplifies descriptions of the physical and cultural characteristics of Oz, confirms the immortality of creatures in Oz (even for recently arriving human beings as well as body parts of humans and animals), and raises philosophical questions about mind versus spirit in the musings of the Tin Woodman with his own humanoid head.

Sequel 12: *The Magic of Oz: A Faithful Record of the Remarkable Adventures of Dorothy and Trot and the Wizard of Oz, together with the Cowardly Lion, the Hungry Tiger and Cap'n Bill, in their successful search for a Magical and Beautiful Birthday Present for Princess Ozma of Oz,* 1919

The action begins on top of Mount Munch, where the Hyups reside. Bini Aru, a Hyup magician, has a disreputable son, Kiki Aru, who has learned the meaning and pronunciation of the word *Pyrzqxgl*—which has been devised by his father as a means of transforming creatures into other beings or inanimate objects. Pronouncing the word, Kiki transforms himself into a hawk and flies east over the Shifting Sands Desert (Baum inconsistently calls this the Deadly Desert, which is more frequently referred to as being on Oz's western border). After resting briefly in Hiland (adjacent to Loland), he continues north past Merryland to Noland for an overnight stay. The next day he continues westerly over the Kingdom of Ix and on into Ev, where he transforms himself back into a Munchkin boy and meets Ruggedo, the deposed ruler of the Land of Ev. After some discussion, the two agree to a diabolical plot that could lead to Ruggedo's conquering Oz.

They are transformed into eagles and fly back over the Deadly Desert to the Forest of Gugu in Gilligan Country. There they are transformed again into Li-Mon-Eags (creatures with lion heads, monkey bodies, and eagle wings) in preparation for meeting with the very large yellow leopard leader, Gugu. In the Gugu Forest, the two Li-Mon-Eags try to convince Gugu and his animal subjects to take part in an invasion of the Emerald City. They tell them the Ozmies wish to enslave the animals of Gugu Forest. In the invasion plan the animals will be transformed into a human army that can conquer the Emerald City, and by converting the Ozmies into animals through the power of the word *Pyrzqxgl*, the new citizens of the Emerald City can enjoy the riches and comforts of the deposed residents. While Gugu is describing this nefarious proposal to his animal subjects prior to a vote, Dorothy, the Wizard, the Cowardly Lion, and the Hungry Tiger arrive. Sensing danger, Kiki transforms the Wizard into a fox and steals the Wizard's black bag of magic devices. Dorothy is transformed into a lamb, and the Cowardly Lion into a Munchkin boy. Aware of Ruggedo's anxiety, Kiki converts him into a goose; the Hungry Tiger is changed into a rabbit; and Gugu is converted into a fat Gilligan woman. Later Ruggedo sidles up to Kiki and convinces him to transform the deposed Nome King back to a Li-Mon-Eag and then begin the transformations to build the invasion army. While Kiki is transforming a group of monkeys into fifty-foot humanoid soldiers, the fox Wizard overhears the magic word and with this power converts Kiki (in his Li-Mon-Eag form) into a hickory nut and Ruggedo into a walnut, neutralizing their power. The Wizard then converts himself back to his humanoid self and transforms Dorothy and crew to their original selves. Dorothy and her friends seek Gugu's cooperation to enlist monkeys who can be made smaller and learn tricks for Ozma's forthcoming birthday party. With the permission of Gugu's colleague, the Great Ape, the Wizard engages a dozen "intelligent and good tempered monkeys." The simian volunteers are each shrunk to four inches and caged for transport to the Emerald City.

Now the traveling crew learns from the Glass Cat, who had joined them sometime earlier, that Trot and Cap'n Bill have run into difficulty during their trip to the Magic Isle, where they tried to obtain a specimen of the Magic Flower, capable of producing several varieties of flowers and fruits on the same plant, as a gift for Ozma on her birthday. Trot and Cap'n Bill have been rooted in soil that causes them to shrink and may ultimately cause them to disappear. Thus, Dorothy and company—guided by the Glass Cat, who has found and returned to the Wizard his bag of magic devices—leave the Gugu Forest to save their colleagues on Magic Isle, which is in the middle of a river in the eastern part of Gilligan Country.

Along the way, they meet the beautiful Lonesome Duck, a magician living in a small diamond palace near Magic Isle. The Duck admits the futility of his magic in saving Trot and Cap'n Bill, but Dorothy and crew—especially the Wizard—are undeterred. Eventually they find the Gilligan River and the island where Trot and Cap'n Bill are trapped. Using the raft the trapped pair used earlier, Dorothy and the Wizard sail to the island while the Glass Cat, who is able to walk on the bottom of the river, accompanies them underwater. Shortly, the three reach their anchored friends. Following some abortive attempts to free Trot and Cap'n Bill with devices from the Wizard's magic bag, Dorothy reminds the Wizard of the "power of the word," which he uses to transform Trot and Cap'n Bill into bumblebees. They fly to shore, where they are transformed into their normal selves. They haven't yet obtained the Magic Flower specimen, but Cap'n Bill, remembering that his peg leg, unlike his other leg, hadn't become rooted on the Magic Isle, wraps the wooden leg in bark and returns to the island to retrieve the Magic Flower.

At the story's end, everyone returns to the Emerald City, where they have a great birthday celebration for Ozma. The miniature monkeys perform, and the wonderful Magic Flower is presented to Ozma. Before the celebration, however, Professor Woggle-Bug, who is now Principal of the Royal Athletic College (located just outside of the Emerald City in Munchkin land), petitions Ozma for help in punishing Royal College students who have rebelled over the food there, which comes in the form of tablets (as in Baum's *The Master Key*). Professor Woggle-Bug has also created tablets for learning to save "paper and books, as well as the tedious hours devoted to study in some of our less favored schools," which permits "the students to devote all their time to racing, base-ball, tennis and other manly and womanly sports." We don't know how Ozma rules in this matter because Dorothy and company, along with several other of Baum's creations, begin Ozma's splendid birthday celebration.

On the day following Ozma's birthday bash, Dorothy and the Wizard, seated by the fountain containing the Waters of Oblivion, are talking to Ozma about their recent adventures when the subject of the last transformations of Kiki and Ruggedo comes up. At this moment, the Wizard remembers that the hickory nut and walnut are still in his pocket, and at Dorothy's suggestion and Ozma's urging, both nuts are transformed in "*Pyrzqxgl*-fashion" to their original selves. They are thirsty when they're brought back, they drink from a cup containing the Waters of Oblivion, and they lose all memory and inclination for evil. Kiki and his former compatriot end up living happily ever after in the Land of Oz.

Sequel 13: *Glinda of Oz: In which are related the Exciting Experiences of Princess Ozma of Oz, and Dorothy, in their hazardous journey to the home of the Flatheads, and to the Magic isle of the Skeezers, and how they were rescued from dire peril by the sorcery of Glinda the Good,* 1920

The story begins with Ozma and Dorothy visiting Glinda in her castle in Quadling Country. The visitors arrive in the Red Wagon pulled by the Sawhorse. As Glinda and Ozma talk about their reigning duties, Dorothy consults Glinda's Magic Record Book. In the "Great Book"—as Baum also calls it—Dorothy learns that the Skeezers have just declared war on the Flatheads. The Skeezers' land is in the northwest corner of Oz in Gilligan Country, just south of the Impassable Desert. The Flatheads are said to live in a mountainous area just south of Skeezer land. However, neither Ozma nor Glinda knows much about the Skeezers or the Flatheads. Glinda goes off to her Room of Magic to investigate and confirms the location of the Skeezers. She discovers that they live on a Magic Isle (different from the one identified in sequel 12) in a lake. Since she also learns that the

Skeezers and their Flathead neighbors appear to be using magic, it behooves Ozma to take action since only she, Glinda, and the Wizard are allowed to practice magic in Oz. Ozma resolves to visit the Skeezers and the Flatheads to quell their turmoil, prevent a war, and see that all "are content and happy" as in other parts of Oz.

Ozma thinks about taking her army, but she has only one soldier. So Ozma and Dorothy return to the Emerald City to make preparations for the peacekeeping mission, but not before Glinda gives Dorothy a Magic Ring she can use to summon the good sorceress for help.

Soon after their return from Glinda's castle, Ozma and Dorothy head north for Gilligan Country in the Red Wagon, Dorothy armed with the Magic Belt and the Magic Ring from Glinda, Ozma carrying the Silver Wand known for its powers of offense and defense. Along the way, they are trapped in a web made by Purple Spiders at the behest of the Spider King, but Dorothy and Ozma are able to defeat the spiders with the help of a crab, who becomes a willing ally when Ozma promises to transform him from the common green variety into a rare white crab. During their escape from the Purple Spiders, Ozma and Dorothy leave the Sawhorse and Red Wagon behind and soon come upon a fog-laden valley, where they are aided by the Mist Maidens who carry them across to a "delightful plain," where they catch sight of their first objective—the Flathead Mountain. They camp overnight on the plain—enjoying a splendidly appointed tent and a sumptuous meal thanks to Ozma's wand. Ozma confesses she enjoys above all using her fairy powers to make others happy and tells Dorothy that if she had "no kingdom to rule, and no subjects to look after . . . [she] would be miserable." Ozma confirms that she is "not as powerful as Glinda the Sorceress, who has studied many arts of magic that I know nothing of." She says, "The Wizard of Oz can do some things I am unable to accomplish, while I can accomplish things unknown to the Wizard. This is to explain that I'm not all-powerful, by any means. My magic is simply fairy magic, and not sorcery or wizardry."

After a long walk the next day, Ozma and Dorothy come to the foot of the Flathead Mountain but are stymied by an invisible wall surrounding it. By trial and error, Ozma finds the entrance to a series of stairways that rise ten steps and descend five. Through persistent climbing and descending, the two sojourners get to the top of the mountain, where they encounter a band of Flathead people who have no features above their ears, no hair on their flat tops, short and stocky noses, and purple eyes. All are adorned in outfits made of precious metals. The all-male reception party carries bows and arrows and battle-axes.

The Flatheads take Ozma and Dorothy prisoner and escort them to a palace where they meet the Supreme Dictator, or Su-dic, who claims to head a democracy in this land. An election takes place each year there, but he is the one who counts the votes. He describes how the Flatheads, born with no brains, were originally stupid. But fairies stopped by one day to give the Flatheads each a can of brains to carry in their pockets. Su-dic and his "first lady"—Rora Flathead—gained power by stealing cans of brains from their subjects, giving the two thieves the cleverness necessary to rule the Flatheads. Su-dic made it a crime to steal another's can of brains; if anyone did, the thief would have to relinquish his or her brains to Su-dic. Rora now has four cans of brains, thereby increasing her inclination to eat fish, which everyone knows is good for you. And in the Land of Skeezers, fish are abundant but protected in the nearby lake. Earlier Rora had been in trouble with the Skeezers when she tried to poison some fish in their lake, which caused the Skeezer leader, Queen Coo-ee-oh, to cast a spell transforming Rora into a brainless, animated Golden Pig. This in turn caused Su-dic to declare war on the Skeezers.

In a discussion with his captives, Su-dic expresses his unwillingness to accede to Ozma's authority or to her suggestions for negotiation with the Skeezers. He threatens to imprison Ozma and Dorothy. Ozma retaliates by using her Silver Wand to make herself and Dorothy invisible. They walk away unnoticed and escape Su-dic's palace. Foiling the pursuit by Su-dic, Rora, and some of their Flathead subjects, Ozma and Dorothy proceed on foot to the Lake of the Skeezers and the Magic Isle.

The Magic Isle is a large land mass surrounded by polished marble in the middle of the Lake of the Skeezers. It is largely composed of glass and has a glass dome. Ozma signals her presence with her Silver Wand, and an automated steel footbridge comes toward them from the Magic Isle. Ozma and Dorothy take the footbridge and enter the domed village on its lower level. They are warmly greeted and directed to a marble platform, which moves them up into the dome where they can see before them an idyllic village. They are escorted to a prominent city center building (later designated as the queen's palace) and directed to a beautiful throne room where they are introduced to the queen of the Skeezers, Coo-ee-oh. The queen—in her mid-teens—is plain in physical appearance but elegantly attired. She is as arrogant and conceited as Su-dic. Coo-ee-oh challenges Ozma's authority over Oz and the Skeezers.

Coo-ee-oh has "done her homework" on Ozma and Dorothy by consulting her Magic Oracle and tells them so, letting them know that she considers herself not only above the Skeezers but also above the two of them. Ozma, however, proclaims, "What and who I am is well established, and my authority comes from the Fairy Queen Lurline, of whose band I was a member when Lurline made all Oz a Fairyland. There are several countries and several different peoples in this broad land, each of which has its separate rulers, Kings, Emperors and Queens. But all these render obedience to my laws and acknowledge me as the supreme Ruler." Despite Ozma's proclamation, Coo-ee-oh is belligerent, determined to assert her power as a Krumbic Witch (with power above all). She holds fast to the commitment she's made for the Skeezers to go to war with the Flatheads. Coo-ee-oh says she thinks Ozma and Dorothy may be imposters, even Flathead spies, and says she has intelligence that the Flatheads intend to invade the Magic Isle the next day.

She intends to be ready and plans to intern Ozma and Dorothy. Coo-ee-oh places them under house arrest in the care of her lady-in-waiting, Lady Aurex, who escorts the two visitors to her home.

Once settled in Lady Aurex's home, Ozma senses the queen's lady-in-waiting might be reasonable, and the two develop a bond of trust. Lady Aurex tells them that the Skeezers are under constant voice surveillance by Coo-ee-oh, and so Ozma must immediately insulate Lady Aurex's quarters from the oppressive reach of the queen. Then Lady Aurex tells Ozma and Dorothy the whole story of Coo-ee-oh's tyrannical rule, including her abuse of Skeezer citizens, her aggressive overtures toward the Flatheads, and her commitment of the inherently peaceful Skeezers to war. Lady Aurex tells them how Coo-ee-oh and Su-dic came into power and about the former benevolent rulers of the Land of Skeezers, the three beautiful maidens known as the Adepts in Sorcery. She recounts how Coo-ee-oh stole the Adepts' instruments of magic and transformed the maidens into fish—one gold, one silver, and one bronze. Fearing the Adepts' threat to make her "shriveled and helpless" if any one of them were killed or otherwise destroyed, Coo-ee-oh had the three precious fish placed in the Lake of the Skeezers, which surrounds the Magic Isle. Now we know why Coo-ee-oh is worried about anyone fishing in Skeezer waters and why she fears Rora's onetime plan to poison the fish in the Lake of the Skeezers. Coo-ee-oh's behavior is the source of much of the enmity between the Flatheads and Skeezers, but their mutual hatred is fueled by the arrogance, conceit, and paranoia of the rulers of both countries.

After Ozma and Dorothy retire, they are awakened by the quaking and swaying of their quarters, which they soon find out is due to Coo-ee-oh's lowering the Magic Isle into the water because of the almost certain prospect of a Flathead invasion. The Flatheads are soon seen on shore, and Coo-ee-oh boards one of her submarines along with several armed Skeezers to meet the Flatheads at the lake's shore. Here Coo-ee-oh encounters Su-dic and a band of Flatheads. As Coo-ee-oh emerges from the submarine, Su-dic douses her with a magic potion from a copper vessel that transforms her into a narcissistic white swan adorned with diamonds. Su-dic is overjoyed that he has disempowered the queen, but in his glee he tips over the second copper vessel, which contains a poison for the lake's fish. The Flatheads, unable to get to the Magic Isle (since the submarine was powered through incantations by Coo-ee-oh), return to their mountain. Coo-ee-oh is so enamored of her newfound beauty as the Diamond Swan that she ignores the Skeezer soldiers' pleas for help and swims away, placing the Magic Isle in danger of remaining sunken because only she can activate the submerging machinery for the island.

Ozma, Lady Aurex, and Dorothy, having witnessed the recent action from the dome of the Magic Isle, are perplexed about their underwater dilemma. When Dorothy asks if

Ozma can use her magic to raise the Magic Isle, the good fairy exclaims that the submerging- and ascending-machine is operated through "witchcraft," which is beyond her powers. Stymied, Dorothy turns the Magic Ring given to her by Glinda right then left, to enlist the aid of the great sorceress. After receiving Dorothy's signal, Glinda sees their predicament through the Magic Record Book. The good sorceress recognizes a big challenge in raising the sunken island because of her failed experiments with models and different recipes. Glinda assembles her advisors, who are organized as the Council of State, to explore what should be done. The Counselors include the Scarecrow, the Tin Woodman, Scraps, the Shaggy-Man, Jack Pumpkinhead, Tik-Tok, Cap'n Bill, Professor Woggle-Bug, Frogman, Uncle Henry (who now lives with Aunt Em in Oz), and of course the Wizard, Glinda's pupil in magic. Although they're at a loss as to how they can raise the Magic Isle, they agree to go as a group to the Lake of the Skeezers, led by Glinda and the Wizard. Betsy, Trot, the Glass Cat, Button Bright, Ojo, and the Cowardly Lion join the group the next morning, and the entourage begins its journey north and west to the Lake of the Skeezers. Button-Bright is lost along the way and some members are threatened by wild animal attack, but Glinda and the crew journey relatively unscathed to the Lake of the Skeezers.

While Glinda and company are on their journey, Ervic, a Skeezer who had traveled in the submarine with Coo-ee-oh, has an encounter with the three magic fish, who encourage him to take them (in the well-washed copper vessel Su-dic used in his attack on the Skeezers) to a cottage on shore. There, Ervic meets and befriends Reera, a Yookoohoo witch related to Mrs. Yoop from *The Patchwork Girl of Oz*. Reera is known for transforming creatures into different forms purely for her own pleasure, but Ervic tricks her into converting the three fish back to the young Adepts of Magic, whose names we learn are Audah, Aurah, and Aujah. While the action with Ervic, Reera, and the Three Adepts is taking place, Glinda and the Wizard try to raise the Magic Isle, but to no avail. The Three Adepts seek out Glinda, and after revealing their identity, they agree to work with the sorceress to rescue Ozma, Dorothy, and the other Skeezers. Using an idea offered by Scraps, Glinda, the Wizard, and the Three Adepts lower the level of the Lake of the Skeezers to expose a few feet of the dome. The group then takes Coo-ee-oh's submarine to the top of the Magic City's dome where they enter the city near the old queen's palace, which Ozma and her friends currently occupy. After celebrating their initial victory, Glinda, the Wizard, Ozma, and Dorothy proceed to Coo-ee-oh's Room of Magic to determine how the Magic Isle can be raised to the surface of the lake. In a brainstorming session, Dorothy suggests that separately enunciating the three components of Coo-ee-oh's name might launch the submarine (coo), actuate the island bridge (ee), and raise the Magic Island (oh). When they enunciate the third magic syllable (oh), the island rises, and with the second (ee), the bridge extends to allow Glinda's traveling companions to cross

to the Magic Isle to celebrate. The Skeezers pledge allegiance to Ozma and her beneficent rule, and Ozma installs Aurex as Queen of the Skeezers. Aurex, in turn, installs Ervic as Prime Minister.

After a night of festivities, Glinda, Ozma, Dorothy, the Wizard, and the traveling
crew—along with the Three Adepts—gather the next day to leave, but first they pledge
to Queen Aurex that they will solve the "Flatheads problem." When the group makes it
to the top of Flathead Mountain, Su-dic commands his followers to attack, but they
throw down their weapons, for they see that the Adepts have returned to rule them be-
nevolently. Su-dic flees but is soon apprehended and imprisoned after having his cans of
brains confiscated.

In the days that follow, and with the Adepts' endorsement, Glinda interviews all the
Flatheads, during which their brains are extricated from their cans and placed on their
heads, and skulls are refashioned around their brainy parts. Glinda also performs her
magic on Su-dic, who is given a single portion of brains with the understanding that he
can no longer create havoc while he is under the watchful eyes of the Adepts. Su-dic's
wife is similarly treated after being transformed from a golden pig back to her original
state. At the end of all these adventures, the "Flatheads" name no longer applies to
Su-dic's former subjects, and so the Adepts rename their people "Mountaineers."

Having completed their mission, Ozma and Dorothy return to the Emerald City,
stopping along the way to retrieve the Sawhorse and the Red Wagon. Upon their return
Ozma reflects on the journey: "I'm very glad I went to see these peoples, . . . for I not
only prevented any further warfare between them, but they have been freed from the
rule of the Su-dic and Coo-ee-oh and are now happy and loyal subjects of the Land of
Oz. Which proves that it is always wise to do one's duty, however unpleasant that duty
may seem to be."

In compiling these synopses of Baum's sequels, I've made use of the following works:
Richard Tuerk's *Oz in Perspective: Magic and Myth in the L. Frank Baum Books*; Rebecca
Loncraine's *The Real Wizard of Oz: The Life and Times of L. Frank Baum*; Michael O. Riley's
Oz and Beyond: The Fantasy World of L. Frank Baum; Katharine M. Rogers's *L. Frank Baum,
Creator of Oz: A Biography*; Edward Bellamy's *Looking Backward, 2000–1887*; William Mor-
ris's *News from Nowhere*; and Michael Patrick Hearn's *The Annotated Wizard of Oz*.

Biographical Chronology: L. Frank Baum, 1856–1919

May 15, 1856: Born Lyman Frank Baum in Chittenango, New York

1861–1863: Family moves to and lives in Syracuse, New York

1866: Father purchases Rose Lawn estate

1866–1868: Is taught at home by English tutors

1868: Is sent to Peekskill Military Academy

1870–1873: Returns to Rose Lawn; publishes *Rose Lawn Home Journal*, *The Stamp Collector*, *Baum's Complete Stamp Dealer's Directory*, *The Empire*

1873–1874: Attends Syracuse Classical School for one year; begins work in the theater as an actor

1875–1876: Takes clerking job in family-owned Neal, Baum & Company dry-goods store in Syracuse

1876–1882: Partners in poultry business with father and brother; publishes *The Poultry Record*; helps establish the Empire State Poultry Association; studies acting; writes for newspapers; manages family-owned theaters in New York and Pennsylvania; forms acting company and writes and stars in his *The Maid of Arran*

November 9, 1882: Marries Maud Gage

1883–1888: Takes *The Maid of Arran* throughout the United States and Canada; moves back to Syracuse; cofounds Baum's Castorine; begins interest in theosophy

December 4, 1883: Son Frank Joslyn born

February 1, 1886: Second son, Robert Stanton, born; Maud is ill for two years after the birth

February 18, 1886: Brother Benjamin dies

February 14, 1887: Father dies

September 1888: Moves family to Aberdeen, Dakota Territory

October 1, 1888: Opens Baum's Bazaar

Spring 1889: Founds Aberdeen Baseball Club and Hub City Nine (professional baseball team)

December 17, 1889: Third son, Harry Neal, born

January 1, 1890: Baum's Bazaar is sold in foreclosure to sister-in-law Helen Gage

January 25, 1890: Begins publication of *The Aberdeen Saturday Pioneer* with "Our Landlady" columns

March 24, 1891: Fourth son, Kenneth Gage, born

1891: Moves family to Chicago; in May begins as reporter for *Chicago Evening Post*, joins Chicago Press Club

Fall 1892: Becomes department store buyer for Siegel, Cooper & Co.

1893: Attends World's Columbian Exposition in Chicago

1893–1897: Works as salesman for Pitkin and Brooks, fine china and glassware firm

1897: Publishes *Mother Goose in Prose*; meets W. W. Denslow

November 1897: Starts journal *The Show Window*

September 1899: Publishes (in collaboration with Denslow) *Father Goose: His Book*

1900: Decides to devote full time to writing fiction; publishes (in collaboration with Denslow) *The Wonderful Wizard of Oz*

1901: Publishes *The Master Key* and *American Fairy Tales*

June 1902: *The Wizard of Oz* stage play opens in Chicago; purchases Macatawa Park summer home

February–March 1904: Tours American Southwest—New Mexico, Arizona, California; discovers the Hotel del Coronado in San Diego

1904–1908: Publishes three Oz sequels (*The Marvelous Land of Oz* in 1904, *Ozma of Oz* in 1907, *Dorothy and the Wizard of Oz* in 1908); publishes twenty-three books in all

1906: Embarks with Maud on five-month international trip to Gibraltar, Egypt, Italy, Switzerland, France

1907: Publishes Maud's letters as *Other Lands than Ours*

1908: Writes and performs in *Fairylogue and Radio Plays*

1908–1911: Publishes fifteen books plus articles, film and stage scripts, poetry, an opera

1909: Sells properties in Chicago and Michigan; moves to rental property in Los Angeles; publishes *The Road to Oz*

1910: Contracts with Selig Studios to produce four works as one-reelers; Maud buys property for Ozcot with inheritance money; publishes *The Emerald City of Oz*

June 1911: Declares bankruptcy

1913: Publishes *The Patchwork Girl of Oz*; develops with Louis Gottschalk the musical production *The Tik-Tok Man of Oz*

1914: Creates The Oz Film Manufacturing Company, which is closed down in 1915

1914–1918: Publishes nineteen books, including *Tik-Tok of Oz* (1914) , *The Scarecrow of Oz* (1915) , *Rinkitink of Oz* (1916), *The Lost Princess of Oz* (1917), and *The Tin Woodman of Oz* (1918), plus movies, plays, articles, and a poem

May 6, 1919: Dies at home with Maud by his side, nine days before his sixty-third birthday

June 7, 1919: *The Magic of Oz* published posthumously

1920: *Glinda of Oz* published posthumously

Bibliographic Essay

I am indebted to many writers and thinkers who have enriched my understanding of L. Frank Baum; his original work, *The Wonderful Wizard of Oz*; the stage play and film based on this work; and his thirteen Oz sequels. In addition, I have benefited from the insights of many authors from diverse fields who have illuminated ideas about personal and professional growth that I've incorporated into my exploration of the learning, loving, and serving paradigm (with its corollaries, wisdom, heart, and courage) that informs *The Way of Oz*. What follows is a list of authors and their works without which I would have been unable to write this book.

For those seeking an understanding of the Way of Oz, the primary source is, of course, Baum's inaugural Oz book *The Wonderful Wizard of Oz*, published in 1900. This work (later titled *The Wizard of Oz*) is available in its original format (online and through booksellers) with W. W. Denslow's illustrations. The thirteen Oz sequels (twelve of which are abstracted in the appendix, with all listed in the bibliography) are also available online or for purchase through booksellers.

In addition to these works, in order to appreciate Baum's classic tale, it is important to view the 1939 film starring Judy Garland—which is readily available on television, online, or in commercial outlets such as Amazon or Netflix.

There are in addition many scholarly works that illuminate the literary and film world of Oz. Among these are Ranjit S. Dighe's *The Historian's Wizard of Oz: Reading L. Frank Baum's Classic as a Political and Monetary Allegory*; Michael Patrick Hearn's *The Annotated Wizard of Oz*; Michael O. Riley's *Oz and Beyond: The Fantasy World of L. Frank Baum*; Salmon Rushdie's *The Wizard of Oz*; Jack Snow's *Who's Who in Oz*; Mark Evan Swartz's *Oz Before the Rainbow: L. Frank Baum's* The Wonderful Wizard of Oz *on Stage and Screen to 1939*; and Richard Tuerk's *Oz in Perspective: Magic and Myth in the L. Frank Baum Books*.

A review of Baum's life and loves, his foibles and frailties, can be found in many memorable biographies, including those of Baum's son, Frank Joslyn Baum, written with Russell P. MacFall, *To Please a Child: A Biography of L. Frank Baum, Royal Historian of Oz*; Martin Gardner and Russel B. Nye's *The Wizard of Oz & Who He Was*; Rebecca Loncraine's *The Real Wizard of Oz: The Life and Times of L. Frank Baum*; Raylyn Moore's *Wonderful Wizard, Marvelous Land*; Katharine M. Rogers's *L. Frank Baum, Creator of Oz: A Biography*; and Evan I. Schwartz *Finding Oz: How L. Frank Baum Discovered the Great American Story*. For perspective on Baum's years in South Dakota, Nancy Tystad Koupal's *Our Landlady* is useful. For an understanding of the rise of populism in Baum's time, Gene Clanton's *Populism: The Humane Preference in America, 1890–1900* is illuminating. Erik Larson's historical novel *The Devil in the White City: Murder, Magic, and Madness at the Fair That Changed America* provides a vivid picture of the Chicago Baum knew in the 1890s. Images and text on the World's Columbian Exposition of 1893 are found at the Paul V. Garvin Library Digital History Collection at the Illinois Institute of Technology.

My concept of integrated learning, inspired by L. Frank Baum's metaphor of the Scarecrow, begins with allusions to the works of various scientists, artists, and scholars across the centuries, including Maimonides's *The Guide for the Perplexed*, Renoir's famous painting "Luncheon of the Boating Party" housed in the Phillips Collection (Washington, DC), a description of Nathaniel Hawthorne's use of time in Alan Lakein's *How to Get Control of Your Time and Your Life*, Albert Einstein's working methods as described in Alan Lightman's *Einstein's Dreams*, more recent scientific collaborations in nanoscience from the National Cancer Institute, and the works of contemporary jazz composer Michael Franks and cartoonist Gary Larson. In later sections, I make references to the Voluntary System of Accountability (APLU, AASCU, 2008) subscribed to by hundreds of accredited universities nationally, and to Blaise Opulente's prescriptions in his seminal work *A Prescription for Intellectual Ills*.

The section on learning and reading begins with a story from Robert Coles's *The Call of Stories: Teaching and the Moral Imagination*, continues with general references to Mortimer J. Adler and Charles Van Doren's *How to Read a Book*, and Kevin Fitzpatrick and Bob Smith, along with papers by Shelia Burkhalter and colleagues, Michael Ferguson, Tamar Lewin, Jackie Mantey, and Andi Twiton on guidelines for common reading programs, all published in *All Things Academic*, archived at the University of Arkansas (http://libinfo.uark.edu/ata/).

In the sections on learning and writing, I found useful Richard J. Light's *Making the Most of College: Students Speak Their Minds*, Hillary Rodham Clinton's *Living History*, and Mortimer J. Adler and Charles Van Doren's *How to Read a Book*. In the sections on note taking and spontaneous inspiration, Julian Jaynes's *The Origin of Consciousness in the Breakdown of the Bicameral Mind* was helpful, as was W. W. Rostow's *The Barbaric Counterrevolution: Cause and Cure*, Salmon Rushdie's *The Wizard of Oz*, J. C. Sheehan's *The Enchanted Ring: The Untold Story of Penicillin*, Garrison Keillor's *The Writer's Almanac*, C. W.

Ceram's *Gods, Graves, and Scholars: The Story of Archaeology*, and Henry David Thoreau's *Walden*. In the section on diaries and journals, I used material from Anne Frank's *The Diary of a Young Girl* and Edward Jablonski's *Gershwin*. In the section on formal writing, I refer to Robert A. Day and Barbara Gastel's *How to Write and Publish a Scientific Paper*; Vernon Booth's *Communicating in Science: Writing a Scientific Paper and Speaking at Scientific Meetings*; William K. Zinsser's *On Writing Well: The Classic Guide to Writing Nonfiction*; William Strunk, Jr., and E. B. White's classic work, *The Elements of Style*; H. J. Tichy's *Effective Writing for Engineers, Managers, Scientists*; Carolyn J. Mullins's *A Guide to Writing and Publishing in the Social and Behavioral Sciences*; and Laurie E. Rozakis's *The Complete Idiot's Guide to Creative Writing*. In the section on plagiarism, I found useful Cal Newport's *How to Win at College: Surprising Secrets for Success from the Country's Top Students*; Patience Simmonds's essay "Plagiarism and Cyber-plagiarism" in *College & Research Libraries News*; Peter Charles Hoffer's articles on plagiarism in *Perspectives*; and Gloria Delamar's "On Rewriting."

In the sections on learning and communicating, I refer to my own earlier work, *Pedestals, Parapets & Pits: The Joys, Challenges & Failures of Professional Life*, and to Lance Morrow's *Time* magazine piece, "The Gravitas Factor." In the section on written communications, I found helpful Corinne David-Ferdon and Marci Feldman Hertz's "Electronic Media, Violence, and Adolescents: An Emerging Public Health Problem" in *Journal of Adolescent Health*; John Fielden's "What Do You Mean I Can't Write?" from *Harvard Business Review*; David W. Ewing's *Writing for Results in Business, Government, the Sciences, the Professions*; J. C. Paradis's "Improving Technical Communications to Improve Productivity" from *Chemical and Engineering News*; and W. I. B. Beveridge's *The Art of Scientific Investigation*. In the discussion of oral communications, I found useful Jeff Scott Cook's *The Elements of Speechwriting and Public Speaking*; Joan Detz's *How to Write and Give a Speech* and *It's Not What You Say, It's How You Say It*; Tony Jeary's *Inspire Any Audience: Proven Secrets of the Pros for Powerful Presentations*; and my own *The Elements of Great Speechmaking: Adding Drama & Intrigue*.

In the sections on learning and traveling I referred to Frederic G. Cassidy and Joan Houston Hall's *Dictionary of American Regional English*; George D. Kuh's *High-Impact Educational Practices: What They Are, Who Has Access to Them, and Why They Matter*; Richard Jackson's article in *Mediterranean Quarterly*, "American Universities around the Mediterranean and Beyond: The Case for the Support by the Obama Administration"; Karin Fischer's "East Carolina U. Uses Simple Technology to Link Students with Peers Overseas" in *The Chronicle of Higher Education*; and Michael DeMers's "The School of Second Life" from a March 2009 broadcast of NPR's *Weekend Edition*.

In writing the sections on love, I found the following books and articles useful: for love of others, Raoul Plus's *God within Us*; Barack Obama's 2009 Cairo speech, "A New Beginning"; Alexander Moseley's article "The Philosophy of Love" from *The Internet En-*

cyclopedia of Philosophy; Debora B. Schwartz's article "Backgrounds to Romance: 'Court-ly Love,'" from *Medieval Literature*; the US Equal Employment Opportunity Commission's *Facts about Sexual Harassment* and *Policy Guidance on Current Issues of Sexual Harassment*; the Centers for Disease Control and Prevention's article "Sexually Transmitted Diseases"; and "Health Benefits to Humans," from the Center for the Human-Animal Bond at Purdue University's School of Veterinary Medicine.

In the section on love of place, I refer to Fawn Brodie's biography, *Thomas Jefferson: An Intimate History*, and to the NPR interview of Junot Díaz, "Junot Díaz on 'Becoming American.'" In the love of learning and self sections, I referred to my own *Pedestals, Parapets & Pits: The Joys, Challenges & Failures of Professional Life*; Glenn R. Schiraldi's *The Self-Esteem Workbook* and his *The Post-Traumatic Stress Disorder Sourcebook: A Guide to Healing, Recovery, and Growth*; and M. Scott Peck's *The Road Less Traveled: A New Psychology of Love, Traditional Values, and Spiritual Growth*.

For integrated perspectives on serving, I've drawn on James E. Sherwood's article for the Berkeley Series, "The Role of the Land-Grant Institution in the 21st Century"; Karen Hughes's essay, "Passion and Perspective," in *All Things Texas Tech*; Scott Pelley's essay, also in *All Things Texas Tech*, "Be Prepared to Test Yourself—Sixty Years from Now"; Americans for a National Service Act; Richard Stengel's 2007 *Time* article, "A Time to Serve"; Scott Simon's NPR *Weekend Edition* interview with Brennan LaBrie, "Kid Reporter Covers 'Worldwide Day of Play'"; Danielle Kovacs's catalogue of the Henry Whittemore Library's Christa Corrigan McAuliffe Papers, 1948–2000; and Juliette Wei-land's "Youth Achievement Award Winners" on the Smart Kids with Learning Disabilities website.

In the sections dealing with a focus on the future, I used these works as references: for integrated perspective and planning, Richard L. Florida's *The Great Reset: How New Ways of Living and Working Drive Post-Crash Prosperity*; Richard J. Light's *Making the Most Out of College: Students Speak Their Minds*; Cathy Wendler and colleagues' *The Path Forward: The Future of Graduate Education in the United States*; and my own *Pedestals, Parapets & Pits: The Joys, Challenges & Failures of Professional Life*. For the sections on diversity, sustainability, and understanding science, I found helpful Anne Fausto-Sterling's *Sexing the Body: Gender Politics and the Construction of Sexuality*; Carl Sagan's *The Dragons of Eden: Speculations on the Evolution of Human Intelligence*; and Chris Mooney and Sheril Kirshen-baum's *Unscientific America: How Scientific Illiteracy Threatens Our Future*.

In the sections on democracy and the power of democratic principles, I used material from the Canadian Charter of Rights and Freedoms (*Legal Rights, Item 7*); Europa's *The Founding Principles of the Union*; and the Club of Madrid's *Club de Madrid: Democracy That Delivers*. In the section on personal responsibility, I used the Advancement Via Individual Determination program website; Evelyn Fox Keller's *A Feeling for the Organism: The Life and Work of Barbara McClintock*; and Alan Lakein's *How to Get Control of Your Time and Your Life*.

In the sections on humility, I relied on Michael O. Riley's *Oz and Beyond: The Fantasy World of L. Frank Baum*; Martin Gardner and Russel B. Nye's *The Wizard of Oz & Who He Was*; Rebecca Loncraine's *The Real Wizard of Oz: The Life and Times of L. Frank Baum*; Raylyn Moore's *Wonderful Wizard, Marvelous Land*; and Katharine M. Rogers's *L. Frank Baum, Creator of Oz: A Biography*. In the discussion of other virtues, I found these works helpful: Christoph Luxenberg's *The Syro-Aramaic Reading of the Koran: A Contribution to the Decoding of the Language of the Koran*; the Gallup Poll "Evolution, Creationism, Intelligent Design"; Edward O. Wilson's *The Creation: An Appeal to Save Life on Earth*; Heather Anne Pringle's *The Master Plan: Himmler's Scholars and the Holocaust*; Martin Benjamin's *Splitting the Difference: Compromise and Integrity in Ethics and Politics*; Stephen L. Carter's *Integrity*; HP Company's "Business Ethics: Guided by Enduring Values;" the University of California's Standards of Ethical Conduct; the Council of International Schools' Code of Ethics and Code of Ethics for Higher Education; the Forum on Education Abroad's Code of Ethics for Education Abroad; International Red Cross and Red Crescent's Code of Conduct; the Institute of Internal Auditors' Code of Ethics; Bertrand Russell's *The Autobiography of Bertrand Russell, 1872–1914*; Pauline Rose Clance's *The Impostor Phenomenon: Overcoming the Fear That Haunts Your Success*; Joan C. Harvey and Cynthia Katz's *If I'm So Successful, Why Do I Feel Like a Fake? The Impostor Phenomenon*; John Graden's *The Impostor Syndrome*; and my own *Pedestals, Parapets & Pits: The Joys, Challenges & Failures of Professional Life*.

Works Cited and Consulted

Ackmann, Martha. *The Mercury 13: The True Story of Thirteen Women and the Dream of Space Flight*. New York: Random House, 2004.

Adiprasetya, Joas. "World Parliament of Religions." In *The Boston Collaborative Encyclopedia of Modern Western Theology*, edited by Wesley Wildman. Boston: Boston University, 2010. http://people.bu.edu/wwildman/WeirdWildWeb/courses/mwt/dictionary/mwt_themes_707_worldparliamentofreligions1893.htm#The_1893_World_Parliament_of_Religions_Adiprasetya.

Adler, Mortimer J., and Charles Van Doren. *How to Read a Book*. New York: Simon & Schuster, 1972.

Algeo, John. "*The Wizard of Oz*: The Perilous Journey." *The American Theosophist*, October 1986.

———. *Theosophy: An Introductory Study Course*. 4th ed. Wheaton, IL: The Theosophical Society of America, 2007.

Americans for a National Service Act. "Our Team." 2010. http://www.nationalservice-act.org/3.html.

Angelou, Maya. *I Know Why the Caged Bird Sings*. New York: Bantam Books, 1991.

Baum, Frank Joslyn, and Russell P. MacFall. *To Please a Child: A Biography of L. Frank Baum, Royal Historian of Oz*. Chicago: Reilly and Lee, 1961.

Baum, Harry. "How My Father Wrote the Oz Books." *American Book Collector*, December 1962, 17.

Baum, L. Frank. *American Fairy Tales*. Chicago: George M. Hill, 1901.

———. *The Art of Decorating Dry Goods Windows and Interiors: A Complete Manual of Window Trimming, Designed as an Educator in All the Details of the Art, According to the Best Accepted Methods, and Testing Fully Every Important Subject*. Chicago: The Show Window Publishing Co., 1900.

———. *The Book of the Hamburgs: A Brief Treatise upon the Mating, Rearing, and Management of the Different Varieties of Hamburgs*. Hartford, CT: H. H. Stoddard, 1886.

———. *Dorothy and the Wizard of Oz*. New York: HarperCollins, 1990. First published 1908 by Reilly and Britton.

———. *Dot and Tot of Merryland*. Chicago: George M. Hill, 1901.

———. *The Emerald City of Oz*. First published 1910 by Reilly and Britton. Project Gutenberg Literary Archive Foundation. http://www.gutenberg.org/ebooks/517.

———. *Father Goose: His Book*. Chicago: George M. Hill, 1899.

———. *Glinda of Oz: In which are related the Exciting Experiences of Princess Ozma of Oz, and Dorothy, in their hazardous journey to the home of the Flatheads, and to the Magic isle of the Skeezers, and how they were rescued from dire peril by the sorcery of Glinda the Good*. First published 1920 by Reilly and Lee. Project Gutenberg Literary Archive Foundation. http://www.gutenberg.org/ebooks/961.

———. *The Lost Princess of Oz*. First published 1917 by Reilly and Britton. Project Gutenberg Literary Archive Foundation. http://www.gutenberg.org/ebooks/24459.

———. *The Magic of Oz: A Faithful Record of the Remarkable Adventures of Dorothy and Trot and the Wizard of Oz, together with the Cowardly Lion, the Hungry Tiger and Cap'n Bill, in their successful search for a Magical and Beautiful Birthday Present for Princess Ozma of Oz*. First published 1919 by Reilly and Lee. Project Gutenberg Literary Archive Foundation. http://www.gutenberg.org/etext/419.

———. *The Marvelous Land of Oz: A Sequel to The Wizard of Oz, Being an Account of the Further Adventures of the Scarecrow and Tin Woodman and also the Strange Experiences of the Highly Magnified Woggle-Bug, Jack Pumpkin-head, the Animated Saw-Horse and the Gump*. First published 1904 by Reilly and Britton. Project Gutenberg Literary Archive Foundation. http://www.gutenberg.org/etext/54.

———. *The Master Key: An Electrical Fairy Tale, Founded upon the Mysteries of Electricity and the Optimism of its Devotees. It Was Written for Boys, but Others May Read It*. Chicago: George M. Hill, 1901.

———. *Mother Goose in Prose*. Chicago: Way & Williams, 1897.

———. *Ozma of Oz: A Record of Her Adventures with Dorothy Gale of Kansas, the Yellow Hen, the Scarecrow, the Tin Woodman, Tiktok, the Cowardly Lion and the Hungry Tiger; Besides Other Good People Too Numerous to Mention Faithfully Recorded Herein*. First published 1907 by Reilly and Britton. Project Gutenberg Literary Archive Foundation. http://www.gutenberg.org/etext/486.

———. *The Patchwork Girl of Oz*. Salt Lake City: Project Gutenberg Literary Archive Foundation. First published 1913 by Reilly and Britton. http://www.gutenberg.org/etext/955.

———. *Rinkitink in Oz. Wherein is recorded the Perilous Quest of Prince Inga of Pingaree and King Rinkitink in the Magical Isles that lie beyond the Borderland of Oz*. First published 1916 by Reilly and Britton. Project Gutenberg Literary Archive Foundation. http://www.gutenberg.org/etext/958.

————. *The Road to Oz: In which is related how Dorothy Gale of Kansas, The Shaggy Man, Button Bright, and Polychrome the Rainbow's Daughter met on an Enchanted Road and followed it all the way to the Marvelous Land of Oz.* First published 1909 by Reilly and Britton. Project Gutenberg Literary Archive Foundation. http://www.gutenberg.org/etext/485.

————. *The Scarecrow of Oz.* First published 1915 by Reilly and Britton. Project Gutenberg Literary Archive Foundation. http://www.gutenberg.org/etext/957.

————. *The Sea Fairies.* New York: Dover, 1998. First published 1911 by Reilly and Britton.

————. *Tic-Tok of Oz.* First published 1914 by Reilly and Britton. Project Gutenberg Literary Archive Foundation. http://www.gutenberg.org/etext/956.

————. *The Tin Woodman of Oz: A Faithful Story of an Astonishing Adventure Undertaken by the Tin Woodman, assisted by Woot the Wanderer, the Scarecrow of Oz, and Polychrome, the Rainbow's Daughter.* First published 1918 by Reilly and Britton. Project Gutenberg Literary Archive Foundation. http://www.gutenberg.org/etext/960.

————. *The Woggle-Bug Book.* Delmar, NY: Scholars' Facsimiles & Reprints, 1978. First published 1905 by Reilly and Britton.

————. *The Wonderful Wizard of Oz.* Library of Congress Digital Collections. First published 1900 by George M. Hill; published as *The New Wizard of Oz* and finally as *The Wizard of Oz* in 1903 by Reilly and Britton. http://lcweb2.loc.gov/cgi-bin/ampage?collId=rbc3&fileName=rbc0001_2006gen32405page.db.

Baum, Robert. "Autobiography." *Baum Bugle,* Spring 1971, 5–6.

Beah, Ishmael. *Long Way Gone: Memoirs of a Boy Soldier.* New York: Farrar, Straus and Giroux, 2007.

Bellamy, Edward. *Looking Backward, 2000–1887.* 1888. Reprint, New York: Signet, 2000.

Benjamin, Martin. *Splitting the Difference: Compromise and Integrity in Ethics and Politics.* Lawrence: University Press of Kansas, 1990.

Beveridge, W. I. B. *The Art of Scientific Investigation,* rev. ed. New York: Norton, 1957.

Black, William. *A Princess of Thule.* 1874. Reprint, Boston: Joseph Knight, 1894.

Bonner, Brian. *Genealogy SF, Stanton and Bonner Families.* S.v. "Lyman Frank Baum." 2008. http://www.genealogysf.com/Stanton-p/p40.htm.

Booth, Vernon. *Communicating in Science: Writing a Scientific Paper and Speaking at Scientific Meetings.* 2nd ed. New York: Cambridge University Press, 1993.

Brodie, Fawn. *Thomas Jefferson: An Intimate History.* New York: Norton, 1974.

Brown, Dee. *Bury My Heart at Wounded Knee.* New York: Holt, Rinehart & Winston, 1970.

Burkhalter, Sheila, Kevin Fitzpatrick, Karen Hodges, David Jolliffe, Bob McMath, Pat

Slattery, and Bob Smith. "What about a Common Reading Program at the University of Arkansas?" *All Things Academic* 9, no. 1 (March 2008). http://libinfo.uark.edu/ata/v9no1/commonreading.asp.

Cahill, Larry. "Why Sex Matters for Neuroscience." *Nature Reviews Neuroscience* 7 (2006): 477–84.

Campbell, Joseph. *The Hero with a Thousand Faces.* 2nd ed. Princeton, NJ: Princeton University Press, 1968.

Canadian Department of Justice. Canadian Charter of Rights and Freedoms. Legal Rights, Item 7. Accessed November 26, 2011. http://laws.justice.gc.ca/en/charter/1.html#anchorbo-ga:l_I.

Capote, Truman. *In Cold Blood.* New York: Random House, 1966.

Carter, Stephen L. *Integrity.* New York: Basic Books/HarperCollins, 1996.

Cassidy, Frederic G., and Joan Houston Hall, eds. *Dictionary of American Regional English.* Vols. 1–4 (Cambridge, MA: Harvard University Press, 1985–2010).

Center for the Human-Animal Bond, Purdue University School of Veterinary Medicine. "Health Benefits to Humans." 2004. http://www.vet.purdue.edu/chab/huben.htm.

Centers for Disease Control and Prevention, US Department of Health and Human Services. "Sexually Transmitted Diseases." Last updated November 17, 2011. http://www.cdc.gov/std.

Ceram, C. W. *Gods, Graves, and Scholars: The Story of Archaeology.* 2nd ed. New York: Knopf, 1982.

City of Peekskill. "Evidence Accumulating Pointing to Peekskill as Inspiration and Home for 'Yellow Brick Road.' Vanished Books May Hold Key." Press release. September 19, 2005. http://64.233.167.104/search?q=cache:M3ASi2C6NAoJ:www.ci.peekskill.ny.us/upload/pr/Peekskill_Yellow_Brick_Road_release_Final_09_19_05.pdf+peekskill+yellow+brick+road&hl=en&ct=clnk&cd=1&gl=us.

Clance, Pauline Rose. *The Impostor Phenomenon: Overcoming the Fear That Haunts Your Success.* Atlanta: Peachtree Publishers, 1985.

Clanton, Gene O. *Populism: The Humane Preference in America, 1890–1900.* Boston: Twayne Publishers, 1991.

Classical Net. "Alexander Porfir'yevich Borodin." Accessed May 2, 2011. http://www.classical.net/music/comp.lst/borodin.php.

Clinton, Hillary Rodham. *Living History.* New York: Simon & Schuster, 2003.

Club of Madrid. "Club de Madrid—Democracy That Delivers." Brochure. 2009. http://www.clubmadrid.org.

Coleridge, Samuel Taylor. *Biographia Literaria.* 1817. Reprint, Princeton, NJ: Princeton University Press, 1985.

Coles, Robert. *The Call of Stories: Teaching and the Moral Imagination.* Boston: Houghton Mifflin, 1989.

Colonial Williamsburg. "Colonial Williamsburg's Rare Breeds Program Complements Living History Interpretation." Accessed November 26, 2011. http://www.history.org/almanack/life/animals/pr_rare.cfm?showsite=mobilesite=mobile.

Cook, Jeff Scott. *The Elements of Speechwriting and Public Speaking.* New York: Macmillan, 1989.

Council for Higher Education Accreditation, US Department of Education. "Database of Institutions and Programs Accredited by Recognized United States Accrediting Organizations." 2004. http://www.chea.org/search/default.asp.

Council of International Schools. Code of Ethics and Code of Ethics for Higher Education, 2009. http://www.cois.org/page.cfm?p=232 and http://www.cois.org/page.cfm?p=309.

Curran, John J. "Peekskill's Origins, Development, and Highlights." Hudson Valley Center for Contemporary Art. 2002. http://www.hvcca.org/aboutpeekskill.html.

David-Ferdon, Corinne, and Marci Feldman Hertz. "Electronic Media, Violence and Adolescents: An Emerging Public Health Problem." *Journal of Adolescent Health* 41 (2007): S1–S5.

Day, Robert A., and Barbara Gastel. *How to Write and Publish a Scientific Paper.* 6th ed. New York: Greenwood, 2006.

Delamar, Gloria. "On Rewriting." Accessed November 26, 2011. http://www.delamar.org/xqrewriting.htm.

DeMers, Michael, and Scott Simon. "The School of Second Life." *Weekend Edition.* NPR. March 7, 2009. http://www.npr.org/templates/story/story.php?storyId=101580485.

Dennett, Daniel C. *Breaking the Spell: Religion as a Natural Phenomenon.* New York: Penguin Group, 2007.

Detz, Joan. *How to Write and Give a Speech.* New York: St. Martin's Griffin, 1992.

———. *It's Not What You Say, It's How You Say It.* New York: St. Martin's Griffin, 2000.

Diamond, Jared. *Guns, Germs, and Steel: The Fates of Human Societies.* New York: Norton, 1997.

Díaz, Junot. "Junot Díaz on 'Becoming American.'" Interview by Steve Inskeep. *Morning Edition.* NPR. November 24, 2008. http://www.npr.org/templates/story/story.php?storyId=97336132.

Dighe, Ranjit S. *The Historian's Wizard of Oz: Reading L. Frank Baum's Classic As a Political and Monetary Allegory.* Westport, CT: Praeger, 2002.

Eliot, T. S. *Four Quartets 4.* 1943. Reprint, New York: Harvest Books, 1968.

Europa: Gateway to the European Union. "The Founding Principles of the Union." Accessed November 26, 2011. http://europa.eu/scadplus/constitution/objectives_en.htm#RIGHTS.

Ewing, David W. *Writing for Results in Business, Government, the Sciences, the Professions.* 2nd ed. New York: Wiley, 1979.

Fausto-Sterling, Anne. *Sexing the Body: Gender Politics and the Construction of Sexuality.* New York: Basic Books, 2000.

Ferguson, Michael. "Creating Common Ground: Common Reading and the First Year of College." *Peer Review* 8, no. 3 (2006). http://www.aacu.org/peerreview/pr-su06/pr-su06_analysis2.cfm.

Fielden, John. "What Do You Mean I Can't Write?" *Harvard Business Review*, May–June, 1966, 144–56.

Fischer, Karin. "East Carolina U. Uses Simple Technology to Link Students with Peers Overseas." *Chronicle of Higher Education* 55, no. 35 (2008): A23. http://chronicle.com/weekly/v55/i35/35a02302.htm.

Fisher, Roger A. *Them Damned Pictures: Explorations in American Political Cartoon Art.* New Haven, CT: Archon Books, 1996.

Fitzpatrick, Kevin, and Bob Smith. "Reading and Life-Long Learning." *All Things Academic* 8, no. 4 (December 2007). http://libinfo.uark.edu/ata/v8n4/reading.asp.

Florida, Richard. *The Great Reset: How New Ways of Living and Working Drive Post-Crash Prosperity.* New York: Harper, 2010.

Forum on Education Abroad, Dickinson College. Code of Ethics for Education Abroad, 2009. http://www.forumea.org/standards-index.cfm.

Frank, Anne. *Anne Frank: The Diary of a Young Girl.* 1947. Reprint, New York: Bantam, 1992.

Franks, Michael. *Barefoot on the Beach.* CD. Palo Alto, CA: Windham Hill, 1999.

Gage, Matilda Joslyn. *Women, Church and State.* 1893. Reprint, New York: Humanities Books, 2002.

Gage, Maud. *Other Lands than Ours.* Shreveport, LA: Pumpernickel Pickle, 2008. First published 1907 by L. Frank Baum with author designation as Maud Gage.

Gallup Poll. "Evolution, Creationism, Intelligent Design." 2010. http://www.gallup.com/poll/21814/evolution-creationism-intelligent-design.aspx.

Gardner, Martin, and Russel B. Nye. *The Wizard of Oz & Who He Was.* East Lansing: Michigan State University Press, 1957.

Graden, John. *The Impostor Syndrome.* Bloomington, IN: Xlibris, 2009.

Haddon, Mark. *The Curious Incident of the Dog in the Night-Time.* New York: Doubleday, 2003.

Harvey, Joan C., and Cynthia Katz. *If I'm So Successful, Why Do I Feel Like a Fake?: The Impostor Phenomenon.* New York: Pocket Books, 1986.

Hearn, Michael Patrick. *The Annotated Wizard of Oz.* Centennial Edition. New York: Norton, 2000.

Hewlett-Packard Company. *Business Ethics—Guided by Enduring Values.* 2010. http://www.hp.com/hpinfo/globalcitizenship/ethics.

Hewlett-Packard Ethics and Compliance Office. *Our Standards of Business Conduct*. 2010. http://h30261.www3.hp.com/phoenix.zhtml?c=71087&p=irol-govConduct.

Hoffer, Peter Charles. "Reflections on Plagiarism: Part 1, A Guide for the Perplexed." *Perspectives*, February 2004: 17–23.

———. "Reflections on Plagiarism: Part 2, The Object of Trials." *Perspectives*, March 2004: 21–25.

Hotel del Coronado. "History." Accessed September 12, 2008. http://www.hoteldel.com/about/history.cfm.

Hosseini, Khaled. *The Kite Runner*. New York: Riverhead Books, 2003.

Hudlin, Edward W. "The Mythology of Oz: An Interpretation." *Papers on Language and Literature* 25 (Fall 1989): 443–62.

Hughes, Karen. "Passion and Perspective." *All Things Texas Tech* 1, no. 2 (2009). http://www.depts.ttu.edu/communications/attt/2009/09/hughes.php.

Inge, M. Thomas, ed. *Agrarianism in American Literature*. New York: The Odyssey Press, 1969.

Institute of Internal Auditors. Code of Ethics. 2009. http://www.theiia.org/guidance/standards-and-guidance/ippf/code-of-ethics/.

International Red Cross and Red Crescent. Code of Conduct. 2009. http://www.ifrc.org/publicat/conduct/code.asp.

Jablonski, Edward. *Gershwin*. New York: Da Capo Press, 1998.

Jackson, Richard. "American Universities around the Mediterranean and Beyond: The Case for the Support by the Obama Administration." *Mediterranean Quarterly* 20, no. 1 (2009): 69–76.

Jaynes, Julian. *The Origin of Consciousness in the Breakdown of the Bicameral Mind*. Boston: Houghton Mifflin, 1976.

Jeary, Tony. *Inspire Any Audience: Proven Secrets of the Pros for Powerful Presentations*. Tulsa, OK: Trade Life Books, 1997.

Keller, Evelyn Fox. *A Feeling for the Organism: The Life and Work of Barbara McClintock*. New York: Freeman, 1983.

Kidder, Tracy. *Mountains beyond Mountains: The Quest of Dr. Paul Farmer, a Man Who Would Cure the World*. New York: Random House, 2004.

Kolbenschlag, Madonna. *Lost in the Land of Oz*. New York: Crossroad, 1994.

Koupal, Nancy Tystad. *Our Landlady*. Lincoln: University of Nebraska Press, 1996.

Kovacs, Danielle. "Christa Corrigan McAuliffe Papers, 1948–2000." Framingham, MA: Framingham State College, Henry Whitmore Library. http://www.framingham.edu/wlibrary/archives/McAuliffe.html.

Kuh, George D. *High-Impact Educational Practices: What They Are, Who Has Access to Them, and Why They Matter*. Washington, DC: Association of American Colleges and Universities, 2008.

Lakein, Alan. *How to Get Control of Your Time and Your Life.* 1973. Reprint, New York: New American Library, 1996.

Langley, Noel, Florence Ryerson, and Edgar Allen. "Movie Script: The Wizard of Oz." *Screenplays Just for You.* http://sfy.ru/sfy.html?script=wizard_of_oz_1939.

Larson, Erik. *The Devil in the White City: Murder, Magic, and Madness at the Fair That Changed America.* New York: Crown Publishers, 2003.

Laufgraben, Jodi Levine. *Common Reading Programs: Going Beyond the Book.* Monograph No. 44. National Resource Center for the First-Year Experience and Students in Transition. Columbia: University of South Carolina, 2006.

Lewin, Tamar. "At Colleges, Women Are Leaving Men in the Dust." *New York Times* online edition, July 9, 2006. http://www.nytimes.com/2006/07/09/education/09college.html.

———. "Summer Reading Programs Gain Momentum for Students about to Enter College." *New York Times,* August 8, 2007. http://www.nytimes.com/2007/08/08/education/08books.html?_r=1&oref=slogin.

Light, Richard J. *Making the Most Out of College: Students Speak Their Minds.* Cambridge, MA: Harvard University Press, 2001.

Lightman, Alan. *Einstein's Dreams.* New York: Warner Books, 1993.

Littlefield, Henry M. "The Wizard of Oz: Parable on Populism." *American Quarterly,* Spring 1964, 48–58.

Loncraine, Rebecca. *The Real Wizard of Oz: The Life and Times of L. Frank Baum.* New York: Gotham Books, 2009.

Luxenberg, Christoph (pseudonym). *The Syro-Aramaic Reading of the Koran: A Contribution to the Decoding of the Language of the Koran.* Berlin: Verlag Hans Schiler, 2007.

"The Maid of Arran." *Wikipedia.* Accessed November 3, 2008. http://en.wikipedia.org/wiki/The_Maid_of_Arran.

Mannix, Daniel P. "Off to See the Wizard." *Baum Bugle,* Autumn 1971, 7.

Mantey, Jackie. "Incoming Freshmen Get Summer Reading Assignments." *U.S. News & World Report,* June 7, 2007. http://www.usnews.com/usnews/edu/articles/070607/7summer.htm?s_cid=rss:7summer.htm.

"Mattydale, New York." *Wikipedia.* Accessed August 25, 2008. http://en.wikipedia.org/wiki/Mattydale,_New_York.

Mayo Clinic. "Angina." 2011. http://www.mayoclinic.com/health/angina/DS00994.

McCarthy, Susan. "Gary Larson." *Salon,* December 21, 1999. http://www.salon.com/people/bc/1999/12/21/larson.

McKee, Donna, and Suzanne Wright. "The Story behind the Masterpiece . . ." Washington, DC: The Phillips Collection, 2008. http://www.phillipscollection.org/html/lbp.html.

Mill, John Stuart. *On Liberty.* Boston: Ticknor and Fields, 1863. http://books.google.

com/books?id=9xARAAAAYAAJ&dq=Mill,+John+Stuart.+On+Liberty&printse
c=frontcover&source=bn&hl=en&sa=X&oi=book_result&resnum=5&ct=resul
t#PPA1,M1.

————. *A System of Logic.* 8th ed. New York: Harper, 1891.

Mooney, Chris, and Sheril Kirshenbaum. *Unscientific America: How Scientific Illiteracy Threatens Our Future.* New York: Basic Books, 2009.

Moore, Raylyn. *Wonderful Wizard, Marvelous Land.* Bowling Green, OH: Bowling Green University Popular Press, 1974.

Morris, William. *News from Nowhere.* 1888. Reprint, New York: Penguin, 1994.

Morrow, Lance. "The Gravitas Factor." *Time* 131, no. 11 (March 14, 1988): 94.

Moseley, Alexander. "The Philosophy of Love." *The Internet Encyclopedia of Philosophy.* 2010. http://www.iep.utm.edu/l/love.htm.

Mullins, Carolyn J. *A Guide to Writing and Publishing in the Social and Behavioral Sciences.* New York: Wiley, 1984.

National Institute of Neurological Diseases and Stroke. "Trigeminal Neuralgia." 2008. http://www.ninds.nih.gov/disorders/trigeminal_neuralgia/trigeminal_neuralgia.htm.

Newport, Cal. *How to Win at College: Surprising Secrets for Success from the Country's Top Students.* New York: Broadway Books, 2005.

Obama, Barack. "A New Beginning." Speech presented in Cairo, Egypt, June 4, 2009. http://www.whitehouse.gov/blog/NewBeginning.

Odyssey Program. "Expanding Your Academic Experiences at UW Oshkosh." 2011. University of Wisconsin, Oshkosh. http://www.uwosh.edu/odyssey/academic-experiences-1.

Opulente, Blaise. "A Prescription for Intellectual Ills." *American Journal for Pharmaceutical Education* 29 (1965): 35–43.

Pais, Abraham. *Subtle Is the Lord: The Science and Life of Albert Einstein.* London: Oxford University Press, 1982.

Paradis, J. C. "Improving Technical Communications to Improve Productivity." *Chemical and Engineering News* 61, no. 11 (1983): 31–32.

Peck, M. Scott. *The Road Less Traveled: A New Psychology of Love, Traditional Values, and Spiritual Growth.* New York: Simon and Schuster, 1978.

Peekskill Military Academy Alumni Association. "Peekskill Military Academy Motto." Accessed November 26, 2011. http://www.pma-alumni.org.

Pelley, Scott. "Be Prepared to Test Yourself—Sixty Years from Now." *All Things Texas Tech* 1, no. 2 (2009). http://www.depts.ttu.edu/communications/attt/2009/09/pelley.php.

Perls, Thomas T., and Margery Hutter Silver. *Living to 100: Lessons in Living to Your Maxi-*

mum Potential at Any Age. New York: Basic Books, 1999.

Plus, Raoul. *God within Us.* New York: P. J. Kennedy and Sons, 1924.

Potter, Jeanne O. "The Man Who Invented Oz." *Los Angeles Times Sunday Magazine,* August 13, 1939, 12.

Pringle, Heather Anne. *The Master Plan: Himmler's Scholars and the Holocaust.* New York: Hyperion, 2006.

Riley, Michael O. *Oz and Beyond: The Fantasy World of L. Frank Baum.* Lawrence: University of Kansas Press, 1997.

Roberge, Pierre R. *Corrosion Basics.* 2nd ed. Houston: NACE International, 2006.

Rockoff, Hugh. "The 'Wizard of Oz' as Monetary Allegory." *Journal of Political Economy* 98 (1990): 739–60.

Rogers, Katharine M. *L. Frank Baum, Creator of Oz: A Biography.* Cambridge, MA: Da Capo Press, 2003.

Rostow, W. W. *The Barbaric Counterrevolution: Cause and Cure.* Austin: University of Texas Press, 1983.

Rozakis, Laurie E. *The Complete Idiot's Guide to Creative Writing.* 2nd ed. New York: Penguin Group, 2004.

Rushdie, Salman. *The Wizard of Oz.* London: The British Film Institute, 1992.

Russell, Bertrand. *The Autobiography of Bertrand Russell, 1872–1914.* Boston: Little Brown, 1967.

Sagan, Carl. *Broca's Brain.* New York: Ballantine, 1974.

———. *The Dragons of Eden: Speculations on the Evolution of Human Intelligence.* New York: Ballantine Books, 1977. Reissue edition, 1986.

Sale, Roger. "L. Frank Baum and Oz." *Hudson Review,* Winter 1972–1973. Revised and reprinted in *Fairy Tales and After.* Cambridge, MA: Harvard University Press, 1978.

"Salina, New York." *Wikipedia.* Accessed August 25, 2008. http://en.wikipedia.org/wiki/Salina,_New_York.

Sample, Steven B. *The Contrarian's Guide to Leadership.* San Francisco: Jossey-Bass, 2002.

———. "Redefining Undergraduate Education for the 21st Century." Presented at The College Board Annual Forum, San Diego, 2006. http://www.usc.edu/president/speeches/2006/college_board.html.

Schiraldi, Glenn R. *The Post-Traumatic Stress Disorder Sourcebook: A Guide to Healing, Recovery, and Growth.* 2nd ed. New York: McGraw-Hill, 2009.

Schwartz, Debora B. "Backgrounds to Romance: 'Courtly Love.'"California Polytechnic State University website. Last updated March 2001. http://cla.calpoly.edu/~dschwart/engl513/courtly/courtly.htm.

Schwartz, Evan I. *Finding Oz: How L. Frank Baum Discovered the Great American Story.* Boston: Houghton Mifflin Harcourt, 2009.

Seaburg, Alan. *Dictionary of Unitarian & Universalist Biography.* S.v. "Horatio Alger."

Accessed November 4, 2008. http://www25.uua.org/uuhs/duub/articles/hora-tioalgerjr.html.

Serve America Act, 111ᵗʰ Cong. (2009).; http://www.govtrack.us/congress/bill.xpd?bill=s111-277.

Sheehan, J. C. *The Enchanted Ring: The Untold Story of Penicillin*. Cambridge: MIT Press, 1982.

Shelley, Mary Wollstonecroft. *Frankenstein*. 1818. Reprint, New York: Dutton, 1963.

Sherwood, James E. "The Role of the Land-Grant Institution in the 21ˢᵗ Century." *Research & Occasional Paper Series: CSHE.6.04*. Center for Studies in Higher Education. Berkeley: University of California, Berkeley, 2004. cshe.berkeley.edu/publications/docs/ROP.Sherwood.6.04.pdf).

———. *The Self-Esteem Workbook*. Oakland, CA: New Harbinger Publications, 2001.

Simmonds, Patience. "Plagiarism and Cyber-plagiarism." *College & Research Libraries News*, June 2003, 385–89.

Simon, Scott. "Kid Reporter Covers 'Worldwide Day of Play.'" Interview with Brennan LaBrie. *Weekend Edition*. NPR. September 26, 2009. http://www.npr.org/templates/story/story.php?storyId=113237133.

Sisson, Richard, Christian K. Zacher, and Andrew Robert Lee Clayton. *The American Midwest: An Interpretive Encyclopedia*. Bloomington: Indiana University Press, 2007.

Smith, Bob. "Farewell and Fare-well University of Arkansas." *All Things Academic* 9, no. 2 (June 2008). http://libinfo.uark.edu/ata.

———. "When Is It Unethical to Copy the Works of Others?" *All Things Academic* 8, no. 1 (2007). http://libinfo.uark.edu/ata/v8no1/default.asp.

———. "Where You Stand Is Where You Sit . . ." *All Things Academic* 5, no. 2 (May 2004). http://libinfo.uark.edu/ata.

———. *See also* Robert V. Smith.

Smith, Red. Radio interview. Washington, DC. NPR, June 1986.

Smith, Robert V. *The Elements of Great Speechmaking: Adding Drama & Intrigue*. Lanham, MD: University Press of America, 2004.

———. *Pedestals, Parapets & Pits: The Joys, Challenges & Failures of Professional Life*. Fayetteville, AR: Phoenix International, Inc., 2005.

Snow, Jack. *Who's Who in Oz*. Chicago: Reilly and Lee, 1954.

Specter, Michael. *Denialism: How Irrational Thinking Hinders Scientific Progress, Harms the Planet, and Threatens Our Lives*. New York: Penguin Press, 2009.

Stengel, Richard. "A Time to Serve." *Time*, August 30, 2007. http://www.time.com/time/specials/2007/article/0,28804,1657256_1657317,00.html.

Sternberg, Robert J. *College Admissions for the 21st Century*. Cambridge, MA: Harvard University Press, 2010.

St. John, Tom. "Lyman Frank Baum: Looking Back to the Promised Land." *Western*

Humanities Review 36, no. 4 (1982): 349–59.

Strunk, William, Jr., and E. B. White. *The Elements of Style.* 4th ed. Boston: Allyn & Bacon, 2000.

Swartz, Mark Evan. *Oz before the Rainbow: L. Frank Baum's* The Wonderful Wizard of Oz *on Stage and Screen to 1939.* Baltimore: Johns Hopkins University Press, 2000.

Thoreau, Henry David. *Walden.* 1852. Reprint, New York: Bantam Books, 1962.

Tichy, H. J. *Effective Writing for Engineers, Managers, Scientists.* New York: Wiley, 1966.

Tolstoy, Leo. *The Death of Ivan Ilych.* Translated by Anthony Briggs. New York: Penguin Classics, 2006. First published in 1886.

Tuerk, Richard. *Oz in Perspective: Magic and Myth in the L. Frank Baum Books.* Jefferson, NC: MacFarland & Company, 2007.

Twiton, Andi. "Common Reading Programs in Higher Education." Folke Bernadottee Memorial Library, Gustavus Adolphus Library, St. Peter, MN. Last updated April 2007. http://gustavus.edu/academics/library/Pubs/Lindell2007.html.

United Nations. "About the United Nations: History." Accessed November 17, 2011. http://www.un.org/aboutun/history.htm.

University of California–Berkeley. Standards of Ethical Conduct. 2005. http://www.ucop.edu/ucophome/coordrev/policy/Stmt_Stds_Ethics.pdf.

Updike, John. "'Oz Is Us.' A Critic at Large." *New Yorker*, September 25, 2000, 84–88.

US Copyright Office. *Copyright Law of the United States and Related Laws Contained in Title 17 of the United States Code*, Circular 92. October 2009. http://www.copyright.gov/title17.

US Equal Employment Opportunities Commission. "Facts about Sexual Harassment." Accessed November 26, 2011. http://www.eeoc.gov/eeoc/publications/fs-sex.cfm.

US Equal Employment Opportunities Commission. "Policy Guidance on Current Issues of Sexual Harassment." 1999. http://www.eeoc.gov/policy/docs/current-issues.html.

Velde, Francois R. "Following the Yellow Brick Road: How the United States Adopted the Gold Standard." *Economic Perspectives*, 4th Quarter, 2002, 42–58.

Vivekanada, Swami. Address to the Parliment of Religions, Columbia Exposition, Chicago, IL, September 11, 1893. http://swamij.com/swami-vivekananda-1893.htm. Original audio recording on YouTube, http://www.youtube.com/watch?v=OSV_jQItkzU.

Walls, Jeannette. *The Glass Castle: A Memoir.* New York: Scribner, 2005.

Watson, Bruce. "The Amazing Author of Oz." *Smithsonian* 31, no. 3 (June 2000): 112–19.

Weiland, Juliette. "2009 Youth Achievement Award Winners." Smart Kids with Learning Disabilities. Accessed November 30, 2011. http://www.smartkidswithld.org/

achievement/success-stories/youth-award-winners/michael-t-sullivan-social-justice-advocate-2009-youth-achievement-award-winner..

Wendler, Cathy, Brent Bridgeman, Fred Cline, Catherine Millett, JoAnn Rock, Nathan Bell, and Patricia McAllister. *The Path Forward: The Future of Graduate Education in the United States.* Princeton, NJ: Educational Testing Service, 2010.

Wilson, Edward O. *Consilience: The Unity of Knowledge.* New York: Knopf, 1998.

———. *The Creation: An Appeal to Save Life on Earth.* New York: Norton, 2006.

Wilson, Robin. "The New Gender Divide." *Chronicle of Higher Education.* Online edition. January 26, 2007. http://chronicle.com/article/The-New-Gender-Divide/33219/.

Woods, Randall Bennett. *Fulbright: A Biography.* New York: Cambridge University Press, 1995.

"World's Columbian Exposition of 1893." 1998. Paul V. Gavin Library Digital History Collection, Illinois Institute of Technology. http://columbus.iit.edu/dreamcity/dctoc.html.

Zinsser, William K. *On Writing Well: The Classic Guide to Writing Nonfiction.* 25th Anniversary Edition. New York: HarperResource, 2001.

Websites

Advancement Via Individual Determination (AVID). http://www.avid.org.

Baum's Castorine. http://www.baumscastorine.com.

Institute for Study Abroad, Butler University, Indianapolis, IN. http://www.ifsa-butler.org.

Michael Franks. http://michaelfranks.com.

Second Life. http://secondlife.com.

The Writer's Almanac. Garrison Keillor. http://writersalmanac.publicradio.org.

Voluntary System of Accountability Program, Association of Public and Land-Grant Universities (APLU) and American Association of State Colleges and Universities (AASCU). http://www.voluntarysystem.org/index.cfm.

Index

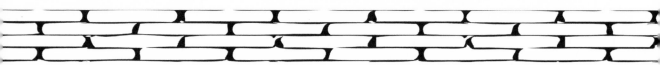

About the Author

Robert V. Smith has pursued a career as faculty member and administrator at five research universities in the United States. Currently serving as the chief academic officer at Texas Tech University, he is the author of several professional development books, including *Where You Stand Is Where You Sit: An Academic Administrator's Handbook* and *Pedestals, Parapets, and Pits: The Joys, Challenges, and Failures of Professional Life.* www.thewayofoz.com